W9-CFJ-033

Placement, Assessment & Reporting Guide

ISBN-13: 978-0-545-32567-7
ISBN-10: 0-545-32567-6

 Pages printed on 10% PCW recycled paper.

Table of Contents

Placement

Assessment

READ 180 Reports

rSkills Tests Reports

SRI Reports

Table of Contents (continued)

About This Guide

The Placement, Assessment, and Reporting Guide is for teachers and leaders.
It provides an overview of the assessment components in *READ 180,* including Teacher and Leadership Dashboards.

This guide will help you:
- Screen, place, and diagnose students appropriately in *READ 180.*
- Assess students throughout the year using screening, progress monitoring, curriculum-embedded, and summative measures.
- Monitor reading progress for students, classes, schools, and districts.
- Use data to drive instruction.

The Placement, Assessment, and Reporting Guide includes four sections:

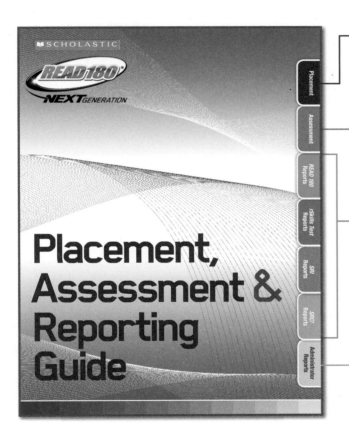

The **Placement and Grouping** section explains how to use the *Scholastic Reading Inventory (SRI)* to identify students who may need intervention, place each student in the appropriate *READ 180* level, group and regroup students throughout the year for targeted instruction, and exit students from the program.

The **Assessment** section describes each *READ 180* assessment and how to use each assessment to monitor progress and performance in all components of the *READ 180* Instructional Model.

The **Teacher Reports** section provides detailed information on how teachers can use data from each *READ 180* assessment component to plan instruction and monitor student progress:
- *READ 180* Reports
- *rSkills Tests* Reports
- *Scholastic Reading Inventory* (*SRI*) Reports
- *Scholastic Reading Counts!* (*SRC!*) Reports

The **Administrator Reports** section explains how school and district leaders can use data captured by each *READ 180* assessment to monitor progress, student response to intervention, and overall program effectiveness.

Comprehensive Assessment

Assessment is an essential part of the teaching and learning process. Effective assessment provides detailed feedback on performance that can inform instruction and enable teachers to target students' needs.

Assessments That Inform Instruction

1. **Screening and Placement Assessments**

   Ensure that students are appropriately targeted for intervention and receive baseline results that can be used to track student reading progress throughout the year.

2. **Curriculum-Embedded Assessments**

   Use as a daily instructional component to maximize student engagement while collecting actionable data that can be used to monitor student progress and inform instructional pacing.

3. **Progress Monitoring Assessments**

   Administer at regular intervals to provide updates on student performance and facilitate targeting of instructional support.

4. **Summative Assessments**

   Gauge student mastery of reading, writing, and listening skills through periodic and comprehensive assessments.

"Thanks to technology, we have the ability to deliver accurate assessments that can be administered to students simultaneously so that we can get on with the critical work of teaching."

— Ted Hasselbring

Feedback for Students and Families

Data from each assessment type is presented in reports to share with students and their caregivers. This feedback helps build student confidence and self-esteem, and enables families to partner in the learning process.

Informative Data for Leaders

Assessment results enable school and district leadership to track performance and assess implementation effectiveness within a school or district.

Assessment in *READ 180*

READ 180 includes a comprehensive array of assessment components. Together, data from these assessments provide a complete picture of student participation, performance, and progress throughout the school year. Some of the assessments can be used on a continuous or as-needed basis. Others are designed for use at specific intervals throughout the year.

1. **Screening and Placement Assessment**

   Scholastic Reading Inventory (SRI) is administered at the beginning of the year to:
   - provide initial screening
   - place students in the appropriate level

2. **Curriculum-Embedded Assessment**

   READ 180 **Topic Software** is used daily. Data from the software is used to:
   - track progress in reading, vocabulary, and writing
   - determine student grouping and instructional pacing

   Scholastic Reading Counts! quizzes are assigned when students complete a book in the Modeled and Independent Reading rotation. Quiz results are used to:
   - monitor independent reading progress
   - provide student motivation

   rBook **Writing and Wrap-Up Projects** are assigned during each *rBook* Workshop to:
   - measure ability to synthesize information
   - gauge ability to articulate responses to reading

3. **Progress Monitoring Assessment**

   Scholastic Reading Inventory (SRI) is administered four times a year to:
   - gauge reading progress
   - ensure appropriate placement

   rSkills Tests are administered at the end of each *rBook* Workshop to:
   - assess mastery of key, standards-aligned skills taught during Whole- and Small-Group
   - group students and determine appropriate instructional pacing

   Oral Fluency Assessments can be administered three times a year to:
   - measure student fluency
   - determine appropriate instructional support

4. **Summative Assessment**

   The rSkills Summative Tests are administered at midyear and end-of-year to:
   - assess mastery of reading, vocabulary, conventions, writing, and listening skills
   - monitor student progress and response to intervention

READ 180 Assessment Time Line

This time line recommends when to administer appropriate assessments for screening, placement, progress monitoring, and instructional planning throughout the course of the school year.

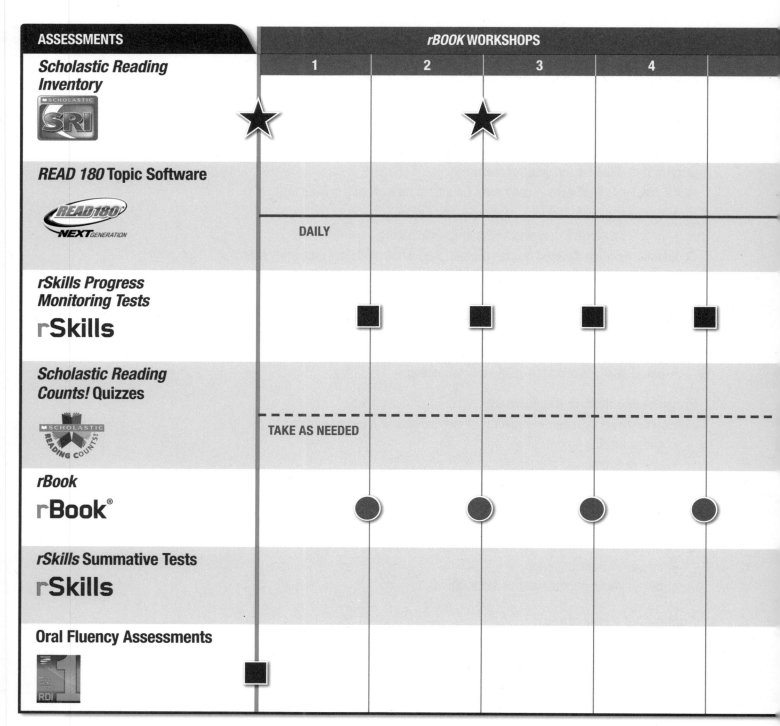

ASSESSMENTS	*rBOOK* WORKSHOPS				
	1	2	3	4	
Scholastic Reading Inventory SRI	★		★		
READ 180 Topic Software	DAILY				
rSkills Progress Monitoring Tests rSkills	■	■	■	■	
Scholastic Reading Counts! Quizzes	TAKE AS NEEDED				
rBook rBook®	●	●	●	●	
rSkills Summative Tests rSkills					
Oral Fluency Assessments	■				

Beginning of the Year

TYPES OF ASSESSMENT IN *READ 180* NEXT GENERATION

Screening and Placement Assessment	Curriculum-Embedded Assessment	Progress Monitoring Assessment	Summative Assessment

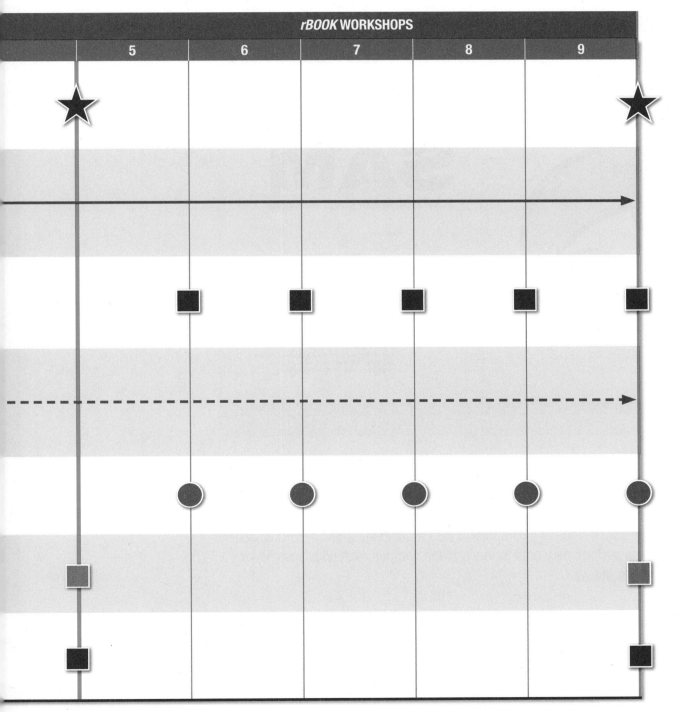

Middle of the Year

End of the Year

Understanding the Scholastic Achievement Manager

READ 180 is strongly grounded in data-driven instruction. The software-based *READ 180* components collect and aggregate data to enable teachers and leaders to monitor student progress and target instruction to meet individual student needs.

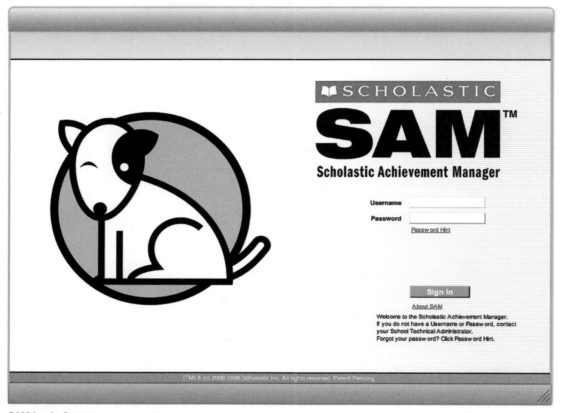

SAM Login Screen

Scholastic Achievement Manager Overview

Access results and supporting resources for *READ 180* assessments through the Scholastic Achievement Manager (SAM). SAM is a computer-based management and reporting system that gathers usage and performance data for each of the computer-based assessments:

- *READ 180* Topic Software
- *rSkills Tests*
- *Scholastic Reading Inventory (SRI)*
- *Scholastic Reading Counts!*

Find step-by-step instructions on how to use SAM in the *READ 180* Software Manual available on the product support website **(www.scholastic.com/read180/productsupport).**

Navigating SAM

The SAM home page includes a SmartBar that lists classes of students enrolled in *READ 180.* Use the five main buttons to access each section of SAM.

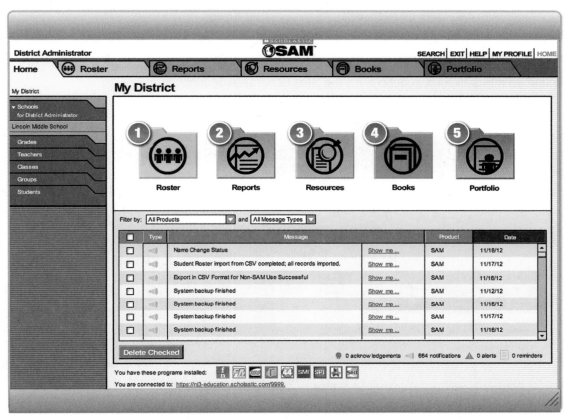

SAM Home Page

① Roster
- Enroll students in software
- Manage student, class, school, and district information

② Reports
- Generate data-driven reports
- Monitor progress
- Diagnose instructional needs

③ Resources
- Locate instructional resources
- Download lesson plans and practice pages
- Link to the Interactive Teaching System (ITS)

④ Books
- Search for instructional texts
- Search for independent reading texts

⑤ Student Digital Portfolio
- Access student oral fluency and writing results
- Use rubrics to digitally assess student performance
- Print and share results with students, families, and school administrators

Understanding the Dashboards

The Teacher Dashboard, Leadership Dashboard, and Student Dashboard provide teachers, leaders, and students with resources and data needed for data-driven differentiated instruction, successful implementation, and daily engagement.

READ 180 Teacher Dashboard

The *READ 180* Teacher Dashboard offers five key functions for the Next Generation Teacher:

1 Schedule Reports and Notifications

Receive alerts and notifications regarding student progress and participation. Schedule SAM reports to be sent to your inbox.

2 Plan Instruction

Link to the *READ 180* Interactive Teaching System (ITS) for daily planning. Generate, save, and print standards-aligned lesson plans.

3 Access Professional Development

Review videos of master teachers, access resources, and review daily instructional tips.

4 Review Performance Results

Monitor student progress in each software component and plan appropriate intervention.

5 Group Students

Use the Groupinator™ to form dynamic groups and differentiate instruction based on student performance results.

Teacher Dashboard Home Page

Navigating the Teacher Dashboard Home Page

Use your SAM login information to log in to the Teacher Dashboard. Navigate to the home page to review student results and accompanying lesson plans for each class period.

Teacher Dashboard Home Page

1 Class Digest

Each class has its own digest that provides overviews of performance results and daily *rBook* instruction. Establish standard class naming conventions in SAM to ensure relevant class names appear on the Teacher and Leadership Dashboard Home Pages.

2 Data Snapshots

At-a-glance views of class performance help drive instructional planning and pacing. *READ 180* Topic Software is the default data snapshot. Click the left and right arrows to review usage and performance results from *SRI*, *rSkills Tests*, and *Scholastic Reading Counts!*

3 Today's Summary

Whole- and Small-Group overviews provide a summary of the day's instruction. The summary links directly to the Interactive Teaching System. Click on **Settings** to select the *rBook* used with each class. Use the left and right arrows to advance through an *rBook* Workshop.

4 Groups

Student groups are generated by the Groupinator and are included on the Today's Summary at each *rBook* CheckPoint. Link directly to accompanying lessons on the Interactive Teaching System from the Summary.

READ 180 Leadership Dashboard

Like the *READ 180* Teacher Dashboard, the Leadership Dashboard streamlines the instructional support and progress monitoring process.

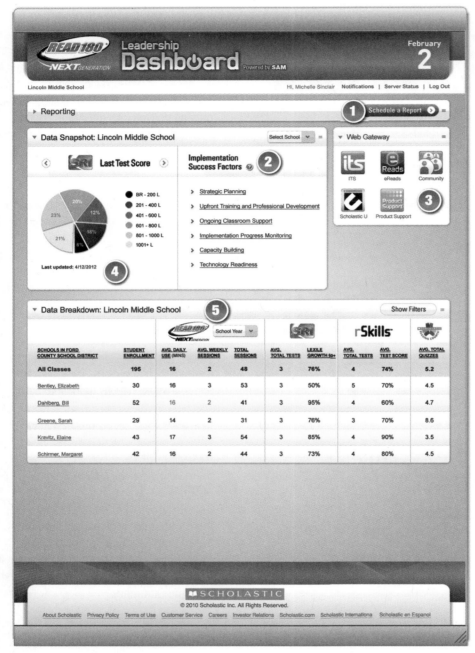

Leadership Dashboard: Home Page

1 Schedule Reports and Notifications

Receive alerts and notifications regarding district, school, or class performance and usage results. Schedule SAM reports to be sent to your inbox.

2 Prepare for Success

Learn how to support a strong *READ 180* implementation.

3 Access Professional Development

Access online support to become familiar with classroom resources and instructional best practices.

4 Review Performance Results

Analyze aggregated data to monitor student progress and plan appropriate intervention.

5 Analyze Detailed Results

Review usage and performance results for each school or class.

READ 180 Student Dashboard

The *READ 180* Student Dashboard motivates students with progress monitoring.

Student Dashboard Home Page

1 **Review Software Progress**

Review current *READ 180* Software Zone performance and work left to complete in each segment.

2 **Track Software Performance**

Review scores for each zone in each software segment, as well as overall scores on *Scholastic Reading Counts!* quizzes.

3 **Monitor** *Scholastic Reading Counts!* **Participation**

Review quizzes passed and average rating for books and eReads.

4 **Highlight Performance Streaks**

Track reading progress and "unlock" trophies for making gains and earning high software scores.

Placement and Grouping

Response to Intervention

Response to Intervention (RTI) is a tiered approach to teaching and learning that optimizes instruction by empowering educators to continuously screen students' skill mastery, identify achievement targets, collect data to monitor student progress, and use data to adjust instruction to match student needs.

Tiers of Intervention

States and districts may define the RTI instructional model according to students' needs. One of the most common structures is the 3-Tier Intervention Model shown here.

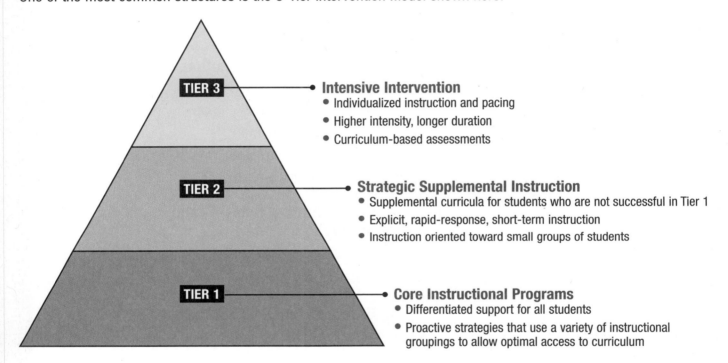

TIER 3

Intensive Intervention
- Individualized instruction and pacing
- Higher intensity, longer duration
- Curriculum-based assessments

TIER 2

Strategic Supplemental Instruction
- Supplemental curricula for students who are not successful in Tier 1
- Explicit, rapid-response, short-term instruction
- Instruction oriented toward small groups of students

TIER 1

Core Instructional Programs
- Differentiated support for all students
- Proactive strategies that use a variety of instructional groupings to allow optimal access to curriculum

RTI in *READ 180*

READ 180 supports and complements the implementation of RTI through its universal screening measures, validated and research-based interventions, and ongoing progress monitoring to facilitate data-based decision-making. The program begins with screening and placement to identify students who need intervention and places them appropriately within the program. *READ 180* then motivates struggling readers with age-appropriate materials at multiple reading levels. Use *READ 180* data to guide instruction and meet key principles of RTI.

For more information, review the "Response to Intervention: An Alignment Guide for *READ 180*" at **www.scholastic.com/administrator/funding/fundingconnection/ pdf/R180_RTI_Alignment.pdf**.

Universal Screening With the *Scholastic Reading Inventory (SRI)*

In an RTI model, all students should be screened three times a year. Universal screening should be brief, reliable, and valid, and should appropriately identify students who require more intense intervention to meet established benchmarks.

Use the *Scholastic Reading Inventory (SRI)* to screen students throughout the year. The Lexile Framework® allows each student's score to be aligned to performance standards that can be used for screening decisions.

Baseline Measure and Placement

Once students have completed their initial *SRI* tests and are placed into *READ 180,* the Scholastic Achievement Manager (SAM) will use their results to place them into the appropriate *READ 180* level. Students build reading proficiency by practicing skills using age-appropriate material at their current reading level. Evaluate students' baseline reading levels to determine if placement in *READ 180* is appropriate. Students with initial Lexile® scores below 400L may benefit from additional screening to determine if placement in a phonics-based program, such as *System 44*, is appropriate.

READ 180 Level	Grade-Level Reading Equivalent		
	Stage A	Stage B	Stage C
Level 1	1.5–2.5	1.5–2.5	1.5–2.5
Level 2	2.5–4.0	2.5–4.0	2.5–4.0
Level 3	4.0–6.0	4.0–6.0	4.0–6.0
Level 4	N/A	6.0–8.0	6.0–12.0

Frequent Monitoring of Student Progress

In an RTI model, data should be regularly collected and analyzed to determine whether instruction is producing the desired academic gains.

READ 180 provides continuous assessment and immediate feedback for students and teachers. SAM gathers and displays quantifiable student performance results in detailed reports that allow teachers to identify and measure student skill mastery.

Data-Driven Differentiation

In an RTI model, classroom instruction should be differentiated to ensure that students will achieve established benchmarks.

READ 180 includes extensive embedded support for differentiating classroom instruction to address students' differing needs. Each *rBook* Workshop includes Scaffolded Support options that promote data-based regrouping and differentiated Small-Group lessons. Students are also placed at appropriate levels and receive individualized support during the Instructional Software and Modeled and Independent Reading Rotations.

Scholastic Reading Inventory (SRI)

The *Scholastic Reading Inventory (SRI)* is an objective, research-based assessment of students' reading comprehension ability that can be used to screen and place students. Based on the Lexile Framework for Reading, the *SRI* can be administered to any reader, regardless of age and grade level. *SRI* is a computer-adaptive test designed for quick administration in an untimed, low-pressure environment.

The Lexile Framework

SRI is based on the Lexile Framework, which measures texts and readers on the same scale. The Lexile Framework is a reliable and tested tool designed to bridge two critical aspects of student reading achievement—leveling text difficulty and assessing the reading skills of each student.

The Lexile scale ranges from Beginning Reader to above 1500L. Any score below 100L is reported as BR, or Beginning Reader. When a reader's Lexile score matches the Lexile measure of a text, the reader experiences confidence and control over the reading process.

READ 180 includes a Lexile Leveled Reading Framework poster that shows text Lexile levels, examples of benchmark literature within each Lexile level, and sample passages. Use this poster to educate students about the Lexile Framework and when matching reader and task.

The *SRI* Read For Life Report also generates a comparison between each student's current Lexile score and sample texts. See **page 212** for more information.

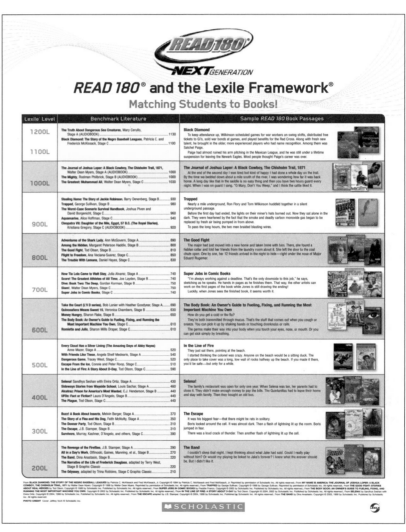

Lexile Framework Poster

SRI Test Items

The *SRI* has a test bank of over 5,000 questions based exclusively on fiction and nonfiction passages from authentic literature, as well as excerpts from young adult and classic literature, newspapers, magazines, and periodicals.

When taking the *SRI*, students answer fill-in-the-blank, or cloze, questions, similar to those found on many standardized tests. These questions measure students' comprehension of the passages they read.

The *SRI* determines the starting level for students in *READ 180*. Over time, results from multiple administrations of the *SRI* are used to measure improvements in reading comprehension.

Adaptive Assessment

SRI is an adaptive test that adjusts to students' responses. As students progress through the test, the difficulty levels of questions change according to students' performance. As the student correctly answers questions, the Lexile of each question increases. When the student answers a question incorrectly, the next question presented is at a lower Lexile level. The test stops once the student has answered a sufficient number of questions to determine an accurate Lexile score.

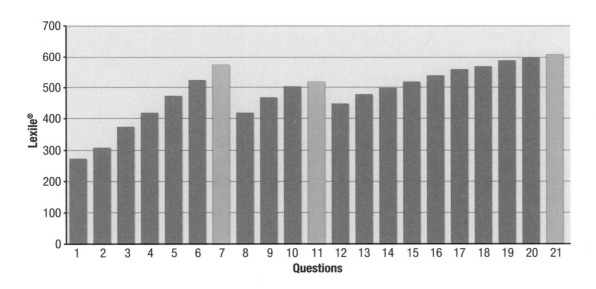

The graph above represents a sample student's performance on one *SRI* test. Each question is numbered. Questions answered correctly are blue; incorrect answers are orange. This graph of *SRI* performance is only a sample. The total number of questions and the Lexile of each question depends on individual student performance.

SRI Validity and Reliability

The *Scholastic Reading Inventory (SRI)* is a research-based assessment that has been field-tested and validated to ensure that it is a reliable indicator of reading comprehension.

Field Testing

The *SRI* is based on the Lexile Framework for Reading. A linking study conducted with the Lexile Framework developed normative information based on a sample of 512,224 students from a medium-to-large state. The sample's distributions of scores on norm-referenced and other standardized measures of reading comprehension are similar to those reported for national distribution.

Validity

Validity indicates whether the test measures what it is supposed to measure. There are several ways to examine the validity of a test like *SRI*. Each type of validation asks an important question about the test.

- **Content Validity** Does the test sample important content related to what the test is supposed to measure?
- **Construct Validity** Does the test measure the theoretical construct (or trait) it is supposed to measure?
- **Criterion-Related Validity** Does the test adequately predict the test-taker's behavior in a specific situation?

Content Validity

The *SRI* test consists of short passages and questions that measure comprehension by focusing on skills readers use when studying written materials from a variety of content areas. These implicit skills include identifying details, drawing conclusions, and making comparisons and generalizations.

Passage Selection

SRI passages are selected from authentic texts that students encounter both in and out of the classroom, such as textbooks, literature, magazines, and newspapers. Passage topics span a variety of interest areas. Each passage develops one main idea or contains information that comes before or after the passage in the source text. No prior knowledge is required to understand a passage.

Item Format

SRI uses an embedded completion item format that has been shown to measure the ability to draw inferences and establish logical connections between ideas. Each item has a statement and four answer choices. Statements are written to enable students to arrive at the correct answer by comprehending the passage. All four answer choices are semantically plausible when the statement is read independently of the text. Item reading levels are controlled to be easier than the most difficult word in the passage.

Below are sample items at various Lexile® levels that might appear on an *SRI* test.

Sample Item	Lexile
Q. When I was talking to Donny Thunderbird, he told me about his relatives all over the reservation. He has cousins with no mother or father, but because they are members of the tribe, they will never be without a home. They will always belong to something. **The tribe is** _____. **A.** lost **B.** huge **C.** famous **D.** supportive	**700L–850L**
Q. Cody's room at home looked like a tornado had hit it. Boxes were piled everywhere. Some were open, with things falling out. Others were still taped shut. **The room was** _____. **A.** messy **B.** small **C.** empty **D.** bright	**400L–550L**
Q. He broke records every week. No one in the state had ever caught more passes. Or gained more yards. Or scored more touchdowns. **He was a** _____ **player.** **A.** great **B.** slow **C.** new **D.** last	**100L–250L**

Construct Validity

SRI was examined for construct validity by analyzing the developmental changes in test scores and the performance between proficient and struggling readers.

Developmental Nature of *SRI*

Reading is a skill that typically develops with age—as students read more, their skills improve, and they are able to access more complex texts. Because growth in reading is uneven, with the greatest growth usually taking place in earlier grades, *SRI* scores should show a similar trend of decreasing gains as grade level increases. Multiple studies indicate that performance on *SRI* increases with grade level. These studies also demonstrate that the growth is uneven; that is, the growth in earlier grades is steeper than growth in later grades. See **Appendix 1** to review growth by grade level.

In addition to the changes in growth expectations on *SRI* from one grade to the next, studies reveal that older struggling readers receive lower scores on the *SRI* than their peers who are reading at grade level, which is also reflected in their performance results on state assessments. This discrepancy between results for struggling readers and grade-level readers supports the construct validity of *SRI*. The studies further clarify that while growth for grade-level readers decreases as students move to higher grade levels, this should not be the case for older struggling readers who receive reading intervention. When compared to grade-level readers, struggling readers should demonstrate greater growth from one *SRI* test to the next, thus closing the reading gap.

Performance Bands and Lexile Correlation

The chart below displays the correlation between *SRI* Lexile levels and their equivalent grade levels. These performance bands are established by the Scholastic Achievement Manager (SAM).

Grade	Below Basic (Far Below Grade Level)	Basic (Below Grade Level)	Proficient (On Grade Level)	Advanced (Above Grade Level)
1	N/A	0L–99L	100L–400L	401L and above
2	0L–99L	100L–299L	300L–600L	601L and above
3	0L–249L	250L–499L	500L–800L	801L and above
4	0L–349L	350L–599L	600L–900L	901L and above
5	0L–449L	450L–699L	700L–1000L	1001L and above
6	0L–499L	500L–799L	800L–1050L	1051L and above
7	0L–549L	550L–849L	850L–1100L	1101L and above
8	0L–599L	600L–899L	900L–1150L	1151L and above
9	0L–649L	650L–999L	1000L–1200L	1201L and above
10	0L–699L	700L–1024L	1025L–1250L	1251L and above
11	0L–799L	800L–1049L	1050L–1300L	1301L and above

Districts or schools that wish to adjust these Lexile performance bands to match district or state performance standards, including the Common Core State Standards, may do so in the *SRI* Settings of the SAM Roster. See the *READ 180* Software Manual for more information (**www.scholastic.com/read180/productsupport**).

Criterion-Related Validity

SRI has been directly correlated with numerous state assessments. All studies reveal statistically significant and positive correlations between the *SRI* to other reading measures. Large-scale correlations have been conducted in Florida, California, and Ohio. Professional Papers published documenting these large-scale and significant results can be found on the *SRI* website (**www.teacher.scholastic.com/SRI**).

In addition to the correlations from SRI to other reading assessments, the Lexile Framework is correlated with a number of other standardized reading comprehension tests. The following norm-referenced and criterion-referenced tests have been correlated to, or linked to, the Lexile Framework:

- TerraNova (CAT/6 and CTBS/5)
- Tests of Adult Basic Education (TABE)
- Stanford Achievement Tests (Ninth and Tenth Editions)
- Metropolitan Achievement Test/8 (MAT)
- ERB: Comprehensive Testing Program, 4th Edition (CTP 4)

- The Iowa Tests (ITBS and ITED)
- Gates-MacGinitie Reading Tests, Fourth Edition
- Dynamic Measurement Group: Dynamic Indicators of Basic Early Literacy Skills (DIBELS)
- Test of English as a Foreign Language (TOEFL)

Many state assessments link to the Lexile Framework, and *SRI* provides extrapolated cut scores for these states. This allows for customized performance standards alignment to state outcome expectations. Information for each assessment can be downloaded from SAM Resources. See **Appendix 2** to review the list of assessments and SAM Keywords.

Reliability

To be useful, assessment results should be reliable—stable, accurate, and dependable. A test's accuracy is estimated by a number called the standard error of measurement (SEM). The SEM provides information about how accurately a test is able to measure a student's ability. Once the SEM in a test score is known, it can be taken into account when reviewing test results.

In reality, all test scores include some measure of error, or level of uncertainty. The SEM is related to three factors: 1) the statistical model used to compute the score, 2) the questions used to determine the score, 3) the condition of the test-taker during testing.

In *SRI*, targeting is a practice that assigns an entry level for first-time test-takers, thereby lowering the SEM. Targeting helps determine the difficulty of the first item that is administered to the students. For more information about targeting, see **Appendix 3**.

The computer algorithm that controls the administration of the *SRI* uses a statistical procedure designed to estimate each student's ability to comprehend text. The algorithm uses prior information about students' level to control the selection of questions and the calculation of each student's reading ability after they respond to each question. Compared to a fixed-item test where all students answer the same questions, a computer-adaptive test produces a different test targeted for each student. When students take a computer adaptive test, they all receive approximately the same raw score, or number of items answered correctly. This occurs because all students answer questions that are targeted for their unique ability—not questions that are too easy or too hard.

SRI Enrollment

The *Scholastic Reading Inventory (SRI)* is a classroom-based assessment that can be administered on the computer. Use SAM to enroll students in *SRI* before administering the first test.

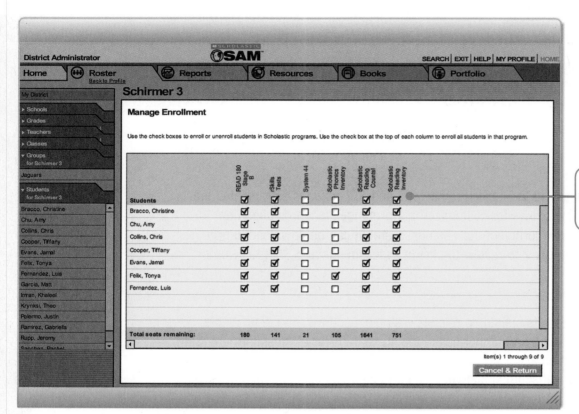

Enrollment Click the top box to enroll all students simultaneously.

SAM Roster: Manage Enrollment Screen

Use SAM for *SRI* Enrollment

1. Navigate to the SAM Roster.
2. Ensure that all students are included on the SmartBar. Click the **Add a Student** link to add students.
3. Click on the teacher name or class name on the SmartBar.
4. Select **Manage Enrollment**.
5. Click the top box to enroll all *READ 180* students in *SRI* simultaneously.
6. Click **Save and Return**.
7. Once students are enrolled, navigate to SAM Reports and print the *SRI* Student Roster Report (p.203).

Data in Action

SRI Testing Windows The *Scholastic Reading Inventory (SRI)* is a classroom assessment that can be used for screening and progress monitoring. It provides immediate reading performance results. *READ 180* students typically take the *SRI* four times a year.

Setting Up the Initial *SRI* Test

Complete enrollment by using the *SRI* Settings to target the estimated reading level of all *READ 180* students for their initial test. Most *READ 180* students should be targeted as Below Grade Level or Far Below Grade Level.

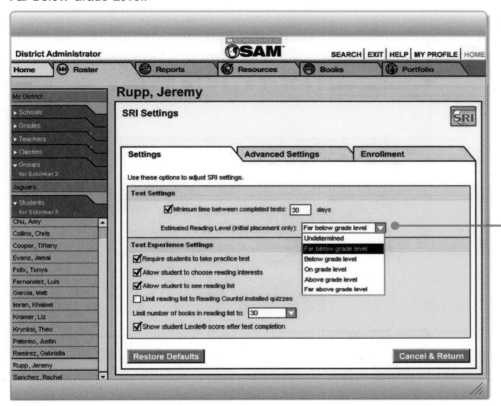

Targeting Select Below Grade Level or Far Below Grade Level from the drop-down menu.

SAM Roster: *SRI* Settings Screen

Target Estimated Reading Levels

1. Navigate to the SAM Roster.
2. Select a student, group, or class on the SmartBar.
3. Select **SRI Settings** in the Program menu at the bottom of the screen.
4. Use the drop-down menu to select the appropriate Estimated Reading Level. When in doubt, it is better to select a reading level below the student's current level.
5. Click **Save and Return**.

Data in Action

Ensure Accurate Results Targeting *READ 180* students for appropriate placement in their initial *SRI* reduces the Standard Error of Measurement (SEM), ensuring more reliable initial *SRI* results.

SRI Student Experience

Once students have been enrolled in *SRI* in SAM, they can log on to the software and take the test. Review the *SRI* testing process with students before administering the test. Directions below are written for student use.

Log in to the *SRI*

1. Launch *SRI* from the Student Gateway.
2. Enter your login information to begin the test.
3. If you receive an error message, check with your teacher to ensure that you are enrolled in the program and are using the correct login information.

SRI **Welcome Screen**

Choose Book Interests

1. Click a colored circle to select a category of interest. You may choose up to three categories.
2. The *SRI* uses these choices to create a customized recommended reading list that corresponds to reading interests and Lexile.
3. Choosing only one or two topics instead of three increases the percentage of books from that genre included on the *SRI* Recommended Reading Report.

SRI **Book Interest Screen**

Preparing for the Test

Practice questions ensure that students understand the test directions and are comfortable using the computer to take the test. Students will answer three practice questions that are formatted like the actual test.

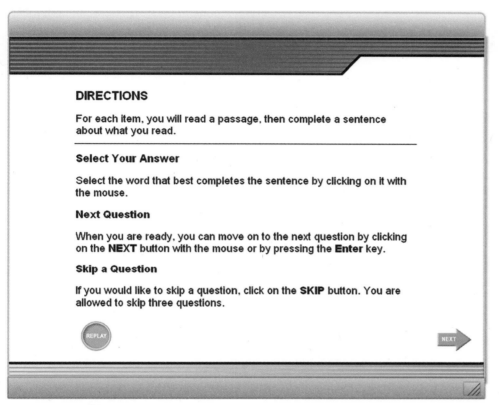

DIRECTIONS

For each item, you will read a passage, then complete a sentence about what you read.

Select Your Answer

Select the word that best completes the sentence by clicking on it with the mouse.

Next Question

When you are ready, you can move on to the next question by clicking on the **NEXT** button with the mouse or by pressing the **Enter** key.

Skip a Question

If you would like to skip a question, click on the **SKIP** button. You are allowed to skip three questions.

REPLAY

NEXT

SRI Test Directions Screen

Answer the Practice Questions

1. Read and listen to test directions.
2. Answer practice questions. Practice questions will be easier than the targeted reading level.
3. If you have difficulty with the practice questions, you will receive a prompt on the screen directing you to seek help from the teacher.

Data in Action

Preparing for *SRI* Before your students take the *SRI* test, review test-taking strategies as a class. See **page 116** for more information about preparing students for assessments.

SRI Student Experience, continued

An *SRI* test consists of brief passages from authentic fiction and nonfiction. After students read each passage, a multiple choice question displays on the screen.

She opened one eye and gasped. Elizabeth was peering over her bunk, her eyes looking like flying saucers. Sidney crouched on the next top bunk with her flashlight on. The girl's mouth hung wide open. "There was a r-ra-raccoon on your bed!"

They were _____.

○ cold
○ laughing
○ thoughtful
○ surprised

NEXT

3 skips left SKIP

SRI Sample Question

Take the Test

1. Select an answer for each question.
2. Change your response by clicking on a different choice before clicking the **Next** button. You cannot return to previous questions.
3. The computer provides questions of increasing challenge as you answer questions correctly.
4. When you miss a question, the computer provides easier questions until it determines the appropriate *SRI* score.
5. During the test, you can choose to skip up to three questions. You may not go back to these questions.
6. Because the test is adaptive, the total number of questions differs for each student.

Data in Action

Recommended Reading Once the test is complete, students receive their scores and can view a customized Recommended Reading Report. This report is based on the student's *SRI* results and the book interest choices made at the beginning of the test.

Completing the Test

Students may not have time to finish an *SRI* test or may become fatigued during the test. If this is the case, they can save an incomplete test and complete it at another time.

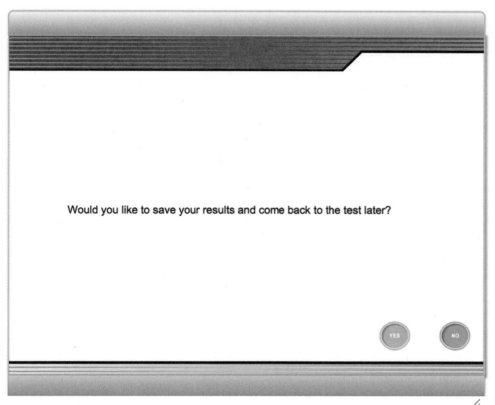

Would you like to save your results and come back to the test later?

YES   NO

SRI Exit Test Screen

Exit the *SRI* Before Completion

1. If you need to exit the test before completion, press the **Escape** key.
2. Click **Yes** to exit the test.
3. At the next login, the *SRI*, will prompt you to complete the unfinished test.

Data in Action

Avoiding Test Fatigue Encourage students to exit the test and resume another day if they begin feeling fatigued. Allowing students multiple days to complete the test will provide a more accurate indication of their true reading ability.

Using *SRI* Results for Placement

Scholastic Reading Inventory (SRI) results help teachers establish a baseline measure, place students in the appropriate level, form groups, and differentiate instruction.

Matching Reading Level in *READ 180* Topic Software

Research has shown that readers make the most progress and develop lifelong reading enjoyment when they are given texts that match their reading level instead of reading material that is too challenging. Once students have completed their initial *SRI*, their baseline results are used to place them into an appropriate *READ 180* Software level. Students will use the software to practice reading skills with texts at their level.

The following table lists the Lexile range for each *READ 180* level in each stage:

READ 180 Level	Stage A	Stage B	Stage C
Level 1	0–400L	0–400L	0–400L
Level 2	401–600L	401–600L	401–600L
Level 3	601–800L	601–800L	601–800L
Level 4	N/A	801L+	801L+

Matching Student to Text in Modeled and Independent Reading

Struggling readers often need assistance in choosing appropriate books and articles to read independently. *READ 180* provides a text complexity measure for every paperback, audiobook, eReads article, and *rBook* reading. Each text has been assessed by multiple reviewers who have considered three key aspects of text complexity: 1) Qualitative Measure, 2) Quantitative Measure, and 3) Reader and Task.

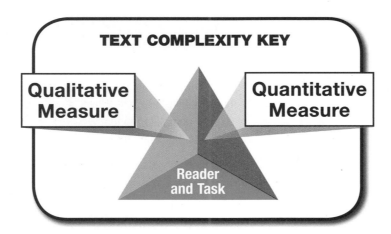

Consider the trajectory of text complexity as you help students select appropriate books in the Modeled and Independent Reading Rotation.

Focusing on Quantitative Measure

The quantitative aspects of a text include its word length or frequency, difficulty of vocabulary, sentence length, and text cohesion. The Quantitative Measure of a *READ 180* text is its Lexile.

Quantitative Measure

The Lexile Framework for Reading provides a common scale for matching reader ability with text complexity, allowing easy monitoring of student progress. Lexiles allow teachers to track student progress and assign each student appropriate reading materials. For example, if a text is too difficult for readers, they may struggle, quickly become frustrated, and give up. On the other hand, if the text is too easy, readers may not be challenged, and become easily distracted or bored.

Students' Lexile scores are the level at which they can read with moderate success— about 75% comprehension. Use *SRI* results to help students select books and eReads at appropriate reading levels during Modeled and Independent Reading. Review the chart below to support students with their independent reading.

Text Difficulty	Lexile Range	Use This Range When
Easy/Fluent	100L–250L below student's *SRI* score	Encouraging reluctant readers.
On-Level	100L below–50L above student's *SRI* score	Assigning independent reading. Most independent reading should be completed at this level.
Challenging	50L–250L above student's *SRI* score	Students have background knowledge or are highly motivated.

For specific information about student reading ranges, review the *SRI* Targeted Reading Report. See **page 200** for more information.

While students should be encouraged to move on to more demanding texts as their skills develop and their *SRI* scores increase, it is not necessary for them to advance to a higher Lexile measure with each new book or article. By reading half a dozen titles within their "On-Level" range, students build reading comprehension before moving on to a higher level.

Using *SRI* Results for Placement, continued

Focusing on Qualitative Measure

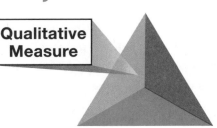

The qualitative measure of a text includes its levels of meaning, structure, language clarity, and background knowledge requirements. For example, a simple text has a clear purpose, literal language, and requires little prior knowledge. A more complex text may have an implied purpose, unconventional structure, and require the reader to have specific background information.

READ 180 provides a text complexity measure for every text, including paperbacks, audiobooks, and eReads found in the Modeled and Independent Reading Rotation. Multiple reviewers have assessed each text and rated the text according to the following scale.

Scale

Simple Moderate 1 Moderate 2 Complex 1 Complex 2

Texts were assigned a Qualitative Measure score based on the following factors:

Purpose/Levels of Meaning

One level of meaning ➡ Multiple levels of meaning (used for fiction texts)
Single, stated purpose ➡ Unstated purpose; multiple purposes (used for nonfiction texts)

Text Structure

Simple, conventional structure ➡ Complex, unconventional structure
Chronological ➡ Interrupted chronology
Simple graphics support text ➡ Sophisticated graphics add essential information

Language

Literal, clear language ➡ Figurative, ironic, or ambiguous language
Current, familiar word choice ➡ Archaic, unfamiliar word choice
Conversational language ➡ Academic language

Knowledge Demands

One simple theme ➡ Complex, sophisticated themes
One perspective ➡ Multiple perspectives
Familiar content or ideas ➡ Unfamiliar content or ideas
No references to other texts ➡ Multiple references to other texts

Quantitative readability formulas give a rough index of the overall difficulty of the text's syntax and vocabulary demands, whereas the qualitative measure of text complexity focuses on dimensions of texts that readability formulas typically cannot capture. In combination, these measures yield an overview of how challenging a text is and in what ways.

Focusing on Reader and Task

Beyond matching students to texts of appropriate reading levels, it is also important to consider reader variables, such as level of motivation and interest, as well as the reading task assigned.

Use the SAM Book Expert to support students with selecting books on topics that interest them. Search for books within a specific Lexile range, and filter those results by interest categories such as genre, culture, theme, or series.

Using the SAM Book Expert

1. Click on the SAM **Books** tab.
2. Use the *SRI* Targeted Reading Report to set the appropriate Lexile range.
3. Review students' book interest surveys completed during the first three weeks to determine topics of interest.
4. Select appropriate book filters.
5. Click **Search**.
6. Once results are displayed, click on a book title to review more information.
7. To only search for books with installed *SRC!* quizzes, use the *Scholastic Reading Counts!* Quiz Manager.

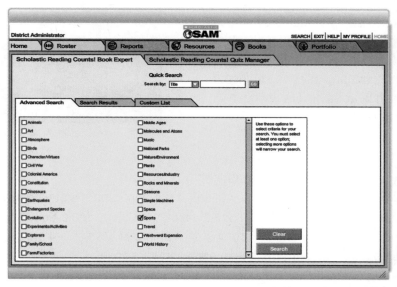

SAM Book Expert Screen

Matching Student to Text in Whole- and Small-Group Instruction

In addition to placing students at appropriate levels in the Instructional Software and Modeled and Independent Reading Rotations, *SRI* results are also used to group students and differentiate instruction during Whole- and Small-Group Instruction.

The Groupinator™ on the Teacher Dashboard places students into groups based on their *SRI* results. These grouping recommendations help determine what level of scaffolding and support to provide during Small-Group Instruction. Access daily Boost and Stretch activities from the Interactive Teaching System to support students at varying reading levels. See **page 40** for more information on grouping and differentiating *rBook* instruction.

Differentiating Instruction in *READ 180*

READ 180 supports differentiated instruction that targets individual student needs in all rotations. *SRI* results are used to place students into appropriate levels, select books, group students, and adjust instruction to support varying student needs.

Differentiating Instruction With Instructional Software

READ 180 software is "intelligent software" that collects data from students' individual responses, continuously assessing each student's progress and adjusting instruction accordingly.

The research-based instructional sequence offers students continuous support and immediate feedback. This feedback is nonjudgmental, private, and encouraging, allowing students to practice at the level they need without embarrassment.

READ 180 Topic Software: Zone Menu

Automatic Software Leveling

The *READ 180* Software uses students' initial *SRI* results to place each student at the appropriate software level. *SRI* scores do not affect a student's level after the initial placement in the Topic Software. Students placed at Level 1 must be manually promoted. Students in Levels 2–4 are promoted in *READ 180* software based on performance in each software zone.

To be promoted to a new level, students in Levels 2–4 must meet the following criteria for four consecutive software segments (a segment includes a passage and accompanying work in each zone).

97%

on Quick Check questions

97%

on Assessment activities

97%

on Assessment activities

96%

on Context Passage

Manually Adjusting Software Levels

At times, you may wish to adjust a student's *READ 180* level based on your observations. Use data from *READ 180* Topic Software reports and the student's classroom performance to determine appropriate student software levels. Consider adjusting a student's Software level when you encounter the following:

- **Students in Level 1**
  Level 1 students use the Topic Software sequentially to cover the complete scope and sequence of phonics skills and word patterns. Since teachers know best when students have mastered these skills, Level 1 students must be promoted manually.

- **Students Who Progress Quickly Through the Software**
  Students should complete a Topic Software segment in 4 to 15 sessions, or school days. If a student is completing segments in less than 3 sessions and is scoring well on software assessments in all zones, consider raising the student's level.

- **Students Who Get "Stuck"**
  Students who spend more than four weeks completing a Topic Software segment may need to be placed at a lower level.

When manually adjusting software levels, the level promotion will not take effect until the student begins the next software segment. Once a student is promoted to a new software level, the student will have access to all 15 software topics at the new level.

Differentiating Instruction With Modeled and Independent Reading

In addition to placing students appropriately in the *READ 180* Software, *SRI* results are used to match readers with appropriate texts in Modeled and Independent Reading.

The *READ 180* Paperback library contains multiple books at each *READ 180* level, written to appropriate levels of readability. These titles span a wide range of genres to appeal to a variety of readers.

Tailor the Modeled and Independent Reading Rotation to meet individual student needs by assisting students in selecting books and eReads at their reading level and interest. Then, vary the level of scaffolding and support you provide based on the text complexity. For example, provide more opportunities for book conferences and completion of written scaffolding such as graphic organizers and QuickWrites when students are reading more complex texts.

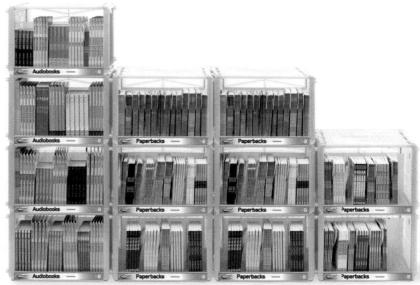

Differentiating Small-Group Instruction

Effective differentiated instruction is based on student performance results. *READ 180* provides support and scaffolding for dynamic and flexible grouping to allow for differentiated instruction within each *rBook* Workshop.

rBook Grouping and Differentiating

Use the Workshop Planning Guide in the *rBook Teacher's Edition* to determine when to regroup students throughout a Workshop. Use the Teacher Dashboard to access student grouping recommendations based on performance results and review targeted instruction recommendations to address student needs.

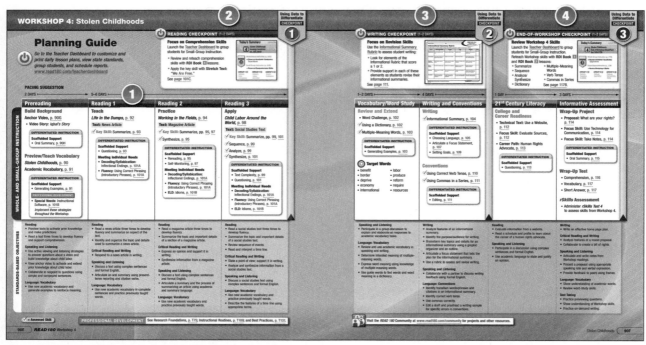

rBook Teacher's Edition: **Sample Planning Guide**

① *rBook* Groups

Throughout each *rBook* Workshop, group students based on reading level. Provide differentiated instruction through daily Boost and Stretch activities designed to provide targeted support.

② Reading CheckPoint Groups

After completing the final reading in each Workshop, regroup students based on comprehension skill performance. Deliver lessons from *Resources for Differentiated Instruction* designed to stretch students with more rigorous texts or reteach key comprehension skills.

③ Writing CheckPoint Groups

After completing the writing process in each Workshop, group students based on reading level or writing skill support needed. Allow students to revise writing based on rubric results.

④ End-of-Workshop CheckPoint Groups

After completing each Workshop and administering the *rSkills Test*, regroup students based on Workshop skill support needed. Deliver lessons from *Resources for Differentiated Instruction* designed to reteach key Workshop skills.

Navigating the Teacher Dashboard Class Page

The Teacher Dashboard streamlines and simplifies the process of differentiating instruction during Small-Group Instruction. At various points within each Workshop, the Groupinator creates three dynamic groups based on student performance data and provides recommendations for strategic instruction tailored to address identified student needs.

Detailed information for each class is available on the Class Page of the Teacher Dashboard. Click on the **Go to Class** button on the Home Page to navigate to the Class Page.

Teacher Dashboard: Class Page

1 Data Snapshots

At-a-glance views of class performance help drive instructional planning and pacing. Review data from the last week, the last four weeks, or the entire year when planning instruction.

2 Today's Summary

Whole- and Small-Group Instruction overviews provide a summary of the day's instruction. The summary links directly to the Interactive Teaching System (ITS). Click on the left or right arrows to advance through the Workshop.

3 The Groupinator

Dynamic and flexible groups are created throughout an *rBook* Workshop, including *rBook* groups and groups for the Reading, Writing, and End-of-Workshop CheckPoints. Review and adjust groups and link directly to accompanying lessons on the ITS.

Grouping for Daily *rBook* Instruction

The *READ 180 rBook* provides comprehensive daily reading, vocabulary, and writing instruction. During each *rBook* lesson, students are placed into three distinct groups for Small-Group Instruction. These groups are based on common areas of instructional focus, which allows for targeted instruction to address specific areas of need.

Using the Groupinator™ to Manage Groups

The Groupinator on the Teacher Dashboard places students into three *rBook* groups based on *SRI* results. Three equal groups are organized by student Lexile. Review *rBook* groups on the Class Page of the Teacher Dashboard.

Groupinator: *rBook* Groups

1 **Adjust Groups**

To move students into a different group in the Groupinator, click on the student's name and drag to a new group.

2 **Refresh Groups**

Student reading levels will change throughout the year as students make reading gains. Click **Refresh Groups** each time your class completes an *SRI* test. The Groupinator will regroup students based on current *SRI* results.

3 **Clear Groups**

To group students using data other than *SRI* results, click **Clear Groups**. All student names will be placed into the ungrouped pool. Click and drag student names into groups.

4 **Save**

Once groups are final, click **Save**. The Groupinator will retain these *rBook* groups until you adjust groups and click **Save** again.

Using Data to Adjust Groups

As students complete additional *SRI* tests, use the Groupinator to regroup students based on students' current reading levels. Click on **Refresh Groups** to automatically regroup students based on the most recent *SRI* results.

You may also choose to incorporate other student data into your grouping decisions. Data from the following reports may help inform grouping decisions:

- *READ 180* Comprehension Skills Report (See page 140.)
- *READ 180* Phonics and Word Study Grouping Report (See page 148.)
- *rSkills Tests* Grading Report (See page 174.)

Providing Appropriate Small-Group Instructional Support

Each *rBook* Small-Group lesson includes opportunities to provide varied supports to meet the needs of a variety of learners. Daily Boost and Stretch activities provide differentiated instruction that targets individual student needs. Use Boost activities with students who need additional scaffolding beyond what is provided in the *rBook Teacher's Edition.* Use Stretch activities with students who are ready for more independent practice of the skills taught in the Workshop. Use the chart below to determine which students would benefit from each type of support.

Stage	Boost	Standard Lesson	Stretch
Stage A	BR–400L	401–600L	601L+
Stage B	BR–600L	601–800L	801L+
Stage C	BR–800L	801–1100L	1100L+

Use the Groupinator to Target Support

1. Click **Save** to finalize *rBook* groups on the Groupinator.

2. Determine which group(s) would benefit from Boost or Stretch activities.

3. Click on the **Lesson Plan** link in Today's Summary to review the Scaffolded Support Boost and Stretch recommendations for the Small-Group lesson.

4. Assign each group the appropriate support in the Lesson Plan. **Print** or **Save** the lesson plan.

Teacher Dashboard: Lesson Plan

Grouping at *rBook* Reading CheckPoints

Each *rBook* Workshop includes three CheckPoints in which teachers take time to regroup students for targeted differentiated instruction. The first CheckPoint of each Workshop appears after students have completed the last reading in each Workshop and is called the Reading CheckPoint.

Understanding Reading CheckPoint Groups

At each Reading CheckPoint, the Groupinator on the Teacher Dashboard places students into three equal groups based on comprehension skills results from the *READ 180* Topic Software. Students are grouped based on common areas of need, and each group is assigned a comprehension skill focus.

As students progress through the *READ 180* Software, you can use the Groupinator to group students based on students' current comprehension results. Click on **Refresh Groups** in the Groupinator to automatically regroup students based on the most recent *READ 180* Software results.

(1) Stretch Groups

Students with strong overall comprehension skill results on the Software may be placed into a **Stretch** group. Students in a Stretch group are assigned a more rigorous text with more independent practice.

(2) Reteach Groups

Students whose software results indicate they need additional support with comprehension skills will be placed into a **Reteach** group. Students in a Reteach group are assigned a scaffolded text and receive more support during Small-Group Instruction.

Teacher Dashboard: Reading CheckPoint Groups

The Groupinator Algorithm

The Groupinator's algorithm creates Reading CheckPoint groups. The algorithm factors a student's current reading level and comprehension skill performance to determine placement within a Stretch or Reteach group. Once each group type has been determined, a comprehension skill focus is assigned to each group. The total number of Stretch or Reteach groups in each class will vary based on students' current comprehension skills performance.

Using the Groupinator to Manage Reading CheckPoint Groups

The Groupinator on the Teacher Dashboard places students into three equal Reading CheckPoint groups based on software results from the *READ 180* Comprehension Skills Grouping Report and targets a specific skill for each group. Review groups on the Class Page of the Teacher Dashboard.

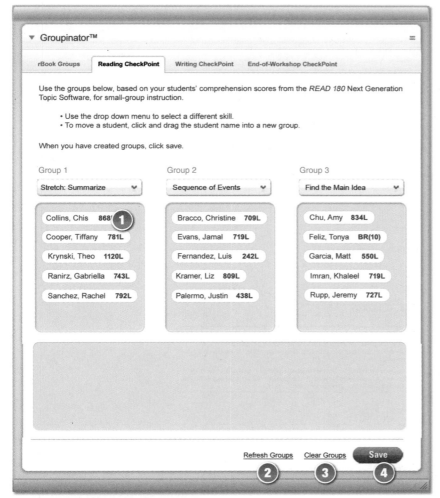

Groupinator: Reading CheckPoint Groups

1 **Adjust Groups**

To move students into a different group in the **Groupinator**, click on the student's name and drag to a new group.

2 **Refresh Groups**

The Groupinator recalculates grouping results each week based on current software progress. Click **Refresh Groups** to review groups based on current progress.

3 **Clear Groups**

To group students using data other than software comprehension results, click **Clear Groups**. All students will be placed into the ungrouped pool. Click and drag student names into each group.

4 **Save**

Once groups are final, click **Save**. The Groupinator will retain Reading CheckPoint groups assigned to each *rBook* Workshop.

Adjusting Reading CheckPoint Groups

The Groupinator recommends Reading CheckPoint groups based on comprehension performance. These groups allow you to differentiate instruction by strategically targeting comprehension skills during Small-Group Instruction.

If you wish to make grouping adjustments on the Groupinator, the *READ 180* Comprehension Skills Report provides a comprehensive summary of results for each comprehension skill assessed on the *READ 180* Topic Software. Use results from this report if making Reading CheckPoint grouping adjustments.

Reviewing CheckPoint Groups

1. Review recommended Reading CheckPoint Groups on the Groupinator.

2. Determine if any students need to be regrouped.

3. Schedule the *READ 180* Comprehension Skills Report to be sent to your e-mail inbox.

4. Review performance on specific comprehension skills when finalizing grouping decisions.

5. If regrouping solely on the current *rBook* Workshop skill, consider specific student performance on that skill, as well as overall performance in reading comprehension.

6. Consider any other relevant data, such as class performance, *rBook* work, and *SRI* results.

7. Once Reading CheckPoint groups have been finalized, click **Save** on the Groupinator. Groups for each Reading CheckPoint will be archived.

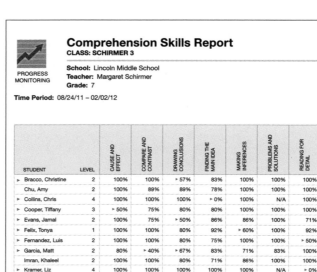

Comprehension Skills Report
CLASS: SCHIRMER 3

PROGRESS MONITORING

School: Lincoln Middle School
Teacher: Margaret Schirmer
Grade: 7

Time Period: 08/24/11 – 02/02/12

STUDENT	LEVEL	CAUSE AND EFFECT	COMPARE AND CONTRAST	DRAWING CONCLUSIONS	FINDING THE MAIN IDEA	MAKING INFERENCES	PROBLEMS AND SOLUTIONS	READING FOR DETAIL	SEQUENCING	SUMMARIZING	TOTAL NUMBER OF SKILLS BELOW 70%
▸ Bracco, Christine	2	100%	100%	▸57%	83%	100%	100%	100%	▸43%	86%	2
Chu, Amy	2	100%	89%	89%	78%	100%	100%	100%	100%	100%	0
▸ Collins, Chris	4	100%	100%	100%	▸0%	100%	N/A	100%	▸50%	100%	2
▸ Cooper, Tiffany	3	▸50%	75%	80%	80%	100%	100%	100%	▸50%	100%	2
▸ Evans, Jamal	2	100%	75%	▸50%	86%	86%	100%	71%	▸57%	100%	2
▸ Felix, Tonya	1	100%	100%	80%	92%	▸60%	100%	92%	100%	91%	1
▸ Fernandez, Luis	2	100%	100%	80%	75%	100%	100%	▸50%	▸0%	▸50%	3
▸ Garcia, Matt	2	80%	▸40%	▸67%	83%	71%	83%	100%	80%	86%	2
Imran, Khaleel	2	100%	100%	80%	71%	86%	100%	100%	75%	86%	0
▸ Kramer, Liz	4	100%	100%	100%	100%	100%	N/A	▸0%	▸0%	▸0%	3
Krynski, Theo	4	100%	100%	100%	100%	100%	100%	100%	100%	75%	0
Palermo, Justin	1	100%	75%	80%	86%	80%	100%	100%	75%	100%	0
▸ Ramirez, Gabriella	3	100%	100%	100%	▸50%	100%	100%	100%	▸67%	▸50%	3
▸ Rupp, Jeremy	3	100%	▸0%	100%	75%	▸0%	100%	100%	N/A	▸50%	3
▸ Sanchez, Rachel	3	88%	▸50%	75%	86%	88%	100%	88%	88%	▸63%	2
TOTAL NO. OF STUDENTS BELOW 70%		1	3	3	2	2	0	3	7	4	25

▸ Indicates score below 70%

Using This Report

Purpose: Students whose names are marked with red flags have comprehension scores of less than 70%. Scan each row for problems with specific skills.

Follow-Up: Plan instructional time targeting specific comprehension skills for small groups. Identify skills for which a large number of students need additional support, and plan Whole-Group Instruction.

READ 180 Comprehension Skills Report

Differentiating Small-Group Instruction at Reading CheckPoints

Each Reading CheckPoint provides an opportunity to deliver targeted reading comprehension lessons to meet the needs of a variety of learners. **Stretch** groups provide opportunities for students with strong performance results to apply the current Workshop skill to an authentic and rigorous text focused on the Workshop theme. **Reteach** groups provide opportunities for students struggling with comprehension to receive additional support targeted to address their specific comprehension challenges.

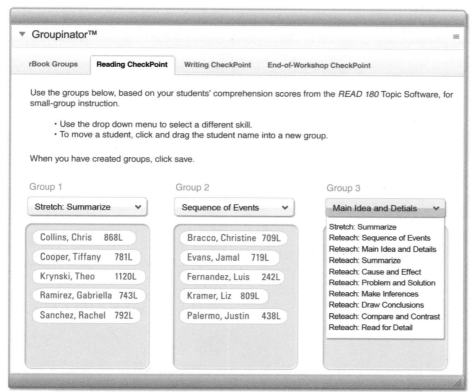

Groupinator: Reading CheckPoint Groups

Assigning Lessons

1. Finalize Reading CheckPoint groups on the Groupinator.

2. Review skills assigned to each group. Adjust if necessary by choosing a different skill from the drop-down menu.

3. Click **Save** to archive results for the current Workshop.

4. Review Small-Group lessons from Today's Summary on the Home Page or Class Page of the Teacher Dashboard.

5. Click on each of the recommended lessons to access the accompanying lesson plan from the *Resources for Differentiated Instruction* on the Interactive Teaching System (ITS).

6. Print and prepare lessons.

Data in Action

Tracking Lesson Assignment Students will be assigned different comprehension skill lessons at each Reading CheckPoint. Track which lessons you have taught to each student by downloading the RDI Lesson Tracker from SAM Resources (**SAM Keyword:** RDI Tracking).

Grouping at *rBook* Writing CheckPoints

Each *rBook* Workshop includes three CheckPoints in which teachers take time to regroup students for targeted differentiated instruction. The second CheckPoint of each Workshop appears after students have completed the writing process and is called the Writing CheckPoint.

Using the Teacher Dashboard to Manage Groups

The Teacher Dashboard Groupinator allows you to arrange students into three groups based on their reading levels or area of writing focus. To group by reading level, maintain *rBook* groups. To group by area of writing focus, review final drafts of student writing to determine common areas of need. Populate the groups in the Groupinator and click **Save.**

1 Adjust Groups

To move students into a group in the Groupinator, click on a student's name and drag to the selected group.

2 Clear Groups

If you wish to begin the grouping process again, click **Clear Groups** to move all student names into the ungrouped pool. Then click and drag student names into groups.

3 Save

Once groups are finalized, click **Save**. The Groupinator will retain the Writing CheckPoint groupings assigned for each Workshop.

Teacher Dashboard Groupinator: Writing CheckPoint

Understanding Writing CheckPoint Grouping

Once students complete their draft of the *rBook* Workshop writing, access the accompanying writing rubric from the ITS or SAM Resources. Use the rubric to assess each student's writing. Once all student work has been assessed, review the rubric results with students and allow them to revise their writing during Small-Group Instruction.

Accessing Writing Results

1. Access the writing rubric for the current *rBook* Workshop from the ITS or SAM Resources.

2. Use the rubric to assess each student's writing.

3. Once all student work has been assessed, review the rubric results to identify common areas of writing support needed.

4. Maintain current *rBook* groups or regroup based on common areas where rubric scores were low.

Sample *rBook* Writing Rubric

Determining Small-Group Lessons

Once you have created three small groups, determine the appropriate Small-Group lesson based on common area of writing need. Plan to spend one to two days providing differentiated support. If multiple students struggled with the same writing area, access corresponding writing skill builder lessons from *Resources for Differentiated Instruction* on the Interactive Teaching System (ITS), or from the Teacher Bookshelf.

Small-Group Writing Support

1. Share rubric results with students.

2. Allow students to revise writing based on rubric feedback.

3. If multiple students struggled with the same aspect of writing, access corresponding writing skill builder lessons from *Resources for Differentiated Instruction*. Assign appropriate lessons to each group.

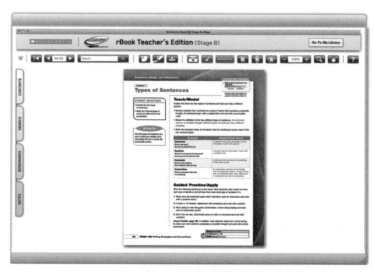

Resources for Differentiated Instruction on the **Interactive Teaching System (ITS)**

Grouping at *rBook* End-of-Workshop CheckPoints

Each *rBook* Workshop includes three CheckPoints in which teahers take time to regroup students for targeted differentiated instruction. The final CheckPoint of each workshop appears after students have completed the Workshop and the accompanying *rSkills Test* and is called the End-of-Workshop CheckPoint.

Understanding End-of-Workshop CheckPoint Groups

Students are grouped based on common areas of need, which are identified by their *rSkills Tests* results. These End-of-Workshop CheckPoint groups provide an opportunity to reteach *rBook* Workshop skills that students have not mastered.

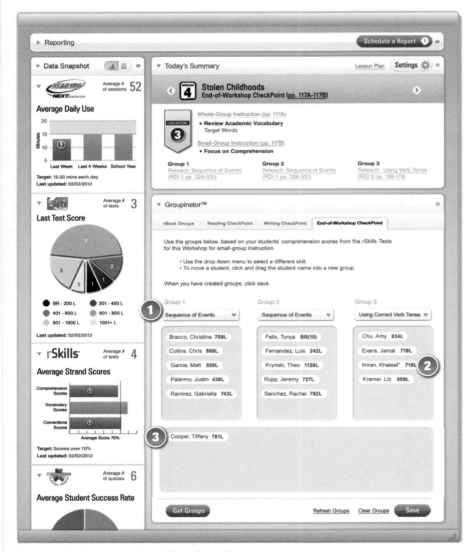

Groupinator: End-of-Workshop CheckPoint Groups

① Skill-Based Groups

Students who received low scores on comprehension, vocabulary/word study, or conventions questions are placed into a group for further instruction on the skills taught during the Workshop.

② Students with Project Assignment

Students who earn perfect scores are placed into a group to maintain three equal groups and are identified within the Groupinator. Assign an *rBook* project (available on the *READ 180* Community Website) for these students to complete independently during Small-Group Instruction while reteaching Workshop skills to the other students in the group.

③ Students with No Test Scores

Students who did not complete the *rSkills Test* on the current Workshop are not included in the three groups. Allow these students to complete the *rSkills Test*.

Using the Groupinator to Manage End-of-Workshop CheckPoint Groups

The Groupinator on the Teacher Dashboard places students into three equal groups at each End-of-Workshop CheckPoint based on *rSkills Test* results from the current Workshop. Students are grouped based on common areas of need, and each group is assigned a skill focus.

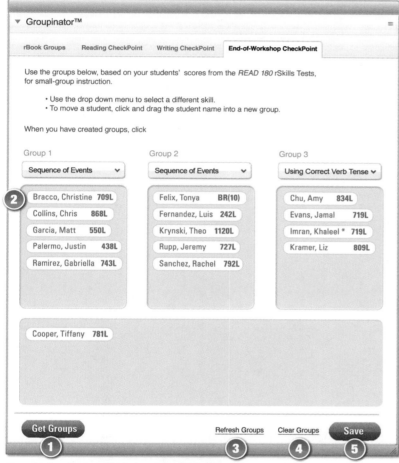

Groupinator: End-of-Workshop CheckPoint Groups

Within the Groupinator panel:

▼ Groupinator™

rBook Groups   Reading CheckPoint   Writing CheckPoint   **End-of-Workshop CheckPoint**

Use the groups below, based on your students' scores from the *READ 180* rSkills Tests, for small-group instruction.

- Use the drop down menu to select a different skill.
- To move a student, click and drag the student name into a new group.

When you have created groups, click

Group 1 — Sequence of Events

Bracco, Christine	709L
Collins, Chris	868L
Garcia, Matt	550L
Palermo, Justin	438L
Ramirez, Gabriella	743L

Group 2 — Sequence of Events

Felix, Tonya	BR(10)
Fernandez, Luis	242L
Krynski, Theo	1120L
Rupp, Jeremy	727L
Sanchez, Rachel	792L

Group 3 — Using Correct Verb Tense

Chu, Amy	834L
Evans, Jamal	719L
Imran, Khaleel *	719L
Kramer, Liz	809L

Cooper, Tiffany	781L

Get Groups   Refresh Groups   Clear Groups   Save

1 Get Groups

Once students have completed their *rSkills Test*, click **Get Groups** to have the Groupinator aggregate SAM results. Check back within an hour to access grouping results. For immediate grouping results, you can also run the *rSkills Test* Grouping Report and manually group students in the Groupinator.

2 Adjust Groups

To move students into a different group in the Groupinator, click on the student's name and drag to a new group.

3 Refresh Groups

Student results will change with each *rSkills Test*. The Groupinator calculates grouping results based on results from the test assigned for the current *rBook* Workshop. Click **Refresh Groups** to review groups based on most recent student results.

4 Clear Groups

To group students using data other than *rSkills Tests*, click **Clear Groups**. All student names will be placed into an ungrouped student pool. Click and drag student names into groups.

5 Save

Once groups are finalized, click **Save**. The Groupinator will retain the End-of-Workshop CheckPoint groups assigned for each *rBook* Workshop.

Adjusting End-of-Workshop CheckPoint Groups

The Groupinator provides targeted groups based on *rSkills Test* performance. These groups support differentiated instruction by strategically targeting and reteaching Workshop skills during Small-Group Instruction.

If you wish to make grouping adjustments on the Groupinator, the *rSkills Tests* Grading Report provides a comprehensive summary of student results for each skill assessed on the *rSkills Test*. Use results from this report when making grouping adjustments.

Steps for Adjusting Groups

1. Review recommended End-of-Workshop CheckPoint groups on the Groupinator.

2. Determine if any groups need to be adjusted.

3. Schedule the *rSkills Tests* Grading Report from SAM to be sent to your e-mail inbox.

4. Review performance on specific Workshop skills when finalizing grouping decisions.

5. Consider any other relevant data, such as *rBook* performance, *READ 180* Software progress, and *SRI* results.

6. Once End-of-Workshop CheckPoint groups have been finalized, click **Save** on the Groupinator. Group assignments for each End-of-Workshop CheckPoint will be archived.

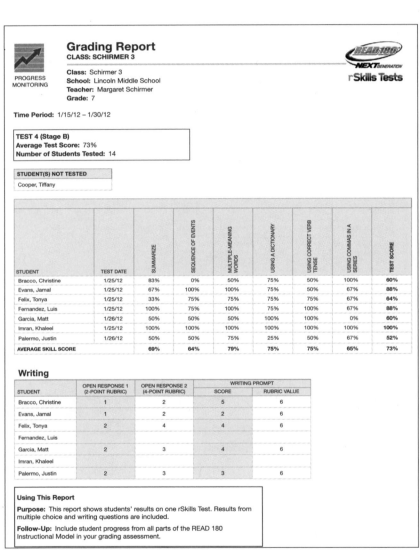

Grading Report
CLASS: SCHIRMER 3

PROGRESS MONITORING

Class: Schirmer 3
School: Lincoln Middle School
Teacher: Margaret Schirmer
Grade: 7

Time Period: 1/15/12 – 1/30/12

TEST 4 (Stage B)
Average Test Score: 73%
Number of Students Tested: 14

STUDENT(S) NOT TESTED
Cooper, Tiffany

STUDENT	TEST DATE	SUMMARIZE	SEQUENCE OF EVENTS	MULTIPLE-MEANING WORDS	USING A DICTIONARY	USING CORRECT VERB TENSE	USING COMMAS IN A SERIES	TEST SCORE
Bracco, Christine	1/25/12	83%	0%	50%	75%	50%	100%	60%
Evans, Jamal	1/25/12	67%	100%	100%	75%	50%	67%	88%
Felix, Tonya	1/25/12	33%	75%	75%	75%	75%	67%	64%
Fernandez, Luis	1/25/12	100%	75%	100%	75%	100%	67%	88%
Garcia, Matt	1/26/12	50%	50%	50%	100%	100%	0%	60%
Imran, Khaleel	1/25/12	100%	100%	100%	100%	100%	100%	100%
Palermo, Justin	1/26/12	50%	50%	75%	25%	50%	67%	52%
AVERAGE SKILL SCORE		**69%**	**64%**	**79%**	**75%**	**75%**	**65%**	**73%**

Writing

STUDENT	OPEN RESPONSE 1 (2-POINT RUBRIC)	OPEN RESPONSE 2 (4-POINT RUBRIC)	WRITING PROMPT	
			SCORE	RUBRIC VALUE
Bracco, Christine	1	2	5	6
Evans, Jamal	1	2	2	6
Felix, Tonya	2	4	4	6
Fernandez, Luis				
Garcia, Matt	2	3	4	6
Imran, Khaleel				
Palermo, Justin	2	3	3	6

Using This Report

Purpose: This report shows students' results on one rSkills Test. Results from multiple choice and writing questions are included.

Follow-Up: Include student progress from all parts of the READ 180 Instructional Model in your grading assessment.

rSkills Tests **Grading Report**

Differentiating Small-Group Instruction at End-of-Workshop CheckPoints

Each End-of-Workshop CheckPoint provides an opportunity to deliver additional instruction in the current *rBook* Workshop skills. Groups will be assigned a focused skill lesson on one of the three test strands—comprehension, vocabulary/word study, or conventions.

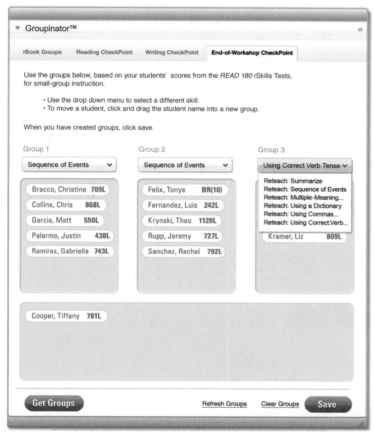

Groupinator: End-of-Workshop CheckPoint Groups

Assigning Lessons

1. Finalize End-of-Workshop CheckPoint groups on the Groupinator.
2. Review skills assigned to each group. Adjust if necessary by choosing a different Workshop skill from the drop-down menu.
3. Click **Save** to archive results for the current Workshop.
4. Review Small-Group lessons from Today's Summary on the Home Page or Class Page of the Teacher Dashboard.
5. Click on each of the recommended lessons to access the accompanying lesson plan from *Resources for Differentiated Instruction* on the Interactive Teaching System (ITS).
6. Print and prepare lessons.

Data in Action

Tracking Lesson Assignment Students will be assigned different skill lessons at each End-of-Workshop CheckPoint. Track which lessons you have taught to each student by downloading the RDI Lesson Tracker from SAM Resources (**SAM Keyword:** RDI Tracking).

Exiting *READ 180*

Most schools establish criteria to assess readiness to move beyond the *READ 180* classroom. Some promote students when they reach a certain performance level—for example, Proficient on *SRI*, Level 4—or when students can successfully read grade-level texts.

Students may also leave *READ 180* when they change schools or to make way for students with greater need. Following are recommendations for evaluating students' readiness to accelerate within *READ 180* or to exit *READ 180* and for support students who make the transition.

Pacing, Differentiating, and Accelerating

READ 180 students may have a wide range of skills and reading levels. As they respond to the program students make gains at their own rates. Some accelerate through the Topic Software but may take longer to increase their *SRI* Lexile scores. Others may be successful using the *rBook* during direct instruction but need more practice to transfer strategies they learned to independent reading or to other classes.

For students who enter *READ 180* reading far below grade level, multiple supports provide necessary scaffolding with developmentally appropriate reading tasks. As students begin making reading gains, *READ 180* offers opportunities to accelerate learning and practice applying reading skills to more complex texts. When students make reading gains and demonstrate success with more advanced content, they may be ready to exit *READ 180*.

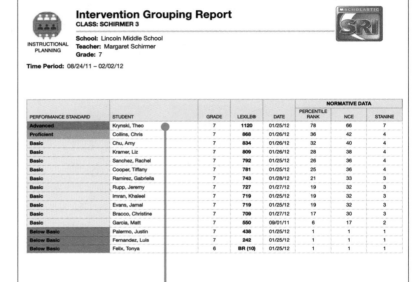

Intervention Grouping Report
CLASS: SCHIRMER 3

School: Lincoln Middle School
Teacher: Margaret Schirmer
Grade: 7

Time Period: 08/24/11 – 02/02/12

PERFORMANCE STANDARD	STUDENT	GRADE	LEXILE®	DATE	NORMATIVE DATA		
					PERCENTILE RANK	NCE	STANINE
Advanced	Krynski, Theo	7	1120	01/25/12	78	66	7
Proficient	Collins, Chris	7	868	01/26/12	36	42	4
Basic	Chu, Amy	7	834	01/26/12	32	40	4
Basic	Kramer, Liz	7	809	01/26/12	28	38	4
Basic	Sanchez, Rachel	7	792	01/25/12	26	36	4
Basic	Cooper, Tiffany	7	781	01/25/12	25	36	4
Basic	Ramirez, Gabriella	7	743	01/28/12	21	33	3
Basic	Rupp, Jeremy	7	727	01/27/12	19	32	3
Basic	Imran, Khaleel	7	719	01/25/12	19	32	3
Basic	Evans, Jamal	7	719	01/25/12	19	32	3
Basic	Bracco, Christine	7	709	01/27/12	17	30	3
Basic	Garcia, Matt	7	550	09/01/11	6	17	2
Below Basic	Palermo, Justin	7	438	01/25/12	1	1	1
Below Basic	Fernandez, Luis	7	242	01/25/12	1	1	1
Below Basic	Felix, Tonya	6	BR (10)	01/25/12	1	1	1

Students may be ready to exit *READ 180* when their *SRI* results indicate that they have reached grade-level proficiency

Using This Report
Purpose: This report groups students under the four SRI performance standards. The report is used to target for additional support students whose performance is Below Basic or Basic.

Follow-Up: Use the information on the report to set goals for students. Plan appropriate instructional support and intervention for students who are reading below grade level. Encourage students to read independently at their reading level.

SRI Intervention Grouping Report

Using Multiple Measures of Success

Multiple formal and informal measures can help determine a student's readiness to leave the *READ 180* program. Formal measures may include the following:

Data	Look For . . .	In The . . .
Lexile scores	Substantial growth	*SRI* Student Progress Report
SRI proficiency	Proficient or Advanced	*SRI* Student Progress Report
SRI normative	NCE, Percentile, or Stanine	*SRI* Student Action Report
Grade-level *rSkills Tests*	Passing scores on Level b tests	*rSkills Tests* Grading Report
Software results	High scores in comprehension and vocabulary	*READ 180* Student Diagnostic Report
Software completion	Multiple segments completed quickly and accurately	*READ 180* Completion Success Report
rBook completion	High scores on *rBook* work	*rBook* Workshop rubric (teacher-completed)
Oral fluency	Increase in performance	Oral fluency rubric (teacher-completed)

Informal measures may include:

- Observation of skill levels, motivation, attitude, and behavior
- *Scholastic Reading Counts!* quiz scores
- Number and level of books read or quizzes passed
- *rBook* writing samples and *rBook* projects
- Student self-evaluation

Supporting Students Beyond *READ 180*

When students leave *READ 180,* it is important to place them into supportive classrooms and monitor their progress as they encounter more difficult content and reading materials. To foster continued success after *READ 180,* encourage students to continue choosing books at the appropriate Lexile levels, especially for independent reading.

Assessment

Effective Assessment for Struggling Readers

Regularly monitoring assessment results ensures that all students are on track for success. Use results to monitor students' performance throughout the year, track response to intervention, identify individual strengths and challenges, and target instruction to meet each student's needs. This will ensure that all students are on track for success.

Types of Assessment

To gain a complete picture of what students understand and can do, it is important to consider results from multiple forms of assessment. The type of assessment to use at any given time depends on the assessment goals, such as evaluating overall reading growth or identifying particular focus skills for Small-Group Instruction.

Formal and informal assessments allow teachers to evaluate student reading progress and performance. Formal assessment usually involves testing in an effort to produce quantifiable data. Informal assessment includes daily appraisal of a student's progress. When used in tandem, formal and informal assessments provide a comprehensive picture of a student's skill mastery and inform instruction by helping to target areas of weakness.

Assessments in *READ 180*

READ 180 provides continuous assessment and immediate feedback for teachers and students. Formal and informal assessments in *READ 180* are powerful tools for initial screening, diagnostic placement, progress monitoring, and progress evaluation.

Assessment data is fed into the Scholastic Achievement Manager (SAM), which continuously gathers data and tracks learning gains for each student. These results are detailed in a variety of reports generated by SAM. Results are also captured on Student Dashboard, Teacher Dashboard, and Leadership Dashboard.

There are four main types of assessment in *READ 180*:
1. **Screening and Placement**
2. **Progress Monitoring**
3. **Curriculum-Embedded**
4. **Summative**

This section provides an overview of the core assessments included in *READ 180*—what they are, when to use them, what they assess, and how to use the results to plan instruction.

Continuous Assessment

READ 180 includes assessments to help inform instruction and track performance in each area of the Instructional Model.

Beginning of Year	During the Year	End of Year
Screening and Placement	**Progress Monitoring, Curriculum-Embedded, Summative**	**Progress Monitoring, Summative**
• *Scholastic Reading Inventory (SRI)*	• *Scholastic Reading Inventory (SRI)* • *READ 180* Topic Software • *rSkills Tests* • *Scholastic Reading Counts! (SRC!)* • *rBook* • *rSkills Summative Tests* • Oral Fluency Assessment	• *Scholastic Reading Inventory (SRI)* • *rSkills Summative Tests* • Oral Fluency Assessment

Scholastic Reading Inventory This assessment uses the Lexile Framework as a screening and diagnostic tool to place students appropriately. *SRI* provides criterion- and norm-referenced comprehension test results for instructional planning, intervention, and progress monitoring.

***READ 180* Topic Software** Each day, students access leveled reading passages that include varying levels of computer support. Students complete work in five zones of the Software. Assessments are embedded in each zone. Results can be used for diagnostic, instructional planning, intervention, and progress monitoring.

rSkills Tests Administer *rSkills Tests* at the end of each *rBook* Workshop, to monitor student performance and understanding of key standards-aligned skills taught during Whole-Group and Small-Group Instruction. Data can be used for intervention, instructional planning, and progress monitoring.

Scholastic Reading Counts! Through computerized quizzes, *Scholastic Reading Counts!* provides information to help monitor student comprehension of books and eReads completed during the Modeled and Independent Reading Rotation. Data can be used for intervention, motivation, and progress monitoring.

rBook Students complete daily instructional tasks, such as reading comprehension, vocabulary and word study, writing, and Wrap-Up Projects in their *rBooks*. Use rubric results to monitor understanding of Whole-Group and Small-Group lessons and pace instruction accordingly.

Oral Fluency Assessments Oral Fluency Assessments may be administered three times a year to monitor student decoding and fluency. Data can be used for intervention, instructional planning, and progress monitoring.

Assessments in *READ 180*

READ 180 includes a variety of assessments designed to inform instruction, monitor progress, and provide continuous diagnosis.

	Assessment Tool	Purpose	What It Assesses	Frequency
SCREENING & PLACEMENT	*Scholastic Reading Inventory (SRI)*	• Screen students for appropriate intervention • Place students appropriately	• Baseline reading level • Placement within *READ 180*	**Once a year**
PROGRESS MONITORING	*Scholastic Reading Inventory (SRI)*	• Monitor student reading progress • Place students appropriately	• Current reading level • Reading gains	**2 times a year** (in addition to initial screening)
	rSkills Tests	• Measure acquisition of *rBook* Workshop skills • Group students for additional support	• Comprehension • Critical reading • Vocabulary/ Word Study • Writing • Conventions	**9 times a year** At the end of each *rBook* Workshop
	Oral Fluency Assessment	Monitor decoding and oral fluency progress	• Word recognition • Decoding speed and accuracy • Oral expressiveness	**3 times a year**
CURRICULUM-EMBEDDED	*READ 180* **Topic Software**	• Monitor student progress • Diagnose reading strengths and challenges • Group students for targeted instruction	• Comprehension • Phonics • Vocabulary • Spelling/ Encoding • Fluency • Writing	**Daily** During Instructional Software Rotation
	Scholastic Reading Counts!	• Assess reading comprehension • Track independent reading progress	• Reading comprehension	When students complete books and eReads in Modeled and Independent Reading
	rBook	• Track mastery of *rBook* Workshop skills • Provide targeted instruction and instructional support	• Comprehension • Conventions • Vocabulary/ Word Study • Critical Reading • Writing	**Daily** Throughout each *rBook* Workshop
SUMMATIVE	*Scholastic Reading Inventory (SRI)*	• Monitor student reading progress • Place students appropriately	• Current reading level • Reading gains	**Once a year** (In addition to screening and progress monitoring)
	rSkills Summative Tests	Measure curriculum mastery	• Comprehension • Critical reading • Vocabulary • Listening • Conventions • Writing	**Midyear End-of-year**

Results	Diagnostic and Intervention Planning
Normative Data NCE, Stanine, Percentile **Performance Standards** Below Basic, Basic, Proficient, Advanced	**IF students are reading at grade level…** …use grade-level curriculum. **IF students are reading below grade level…** …begin *READ 180* at the designated level.
Normative Data NCE, Stanine, Percentile **Performance Standards** Below Basic, Basic, Proficient, Advanced	**Use results to…** …group students with similar Lexile levels for Small-Group rotations. …assign appropriate instructional and independent reading materials.
Test Results Comprehension, Vocabulary, Word Study, Conventions, Open Response: Critical Thinking, Writing Prompt	**IF students need further support/challenge…** … review *READ 180* Reports to cross-reference results. …regroup students and provide targeted support during Small-Group rotations.
Oral Fluency Results Percentile based on WCPM (Words Correct Per Minute)	**IF students need further support…** …provide phonics or fluency support from *Resources for Differentiated Instruction* at *rBook* CheckPoints
Comprehension Results Reading for Detail, Sequencing, Finding the Main Idea, Summarizing, Cause and Effect, Compare and Contrast, Problem and Solution, Making Inferences, Drawing Conclusions **Other Results** Phonics, Spelling, Fluency, Writing, Time On-Task	**IF students need further support…** …regroup students to provide targeted support during Small-Group rotations. …monitor software usage. **IF students need challenge…** …provide opportunities to apply skills with less scaffolding. …ensure appropriate software level.
Quizzes passed Number of quizzes attempted Percentage of goal achieved	**IF students are not meeting individual goals…** …provide additional support in daily independent reading
Writing Rubric Results Results align to writing type assessed **Wrap-Up Project Rubric Results** Results align to project type assessed **Workshop Rubric Results** Progress and performance on *rBook* tasks	**USE writing rubric results to…** …provide support in revision during each Writing CheckPoint **USE Wrap-Up Project rubric results to…** …provide feedback on project performance and track progress **USE Workshop rubric results to…** …monitor overall performance and share results with students
Normative Data NCE, Stanine, Percentile **Performance Standards** Below Basic, Basic, Proficient, Advanced	**IF students are reading at grade level…** …use grade-level curriculum. **IF students are reading below grade level…** …begin *READ 180* at the designated level.
Test Results Comprehension, Vocabulary, Word Study, Conventions, Open Response: Critical Thinking, Writing Prompt	**IF students need further support/challenge…** … review *READ 180* Reports to cross-reference results. …provide targeted support during Small-Group rotations.

Using *SRI* for Progress Monitoring

READ 180 begins with a screening and placement assessment called the *SRI* that provides results to identify intervention needs and place students in the appropriate *READ 180* level. Through appropriate screening and placement, students build skills and practice reading with texts that match their individual reading levels.

Use *SRI* to screen and place students in *READ 180,* monitor reading growth throughout the year, plan differentiated instruction to meet changing needs, and match readers to appropriately leveled texts.

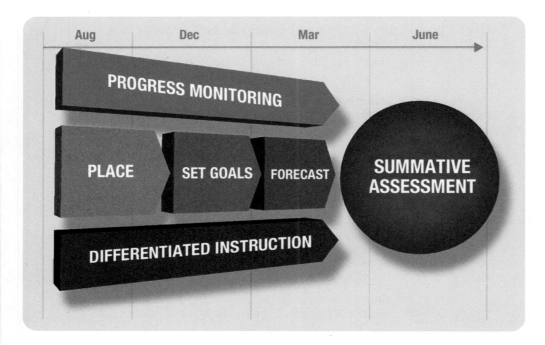

What *SRI* Measures

Reporting on a developmental scale, *SRI* supports universal screening for all instructional levels. *SRI* measures a reader's ability to comprehend narrative and expository texts of increasing difficulty. *SRI* results help locate a reader's comprehension level on the Lexile Framework, which measures readers and texts using the same scale. Once a reader's comprehension level is measured, it is possible to forecast how well the reader will comprehend reading materials that have also been measured with the Lexile Framework. Use results to establish growth goals and track progress over time as additional *SRI* tests are administered to students.

Establishing an *SRI* Testing Cycle

SRI can be administered at any time within the school year. The test is untimed. Typically, students take 20–30 minutes to complete the test. Most classrooms choose to administer the *SRI* during the Instructional Software rotation. Alternately, schools with a computer lab may utilize the lab to administer the *SRI* to the entire class simultaneously. If students do not complete the test by the end of the rotation, they may exit out of the software and resume the test the next day.

It is recommended that *READ 180* students take the *SRI* four times each year, with each test administration at least 30 days apart. Spacing the assessments in this way allows time between tests for students to make gains through instruction and practice and for teachers to make informed instructional decisions.

It is typical to front-load the *SRI* test by administering two tests in the fall, followed by one test in the winter and a final summative test in the spring. In this way teachers and administrators can ensure a reliable fall score for determining instructional plans and appropriate placement within the program. Subsequent *SRI* administrations are completed to monitor reading growth.

Sample *SRI* Testing Administration Cycle

The chart below provides a sample of an annual *SRI* testing cycle.

Test	Time of Year	Purpose
1	First three weeks of instruction	Determine initial placement
2	Fall	Establish goals
3	Winter	Forecast annual growth
4	Spring	Summative assessment

Establishing *SRI* Testing Windows

In addition to establishing the total number of *SRI* administrations for a school year, schools and districts often establish testing "windows"—specific periods of time to administer each round of *SRI* testing. Establishing a range of testing dates for each *SRI* administration enables teachers and students to prepare for an optimal testing experience and address any challenges that may occur with the testing experience.

Establishing school- or district-wide testing windows also ensures that accurate growth comparisons can be made. Many schools and districts establish common testing windows of two to four weeks.

Understanding *SRI* Growth Targets

As students develop stronger comprehension skills, their reading growth is reflected in their *SRI* results. When readers are young or just learning to read, their growth rate will be higher. As they become fluent, the rate of growth decreases. For example, when you were learning to read, you likely made large gains in reading comprehension initially. Now that you are a fluent reader, your gains are likely very small.

Understanding *SRI* Growth Expectations

Determining appropriate growth expectations depends on the student's grade level and current Lexile score. The expected growth rate chart below is based on students whose results indicate that they are reading at the 25th percentile.

Grade	Average Annual Lexile Growth (Based on Students at the 25th Percentile)[1]
3–5	140L
6–8	70L
9–11	50L

When implemented with fidelity, *READ 180* students often achieve more than one year's reading growth. Students with lower initial Lexile scores may take longer to reach proficiency. Compare students' initial Lexile and grade-level growth expectations to determine how much growth is needed and the length of time it may take for students to reach proficiency.

Setting Individual Growth Targets

Students who understand established *SRI* growth targets are more likely to be motivated to do whatever it takes to succeed. Use individual student *SRI* reports, performance standard information, and *rBook* Student Logs to discuss growth with students.

DATA STORY

Student: Andy Sullivan
Grade: 4
Initial Lexile: 589L
Performance Standard: Basic
Final Lexile: 907L
Performance Standard: Advanced

Andy began the year with a Lexile in the Basic range. His teacher helped him set and track his goals, and also encouraged him to complete eReads articles to stretch his comprehension. By the end of the year, Andy moved to the Advanced performance standard and is eligible to exit READ 180.

DATA STORY

Student: Lydia Gonzalez
Grade: 10
Initial Lexile: 640L
Performance Standard: Below Basic
Final Lexile: 740L
Performance Standard: Basic

Lydia began the year with a Lexile in the Below Basic range. Her teacher helped her set a goal to move up one performance standard by the end of the year. By tracking her growth and providing additional support during Modeled and Independent Reading, Lydia moved to the Basic performance standard by the end of the year.

SRI Growth Case Study: What Growth Should I Expect?

Review the case study below to learn how to set and track student *SRI* growth expectations. Use these steps when communicating growth targets to your students.

1. **Administer an initial *SRI* test.** Chris completed his initial *SRI* test and scored a 784L.

2. **Use *SRI* test results to determine performance standard.** The *SRI* Intervention Grouping Report reveals that Chris falls within the Basic Performance Standard for 7th grade.

DATA STORY

Student: Chris Collins
Grade: 7
Initial Lexile: 784L
Performance Standard: Basic

3. **Identify Lexile needed to reach a higher performance standard by next school year.** Review of the Performance Bands and Lexile Correlation chart on **page 24** indicates that to reach Proficient, an 8th grader would need a fall Lexile of 900L. To achieve this Proficient performance standard by the fall of 8th grade, Chris needs to score at least a 900L on his spring test.

4. **Review average annual Lexile growth for current grade level to set growth expectations.** Based on his initial *SRI* results, Chris would need a Lexile gain of 116L to reach the Proficient performance standard by the fall of 8th grade. The chart on **page 62** indicates that the average expected Lexile growth for a student in 7th grade is 70L. Since many *READ 180* students achieve more than one year's *SRI* growth during a school year, a Lexile gain of 116L is achievable.

5. **Communicate growth expectations to students.** In a conference with Chris, help him understand his growth goal of 116L. Use the *SRI* Student Log in the *rBook*, as well as the *SRI* Student Progress Report or SRI Read for Life Report to help Chris track his initial results and subsequent growth. Tailor resources and instruction to help Chris stretch his reading fluency by offering eReads, Stretch texts, and appropriately leveled books.

6. **Monitor growth throughout the year and provide guidance and support.** Use the *SRI* Student Log in the *rBook* to help Chris set growth goals from one *SRI* test to the next, making his annual growth goal more achievable. Track and celebrate growth after each test, and adjust the end-of-year growth goal if necessary, depending on test results throughout the year.

1 In July 2008, *SRI* fall-to-spring growth expectations were recalculated based on seven years of student data from a large urban school district in South Florida. In the data set, each grade level grouping included all pre- and posttest *SRI* scores collected for that grade over the seven years studied. Expected growth on *SRI* was calculated based on students reading at the 25th percentile. A total of 82,954 students were included in the sample.

How *SRI* Results Are Reported

Teachers administer *SRI* tests throughout the school year to monitor student progress. Results can be compared against the original (norm) group that took the test. SAM Reports for individual students, classes, schools, or districts display *SRI* results with the following metrics:

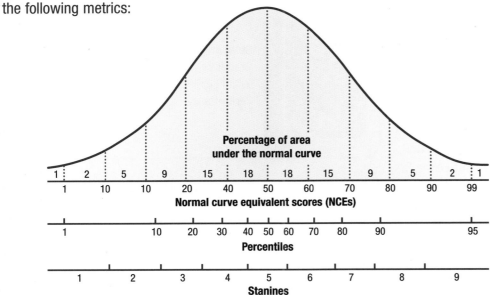

Percentile Rank A student's percentile rank is a score that tells the percent of students in a particular group that received lower scores on a test than the student did. It shows the student's relative position, or rank, in a group of students who are in the same grade. For example, if a student scores at the 65th percentile, it means that the student performed as well or better than 65% of the norm group.

Stanine A stanine is a standardized score ranging from 1 to 9. Unlike percentile rank, stanine scores are equally distributed across the entire bell curve for all grade levels. Stanines represent a range of scores. Stanines 1–3 are considered below average, stanines of 4–6 are considered average, and stanines of 7–9 are considered above average. Like percentiles, stanines indicate a student's standing in comparison with the norm group.

Normal Curve Equivalent (NCE) The NCE is a way of measuring where a student falls along a normal bell curve. NCE's range from 1 to 99. If a student was to make exactly one year of progress after one year of instruction, his NCE score would remain the same and his NCE gain would be zero, even though his Lexile would increase. Students who make more than a year's progress will have made a larger gain, resulting in a larger NCE score.

Grade Level The grade level indicates how close to grade-level proficiency a student's reading level is, based on his Lexile and associated grade-level Lexile range. Grade level equivalencies range from Far Below Grade Level to Far Above Grade Level.

Performance Standard A performance standard associates a student's Lexile with one of four performance standards: Below Basic, Basic, Proficient, and Advanced. These performance standards include a range of Lexile scores which vary by grade level.

Variations in *SRI* Results

It is expected that over the course of the year, students' Lexile scores will increase, with most students who fully participate in *READ 180* averaging between one and two year's reading growth. Declines in scores between administrations of *SRI* may be based on a variety of factors.

External Factors

- The student's state of mind at the time of testing can affect the test score. The student may be tired, hungry, or distracted during an administration, which can impact performance.
- The testing environment may not be conducive for the student. If the classroom environment is noisy or the student feels pressured to complete the test within a set time period, the environment may impact performance.

Internal Factors

- Targeting a *READ 180* student's initial reading level as Below Grade Level or Far Below Grade Level in SAM enables the test to set initial questions at the appropriate reading level. If a student is significantly below the 50th percentile and is not targeted, it may take longer than one test administration for the *SRI* to adapt the difficulty of the questions to the students' appropriate level.
- Since *SRI* is adaptive, retesting the student too often diminishes the accuracy of the *SRI* score. Retaking *SRI* several times in rapid succession will continue to reduce the possible Lexile gains that a test may reflect, since the gain from item to item gets smaller and smaller with each test within the 30-day window. Severe over-testing can lead to miniscule maximum gains between items, which means that a student's final score could be the same from test to test, regardless of increased performance.

Reviewing *SRI* Score Variations

When a student's *SRI* score...	This may be due to...	Scholastic recommends...
...shows a slight decline or flatlines.	...the test adapting to a student's true reading level.	...reviewing the test score in context of the student's overall *SRI* performance. ...waiting for the next *SRI* testing window to administer another test.
...shows a decline on the second *SRI* test.	...not appropriately targeting the initial *SRI* test.	...removing the initial *SRI* test score using the Delete test function in the *SRI* Settings in SAM Roster. ...using the 2nd *SRI* score as the fall benchmark.
...shows a decline of more than 60 Lexile points and the tests have been administered at least 30 days apart.	...external factors affecting a student's test experience.	...removing the initial *SRI* test score using the Delete test function in the *SRI* Settings in SAM Roster. ...retesting the student within the established testing window.
...shows a decline of more than 60 Lexile points and the tests have been administered less than 30 days apart.	...overtesting.	...establishing testing windows that are at least 30 days apart. ...removing the extra *SRI* test score using the Delete test function in the *SRI* Settings in SAM Roster.

Using *SRI* Results

As students take *SRI* tests throughout the year, use results to track student progress and plan appropriate instruction. Results can be used to determine appropriate placement, track reading growth, and provide appropriate instructional support.

Using *SRI* Results For Progress Monitoring

Use the Dashboard and SAM reports to monitor *SRI* results. Use the Dashboard to track reading progress and plan appropriate intervention. Review detailed progress monitoring reports in SAM.

Use the Teacher Dashboard to Monitor Student Progress

The Teacher Dashboard aggregates *SRI* data to provide a snapshot of student performance after each test.

Home Page: *SRI* Data Snapshot

- Results for each Lexile range are listed in a pie chart. Click each section of the pie chart to review a list of students whose results fall within each Lexile range.
- Use results to monitor reading performance for each class.

Class Page: *SRI* Data Snapshot

- The summary lists the average number of test administrations completed, as well as providing a graph or chart of total students within each Lexile range.
- Use results to track recent performance (last week or last four weeks) or compare current performance against previous performance (all year).

Use SAM Reports to Monitor Student Progress

SAM reports help track student reading progress. Use these results to determine baseline results, establish growth expectations, provide individual feedback and support, and discuss reading progress with students.

- **SRI Student Progress Report**
  Trace performance on all *SRI* tests
- **SRI Growth Report**
  Monitor progress for an entire group or class
- **SRI Student Test Printout**
  Review specific test questions and student responses

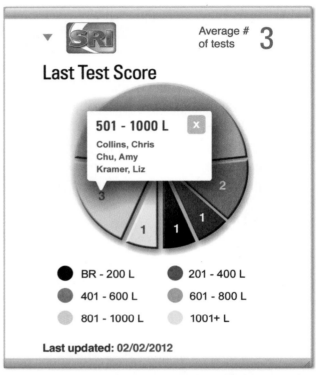

Teacher Dashboard: *SRI* Data Snapshot

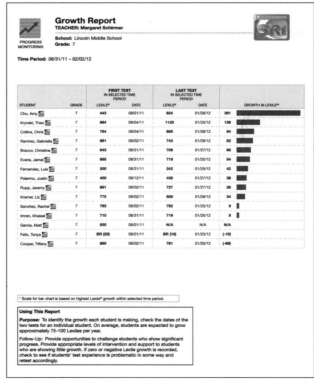

SRI Growth Report

Using *SRI* Results For Instructional Planning

Use the Teacher Dashboard to group students and plan appropriate instructional support. Review detailed instructional planning reports in SAM.

Use the Teacher Dashboard to Plan Instruction

The Class Page of the Teacher Dashboard provides instructional guidance based on *SRI* results.

Grouping Results

- Use the Groupinator on the Class Page of the Teacher Dashboard to view recommended *rBook* groups based on *SRI* results.
- Adjust groups as necessary in the Groupinator and save results.

Recommended Lessons

- Boost and Stretch activities are available on the Interactive Teaching System for each day's *rBook* lesson.
- Use *SRI* results to determine which students would benefit from each type of scaffolding.

Use SAM Reports to Plan Instruction

Use *SRI* reports to establish groups, assist students with book selection, and provide appropriate support during Whole-and Small-Group Instruction. Use report results to gauge reading progress and determine necessary intervention.

- **SRI Intervention Grouping Report**
  Group students for appropriate intervention

- **SRI Targeted Reading Report**
  Assist students with selecting books within appropriate reading ranges

- **SRI Student Action Report**
  Review instructional recommendations based on student's current Lexile score

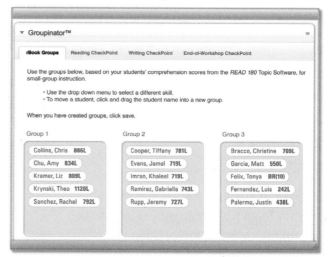

Groupinator: *rBook* Groups

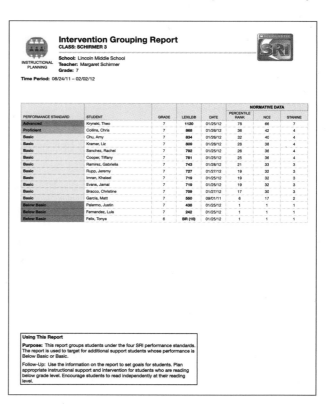

SRI Intervention Grouping Report

READ 180 Topic Software

The *READ 180* Topic Software provides individualized instruction and practice using high-interest reading materials and anchored instruction. The software presents a carefully planned sequence of instruction and practice activities broken into five "zones" and continuously assesses and adjusts according to students' skill needs and mastery.

Five Software Zones Continuously Assess Progress

- **Reading Zone**
- **Word Zone**
- **Spelling Zone**
- **Success Zone**
- **Writing Zone**

Students receive immediate and encouraging feedback as the Topic Software gathers information about their proficiency in comprehension, vocabulary, fluency, phonics, spelling, and writing. Use Topic Software results throughout the year for continuous diagnostic assessment to monitor students' reading progress and group students for targeted instruction.

READ 180 Topic Software: Zone Menu

Understanding Reading Zone Assessments

Students begin each software session in the Reading Zone, where they watch an anchor video designed to help students build mental models of key concepts, then read a related passage at their reading level. Each passage provides individualized support in building targeted comprehension, vocabulary, and word study skills. Once students complete the reading, they answer Quick Check comprehension and vocabulary questions.

Comprehension Assessment

Core comprehension skills are assessed through daily **Quick Check Comprehension Questions**, a total of 10 per segment (text).

Vocabulary Assessment

High-use vocabulary words are taught and assessed through daily **Quick Check Vocabulary Questions**, a total of 5 per segment.

Reading Zone: Quick Check Comprehension Question

Using Reading Zone Results for Progress Monitoring

As students participate in the Reading Zone each day, use the Teacher Dashboard to track participation and performance. Review more details in SAM reports.

Use the Dashboard to Monitor Student Progress

The Dashboard aggregates *READ 180* data to provide a snapshot of student participation.

Home Page: *READ 180* Data Snapshot

- Average participation results for each class are listed in a bar graph. Review time on-task for the last week, last four weeks, or entire school year.
- Click a red bar in the bar graph to review individual student results.

Class Page: *READ 180* Data Snapshot

- The summary lists the average number of sessions completed, as well as providing a chart of average comprehension, vocabulary, and participation results.
- Schedule a SAM report or opt in to receive an alert if student participation does not meet expected benchmarks.

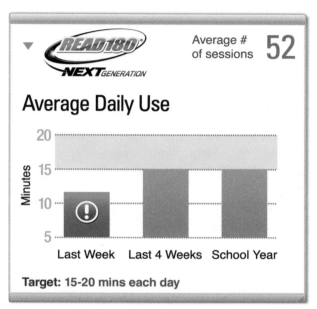

Teacher Dashboard: *READ 180* Data Snapshot

Use SAM Reports to Monitor Student Progress

Run and analyze SAM reports to review detailed class or student performance results.

- *READ 180* **Reading Progress Report**
  Monitor progress and participation for an entire group or class
- *READ 180* **Student Reading Report**
  Monitor progress and participation for an individual student
- *READ 180* **Comprehension Skills Grouping Report**
  Use results to create *rBook* Reading CheckPoint groups

Using Reading Zone Results for Instructional Planning

Assessment results are most powerful when used to facilitate instructional planning. Use Reading Zone results to drive instruction in the following ways:

- Use Groupinator recommendations for providing comprehension support at *rBook* Reading CheckPoints.
- Use vocabulary results to provide targeted instruction during Whole-Group at *rBook* Reading CheckPoints.
- If a student appears to struggle with a specific comprehension skill, provide scaffolded support by assigning accompanying comprehension graphic organizer from *Resources for Differentiated Instruction* as reading support during Modeled and Independent Reading.

READ 180 Topic Software, continued

Understanding Word Zone Assessments

After completing questions in the Reading Zone, students work in the Word Zone. Students receive systematic instruction in decoding and word recognition as they build automaticity. Students work with words included in the Reading Zone passage in an assessment activity, then move on to a study cycle of activities.

"Pretest" Assessment

Students complete a pretest, then receive individualized support and instruction for words they missed or were slow to recognize in the **Word Assessment**.

"Post-test" Assessment

The **Speed Challenge** builds students' word recognition and fluency with timed activities for independent practice in identifying Study and Review words. Students who identify less than 80% of their Review Words correctly must complete extra practice in a Review activity.

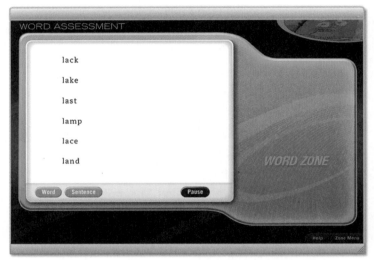

Word Zone: Word Assessment

Understanding Spelling Zone Assessments

After completing daily activities in the Word Zone, students move on to the Spelling Zone. The Spelling Zone provides students with activities that build spelling and phonics skills. Students receive extra support and instruction, as well as guided and independent practice, culminating in a proofreading activity designed to help them identify and correct misspelled words.

"Pretest" Assessment

The **Spelling Assessment** helps students see which words from the Assessment List they need to study. Students work with 10 words per round, taken from the Reading Zone passages.

"Post-test" Assessment

In the **Spelling Challenge**, students hear a word pronounced, then type their spelling of the word. If a word is spelled correctly, students move on to the next word. If a word is misspelled, students receive corrective feedback.

Spelling Zone: Spelling Assessment

Using Word Zone and Spelling Zone Results for Progress Monitoring

As students participate in the Word and Spelling Zones each day, use the Teacher Dashboard and SAM reports to monitor progress, track participation, and make instructional decisions. Use the Teacher Dashboard to track participation and performance. Review detailed reports for progress monitoring in SAM.

Use the Teacher Dashboard to Monitor Student Progress

The Dashboard aggregates *READ 180* data to provide a snapshot of student participation.

- **Home Page: Report Scheduler** Schedule a SAM report that includes Word Zone and Spelling Zone performance results. Review results and provide appropriate intervention.

Teacher Dashboard: Report Scheduler

Use SAM Reports to Monitor Student Progress

Run and analyze SAM reports to review detailed class or student performance results.

- *READ 180* **Reading Progress Report**
  Monitor Word Zone and Spelling Zone Assessment Activity results for a group or class
- *READ 180* **Grading Report**
  Monitor Word Zone and Spelling Zone Challenge Activity results for a group or class
- *READ 180* **Student Diagnostic Report**
  Monitor individual student Word Zone and Spelling Zone results

Using Word Zone and Spelling Zone Results for Instruction

Assessment results are most powerful when used to facilitate instructional planning. Use Word and Spelling Zone results to drive instruction in the following ways:

- Use the grouping reports to identify students who chronically struggle with fluency and phonics and address their challenges during Small-Group Instruction at the Reading CheckPoint. Use *Resources for Differentiated Instruction* lessons to facilitate instruction in phonics and fluency.
- Print and share the *READ 180* Student Diagnostic Report. Ask students to use words from these reports when completing *rBook* Writing assignments.
- For additional practice, send home the *READ 180* Student Word Zone Report and/ or *READ 180* Student Spelling Zone Report. Ask students to practice spelling and pronouncing words with family members or ask students to complete additional writing activities with these words.

READ 180 Topic Software, continued

Understanding Success Zone Assessments

Students reach the Success Zone after they achieve all of the requirements of the Reading Zone, Word Zone, and Spelling Zone. In the Success Zone, comprehension is the main focus. Students demonstrate oral fluency in a final recording.

To enter the Success Zone, students must:

- Answer all 15 Quick Check questions in the Reading Zone.
- Make a self-assessment oral recording in the Reading Zone.
- Master all of the words on their Assessment List in the Word Zone.
- Master the minimum amount of words for their level in the Spelling Zone.

Although students may receive more than the minimum words to study in the Spelling Zone, they only need to master the minimum required words for their level in order to unlock the Success Zone. The minimum amount of words a student must master in the Spelling Zone depends on the student's level:

READ 180 Software Level	Minimum Words Mastered
Level 1	6 words
Level 2	12 words
Level 3	18 words
Level 4	24 words

Once in the Success Zone, students complete three activities.

Discrepancy Passage

The **Discrepancy Passage** builds comprehension skills and focuses attention on main ideas and details.

Context Passages

The **Context Passages** ask students to apply comprehension and vocabulary strategies to complete a cloze activity.

Final Recording

The **Final Recording** provides students with the opportunity to practice fluency and demonstrate their learning.

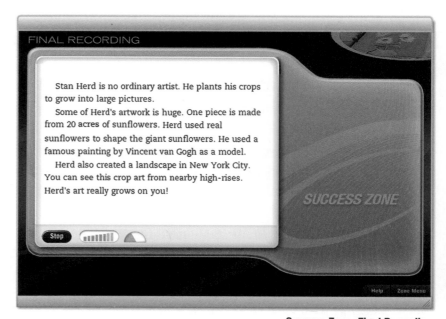

Success Zone: Final Recording

Assessing Oral Fluency Practice

When students complete their final oral fluency recordings in the Success Zone, their recordings are stored in SAM for your review. Access the SAM Student Digital Portfolio to review student recordings using an oral fluency rubric.

1. Log in to SAM and navigate to the SAM Student Digital Portfolio.

2. Click a student's name to access oral fluency results.

3. Click a student's level to open the associated reading passage.

4. Click the **Play** button to listen to the student's recording.

5. Use the accompanying rubric to determine fluency level.

6. Click the appropriate score (on a 1–6 scale).

7. Enter any comments or feedback.

8. Click **Save**. Print results or access results in *READ 180* reports.

Use the Teacher Dashboard to Schedule Reports

Use the Teacher Dashboard to schedule a SAM Report to help monitor student performance and progress. Schedule a SAM Report that contains Success Zone information. The scheduled report will be sent to your e-mail inbox.

Use SAM to Access Results

Review Success Zone results in the *READ 180* Reports. Both student and class reports include information on Success Zone performance.

Recommended reports for reviewing Success Zone results include:

- *READ 180* Grading Report
- *READ 180* Student Reading Report
- *READ 180* Student Segment Status Report

SAM Digital Portfolio: Oral Fluency

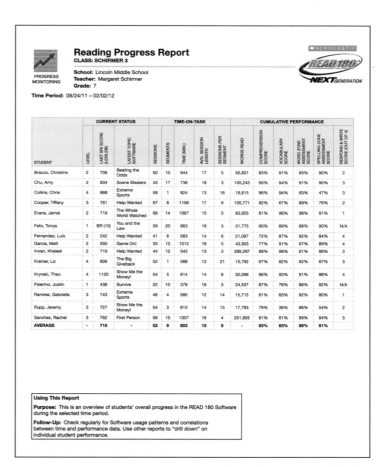

READ 180 Reading Progress Report

READ 180 Topic Software, continued

Understanding Writing Zone Assessments

After students have completed work in the Success Zone, they have the opportunity to respond in writing to their reading. In the Writing Zone, students write and support an argument in response to a leveled prompt related to the topic of their current segment.

Writing Zone Options

The Writing Zone is an optional zone that teachers can turn on or off for individual students or the entire class. There are three Writing Zone options:

- Complete Writing Zone work for each segment.
- Complete Writing Zone work for every other segment.
- Do not complete Writing Zone work.

Writing Zone Activities

Once in the Writing Zone, students must complete a Respond & Write activity. Students read a prompt, form an opinion, use sentence frames to write a structured response, revise their writing, and publish a final draft.

Respond: Take a Stand

Students use frames to form an argument and review other students' opinions.

Write: State and Support an Opinion

Students are asked to read a prompt and use sentence frames to craft a response with supporting details and a conclusion.

Revise: Self-Check

Students are prompted to use a rubric to revise their writing. The software highlights potentially misspelled words and "overused" words.

Publish: Edit, Record, and Send

Students have a final opportunity to edit their writing. They will then make an oral recording of their writing and publish their response by clicking **Send**. Their final draft will be sent to the SAM Student Digital Portfolio.

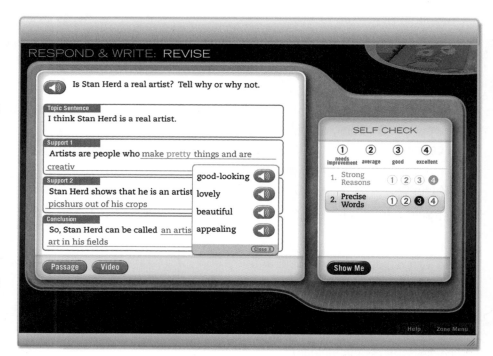

READ 180 Writing Zone: Revise Screen

Assessing Writing Zone Response Results

When students complete their writing from the Writing Zone, their published responses are stored in SAM for your review. Use the SAM Student Digital Portfolio to review their writing using an accompanying 4-point rubric.

1. Log in to SAM and navigate to the SAM Student Digital Portfolio.

2. Click on a student's name to access published writing.

3. Review the student's draft response and final response.

4. Score the writing using the accompanying rubric.

5. Enter any comments or feedback.

6. Click **Save**. Print results from the SAM Student Digital Portfolio or access results in *READ 180* reports.

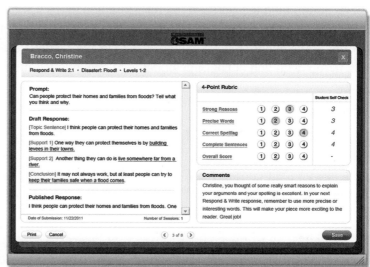

SAM Digital Portfolio: Respond & Write

Accessing Results on the Teacher Dashboard

Use the Dashboard to set up notifications or schedule a SAM Report to monitor progress.

Home Page: Report Notifications

- Opt in to receive notifications alerting you when students complete a segment.
- Once you receive the notification, assess oral fluency and writing results in the SAM Student Digital Portfolio.

Home Page: Report Scheduler

- Schedule a SAM Report that contains Success Zone information. The scheduled report will be sent to your e-mail inbox.

Accessing Results on SAM

Review Writing Zone results in *READ 180* Reports. Both student and class reports include information on writing zone responses.

Recommended reports for reviewing Writing Zone results include:

- *READ 180* Grading Report
- *READ 180* Reading Progress Report
- *READ 180* Student Diagnostic Report
- *READ 180* Student Segment Status Report

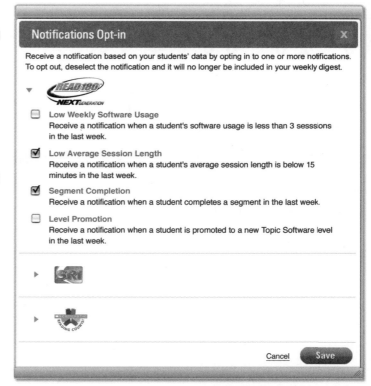

Teacher Dashboard: Notifications

Accessing Results on the Student Dashboard

When students understand the purpose of their work and can track their progress toward proficient reading, they are more likely to fully engage in the learning process. The *READ 180* Student Dashboard allows students to chart their software progress and uses those results to motivate and encourage students to continue learning.

Monitoring Progress

When students log in to the *READ 180* Topic Software each day, they are given a limited amount of time to use the Student Dashboard to explore their progress. They can review their performance on their current *READ 180* software topic, explore results from previous topics and segments, and check on their participation in *Scholastic Reading Counts!* quizzes.

Student Dashboard: Home Page

1 **Monitor Progress**

Students can monitor how much work they have left to complete in each *READ 180* software zone.

2 **Review Study Words**

Students can review their study words in the Spelling and Word Zones.

3 **Track Progress and Performance**

Students can track their total words read in the *READ 180* software and *Scholastic Reading Counts!* and monitor the amount of time they spend on the software each day.

Using Results for Student Motivation

The *READ 180* Student Dashboard also provides students with motivating results. By tracking individual high scores, performance streaks, and earning "trophies" for strong performance, students receive immediate feedback. Ownership of results empowers students to determine the best way to strengthen their performance.

Student Dashboard: My Personal Best Screen

1 Review Performance
Accuracy of responses in each *READ 180* zone is tracked. The total number of questions answered correctly in a row is compiled those into **Current** and **Best** performance streaks.

2 Track High Scores
The Student Dashboard also displays each student's **highest score** in the *READ 180* Topic Software Reading Zone, Word Zone, and Spelling Zone.

3 Collect Trophies
Students unlock **Trophies** as they achieve performance benchmarks in *READ 180*, *Scholastic Reading Counts!,* and *SRI.*

rSkills Tests

rSkills Tests are curriculum-based assessments that align to each rBook Workshop. Each test assesses students' ability to demonstrate understanding of specific reading skills. These tests are designed to monitor skill mastery and support instruction, and are aligned to key Reading and Language Arts content standards.

Purpose of rSkills Tests

The rSkills Tests enable you to assess students' transfer of specific reading skills taught in each rBook Workshop. These tests are designed to be used flexibly to meet assessment, grading, reporting, and instructional needs.

Progress Monitoring Tests

Each READ 180 stage includes nine Progress Monitoring tests that are designed to assess the Comprehension, Vocabulary/Word Study, Conventions, Critical Reading, and Writing skills taught in the rBook Workshops.

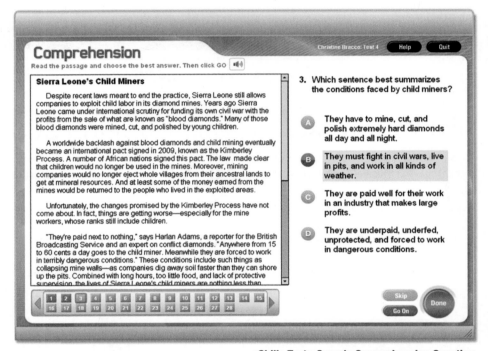

rSkills Tests: Sample Comprehension Question

Summative Tests

In addition to assessing the same skills on the Progress Monitoring tests, two Summative Tests also assess Listening Comprehension.

Test Formats

The rSkills Progress Monitoring Tests are available as online or print assessments. rSkills Progress Monitoring Tests administered on the computer include automatic scoring and reporting. The rSkills Summative Tests are available on SAM as print tests only.

What the rSkills Tests Assess

The rSkills Progress Monitoring Tests are designed to be administered at the end of each rBook Workshop. rSkills Summative Tests are designed to be administered at midyear and end of year. All skills are tested in the manner in which they are taught in the rBook and the reading comprehension passages assume some background knowledge based on the rBook Workshops. Review the following chart for strand types assessed and total questions assigned per strand.

Test Strand	Total Items (Progress Monitoring)	Total Items (Summative)
Comprehension	10 text-based multiple-choice questions	20 text-based multiple-choice questions
Vocabulary/Word Study	8 multiple-choice questions	10 multiple-choice questions
Conventions	7 multiple-choice questions	10 multiple-choice questions
Writing (optional)	2 open response questions 1 writing prompt	2 open response questions 1 writing prompt
Listening (Summative Tests only)	N/A	10 listening comprehension questions

rSkills Tests Levels

Each *rSkills Test* is available at below grade-level (Level a) and at grade-level (Level b). The level assigned will depend on assessment goals and students' reading levels. Both levels assess the same skills and have the same test format. However, as the table shows below, the levels differ in Lexile range, passage length, and sentence structure.

Leveling Criteria	Below Grade-Level Tests (Level a)	Grade-Level Tests (Level b)
Lexile	**Stage A:** 250–599L **Stage B:** 250–699L **Stage C:** 250–799L	**Stage A:** 600–950L **Stage B:** 700–1075L **Stage C:** 800–1100L
Length	**Stage A:** 150–200 words **Stage B:** 150–300 words **Stage C:** 150–300 words	**Stage A:** 200–600 words **Stage B:** 300–700 words **Stage C:** 300–800 words
Structure	Shorter, simpler sentences	Longer, more complex sentences

Below Grade-Level Tests (Level a) Use below grade-level tests for struggling readers, English Language Learners, or students in *READ 180* Levels 1 and 2. If a student scores consistently well, consider administering a grade-level test later in the year. Be sure to prepare the student for the change in difficulty and allow for additional testing time.

Grade-Level Tests (Level b) Use the grade-level tests for students reading at or near grade level. Level b tests will assess students' performance against grade-level standards or can be used informally for test-taking practice. Consider moving more of your class to the grade-level tests as the year progresses.

Assigning Tests in SAM When assigning *rSkills Tests* to students in SAM, you can assign the entire class to a particular *rSkills* Test level or you can assign levels to individual students. By selecting "Automatic Leveling," SAM will assign below grade-level tests to Level 1 and Level 2 students and will assign grade-level tests to Level 3 and Level 4 students.

rSkills Tests Open Response and Writing Questions

Each *rSkills Test* includes two optional open-response questions designed to elicit short, constructed responses. These questions assess a student's ability to respond to a text using the critical reading skills of Synthesize, Evaluate, and Analyze. Each *rSkills Test* also includes a writing prompt. These prompts assess the kinds of writing students have learned and practiced in the *rBook* Workshops.

Include these questions as part of the formal test, use them for review, or assign them as an on-demand writing opportunity.

Reviewing *rSkills Tests* Results

Students typically complete *rSkills Progress Monitoring Tests* on the computer. Use SAM to assign students the appropriate test. Select the test aligned with the current *rBook* Workshop and then select the appropriate test level. You can assign tests to students individually or as a class.

Multiple Choice Responses

Once students have completed the test, the software will automatically score students' multiple-choice responses. These results will be included on *rSkills Tests* reports.

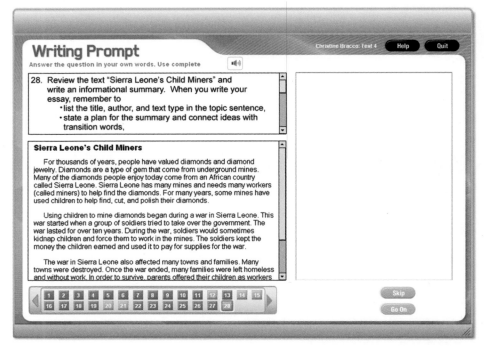

rSkills Test **Sample Writing Prompt**

Open Response and Writing Responses

When students complete open response and writing questions on the *rSkills Tests*, their responses are sent to the SAM Student Digital Portfolio. From there you can access the prompt, the student's response, and the accompanying rubric for each question. Use the SAM Student Digital Portfolio to assign grades and add comments for each student response. Grades and comments for each response can be printed from the SAM Student Digital Portfolio and are included in some of the *rSkills Tests* reports.

Using SAM Student Digital Portfolio to Assess *rSkills Tests* Written Responses

1. Log in to SAM and navigate to the SAM Student Digital Portfolio.
2. Click on a student's name to access completed Open Response and Writing Prompt.
3. Score the responses using the accompanying rubric.
4. Enter any comments or feedback.
5. Click **Save.** Print results or access results from *rSkills Tests* reports.

Assessment

SAM Digital Portfolio: Sample *rSkills Tests* Writing Rubric

Scoring Print *rSkills Tests*

To score a print test, use the answer key found at the end of each test. The answer keys include answers for each multiple-choice question, as well as sample responses for open response questions. When scoring a print test, you may wish to use a Scoring Chart to record and calculate student test scores (**SAM Keyword:** rSkills Tests Overview).

To use a Scoring Chart, make a copy of the appropriate chart for each student. For multiple-choice questions, mark each correct answer by circling the item number. Mark each incorrect answer by crossing out the item number. To find the score for each subtest of the total test, count the number of items answered correctly. To find a percentage score, divide the number of correct items by the total number of items and multiply by 100.

For Open Response questions, use the *rSkills* Open Response Rubric (**SAM Keyword:** rSkills Tests Overview) to assess student responses. Then, mark the number of points earned by each response. To assess Writing results, download the appropriate Writing Rubric from SAM Resources. Complete the rubric by marking the number of points for the student's writing.

Using *rSkills Tests* Results

As students complete *rSkills Tests*, track student mastery of Workshop skills and plan appropriate instruction. Results are available on the Teacher Dashboard and through SAM reports.

Using *rSkills Tests* Results for Progress Monitoring

Use the Teacher Dashboard to track reading progress and plan appropriate intervention. Review additional details for progress monitoring in SAM reports.

Use the Dashboard to Monitor Progress

The Teacher Dashboard aggregates *rSkills Tests* data to provide a snapshot of student performance after each test.

Home Page: *rSkills Tests* Data Snapshot

- Results for each test are listed in a bar graph. Review performance results from each strand of the *rSkills Test*.
- Use results to track recent performance or compare current performance against previous performance. Click on a red bar to review individual student strand results.

Class Page: *rSkills Tests* Data Snapshot

- The summary lists the average number of tests completed, as well as providing a graph or chart of performance in comprehension, vocabulary/word study, and conventions.
- Use results to track how well each class mastered Workshop skills.

Use SAM Reports to Monitor Student Progress

Use *rSkills Tests* reports to monitor overall class performance, provide individual feedback and support, and discuss reading progress with students.

- **rSkills Tests Grading Report**
  Details skill performance for a group or class on one test
- **rSkills Tests Student Progress Report**
  Tracks performance from one test to the next
- **rSkills Tests Student Skills Report**
  Lists performance for each test strand and skill

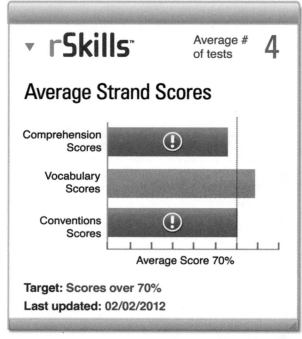

Teacher Dashboard: Data Snapshot

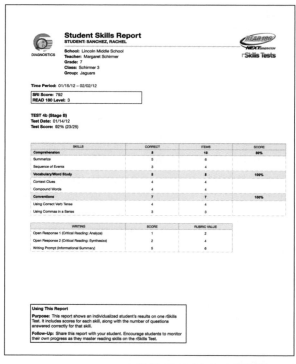

rSkills Tests Student Skills Report

Using *rSkills Tests* Results for Instructional Planning

Use *rSkills Tests* results to determine instructional pacing and identify skills to reteach before moving on to the next *rBook* Workshop.

Use the Dashboard to Plan Instruction

The Class Page of the Teacher Dashboard provides instructional guidance based on *rSkills Tests* results.

- **Grouping Results** Use the Groupinator on the Class Page of the Teacher Dashboard to view recommended End-of-Workshop CheckPoint groups based on *rSkills Tests* results. Adjust groups as necessary in the Groupinator and **Save** results.

- **Recommended Lessons** The Groupinator recommends lessons from *Resources for Differentiated Instruction* based on grouping results. Use these lessons during Small-Group Instruction at End-of-Workshop CheckPoints. Launch the Interactive Teaching System (ITS) from the Teacher Dashboard to access appropriate lessons.

Use SAM Reports to Plan Instruction

Use *rSkills Tests* reports to to gauge reading progress and determine what intervention is necessary.

- **rSkills Tests Grouping Report** Groups students for differentiated instruction at *rBook* End-of-Workshop CheckPoints
- **rSkills Tests Summary Skills Report** Aggregates results for each strand and skill

Assess Cumulative Mastery

Assign *rSkills Summative Tests* at the end of Workshop 5 and Workshop 9 to gauge overall student mastery of skills taught during Whole- and Small-Group.

Groupinator: End-of-Workshop CheckPoint Groups

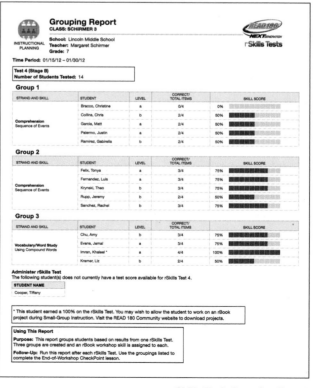

rSkills Tests Grouping Report

Implementing *rSkills Tests*

rSkills Progress Monitoring Tests are designed to be administered at the end of each *rBook* Workshop. Results from these tests are used to review how well students have mastered the content taught during the Workshop.

Administering *rSkills Tests*

rSkills Tests were designed to be administered on the computer. When students complete *rSkills Tests* on the computer, their results are calculated on the computer and included in SAM reports.

Use SAM to Assign *rSkills Tests*

1. Log in to SAM and navigate to the SAM Roster.
2. Select a class, group, or student from the SmartBar on the left side of the screen.
3. Click on *rSkills Tests* Settings.
4. Select the appropriate Stage and *rBook*.
4. Select the current Workshop.
5. Select the appropriate test level and click **Save**.
6. To assign Open Response questions and the Writing Prompt.
7. Click on the Settings tab and select appropriate questions to assign.
8. Click **Save and Return.**

Implementing *rSkills Tests* in the *READ 180* Classroom

Students who are using the computer to take an *rSkills Test* can complete the test during the Instructional Software rotation. Alternately, if a computer lab is available, the entire class can take the *rSkills Test* on the computer simultaneously. In this case, shorten Whole-Group Instruction and do not implement rotations. Instead, when students complete their test, instruct them to continue reading the book they have selected for Modeled and Independent Reading.

Both implementation options are available as part of daily lesson plans in the Teacher Dashboard. Select the appropriate implementaiton type when clicking on the Lesson Plan link for days when administering *rSkills Tests*.

Preparing Students for an *rSkills Test*

READ 180 students may not have had successful test-taking experiences in the past. Many lack the skills and self-esteem needed to experience success on tests. However, you can help your students success on the *rSkills Tests* by creating a supportive testing environment.

Test Structure

Explain to your students that they will be taking an *rSkills Test*. The test is divided into five sections. Each section contains questions based on skills they learned during the *rBook* Workshop.

1. Comprehension
2. Vocabulary and Word Study
3. Conventions
4. Open Response (optional)
5. Writing (optional)

Completing *rSkills Tests* on the Computer

To take an *rSkills Test* on the computer, each student will need to log on to the *rSkills Tests.* Encourage students to answer the onscreen sample questions. Check in with students after they have answered the sample questions to make sure they are comfortable using the software.

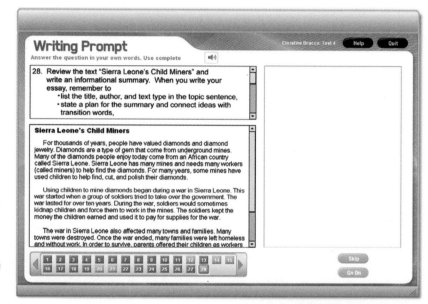

Sample *rSkills Test* Writing Question

Share these tips with students:

1. Follow the prompts on each screen.
2. Answer the sample questions before beginning the test.
3. You can skip a question and return to it later.
4. Use the scroll bar to view a complete comprehension passage.
5. If you run out of time, you can save your work and exit from the program. When you return, the test will resume where you left off.

Completing Print *rSkills Tests*

You can also choose to administer print *rSkills Tests*. Print a copy of the test and accompanying answer key from the ***rSkills Tests* Settings** in the SAM Roster. You can choose to administer print tests during Whole-Group and Small-Group Instruction or can suspend rotations and administer the test to all students simultaneously. Students can mark or write their answers on the test or on a separate Test Answer Document included with each test.

Scholastic Reading Counts!

Scholastic Reading Counts! (SRC!) is a comprehensive, computerized program that provides resources to assess student progress in the Modeled and Independent Reading Rotation. *SRC!* is based on the positive correlation between reading frequency and reading achievement.

Purpose of *Scholastic Reading Counts!* Quizzes

Scholastic Reading Counts! (SRC!) quizzes assess whether a student has read and understood a book or eRead. If students are reading appropriately leveled books, they should be able to pass the quizzes and their success will motivate them to read more. The program includes quizzes for all *READ 180* paperbacks, audiobooks, and eReads.

Scholastic Reading Counts! Welcome Screen

After completing each book or eRead, students take a *Scholastic Reading Counts!* quiz to demonstrate understanding of what they read. Ten multiple choice questions are selected from a bank of 30 questions, allowing students to retake a quiz with fresh questions, if necessary.

How *Scholastic Reading Counts!* Works

Familiarize your students with the format of *SRC!* before they take their first quiz.
You may want to review and model strategies for answering different types of questions.

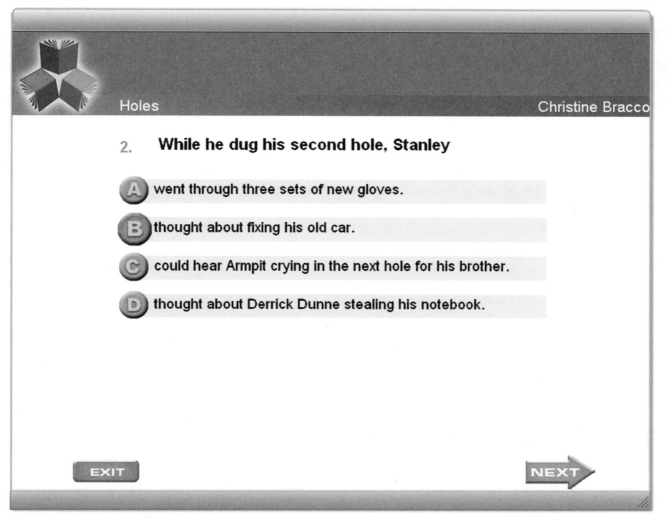

Holes   Christine Bracco

2.   **While he dug his second hole, Stanley**

A   went through three sets of new gloves.

B   thought about fixing his old car.

C   could hear Armpit crying in the next hole for his brother.

D   thought about Derrick Dunne stealing his notebook.

EXIT   NEXT

Scholastic Reading Counts! Sample Quiz Question

When taking a quiz, students:

- Receive 10 randomly selected questions from a database of 30 test questions. You can adjust the number of questions per quiz in the *SRC!* Settings of the SAM Roster.
- Answer modified cloze, embedded cloze, and direct questions.
- See highlighted answer choices that allow students to check their answer selection before moving on to the next question.
- View a personalized congratulations screen and rate their book upon passing the quiz.
- Have the option to view wrong answers. The correct answers will not be shown.
- Retake a different version of the quiz if they score below 70%.
- Once beginning a quiz, students should complete all questions. Exiting a quiz early will count as a quiz attempt.

Scholastic Reading Counts!, continued

What *Scholastic Reading Counts!* Quizzes Assess

Scholastic Reading Counts! quizzes enable students to demonstrate comprehension of the books and eReads they read in the Modeled and Independent Reading Rotation.

Each quiz includes 5 to 30 questions selected randomly from a set of 30. No two quizzes are alike. You can specify the number of questions that will appear; the default is 10. Varied quiz formats prepare students for types of questions they will encounter on standardized tests.

When to Use *Scholastic Reading Counts!*

Scholastic Reading Counts! quizzes are most effective when used as a culminating measure of written accountability for the Modeled and Independent Reading Rotation. Prior to taking a quiz, students should complete other comprehension checks, such as daily reading logs, graphic organizers, QuickWrites, and/or one-on-one reading conferences. Before allowing students to take a quiz, check in with students to ensure that they have completed their book and have comprehended the content.

Some classrooms install one extra computer in the Instructional Software rotation to be used for eReads and *Scholastic Reading Counts!* quizzes. Students can then take a quiz during the Modeled and Independent Rotation. If no extra computers are available, students can take a quiz when they rotate to the Instructional Software area. Once they have completed their quiz, they can spend the remainder of the Instructional Software rotation working on the *READ 180* Topic Software.

Using *Scholastic Reading Counts!* to Monitor Progress

Scholastic Reading Counts! quizzes enable monitoring of student progress in the Modeled and Independent Reading rotation. SAM reports provide actionable, quantitative data that allow for evaluation of student progress in order to raise student achievement.

- Student progress can be tracked by quizzes passed, points earned, and/or words read.
- Student progress can be evaluated by an increase in Lexile, performance standard, or other normative data.
- Student progress can be measured against quantifiable reading goals that are customizable in SAM.

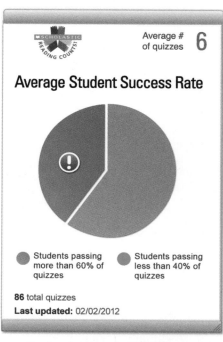

Teacher Dashboard: *SRC!* Data Snapshot

Using the Dashboard to Monitor Student Progress

The Teacher Dashboard aggregates *Scholastic Reading Counts!* data to provide a snapshot of student performance, student participation, and results.

Home Page: Data Snapshots

- Average quiz success rate for each class is displayed in a pie chart. Review information about students who are passing less than 70% of quizzes attempted.
- Click on the red section of the pie chart to review a list of all students whose quiz success rate is below 70%.

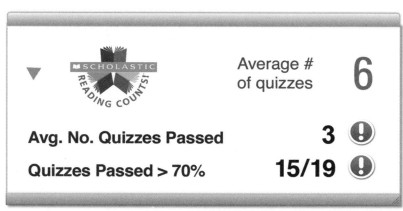

Teacher Dashboard *SRC!* Data Snapshot

Class Page: Data Snapshots

- The summary lists the average number of quizzes attempted per student, the total average quizzes passed per student, and the overall average quiz success rate.
- Opt in to receive a notification when students pass a *Scholastic Reading Counts!* quiz.

Use SAM Reports to Monitor Student Progress

Run and analyze SAM reports to review detailed class or student performance results.

- **_SRC!_ Books Read Report**
  Monitor progress and participation for an entire group or class
- **_SRC!_ Reading Progress Report**
  Monitor quiz success for an entire group or class
- **_SRC!_ Student Reading Report**
  Review individual student quiz results

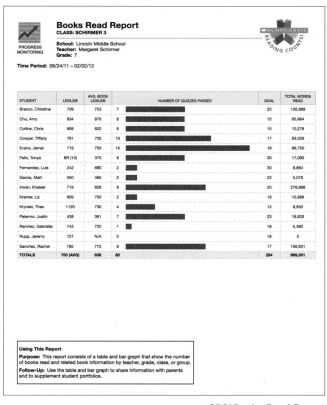

SRC! Books Read Report

Managing *SRC!* Settings in SAM

The Scholastic Achievement Manager (SAM) enables you to manage *Scholastic Reading Counts!* quiz settings for individual students, groups, or classes. Use SAM to adjust settings and assist students with finding appropriate books and eReads to read during the Modeled and Independent Reading Rotation.

Adjusting *Scholastic Reading Counts!* Settings in SAM

Scholastic Reading Counts! settings can be adjusted in the SAM Roster to meet individual student needs.

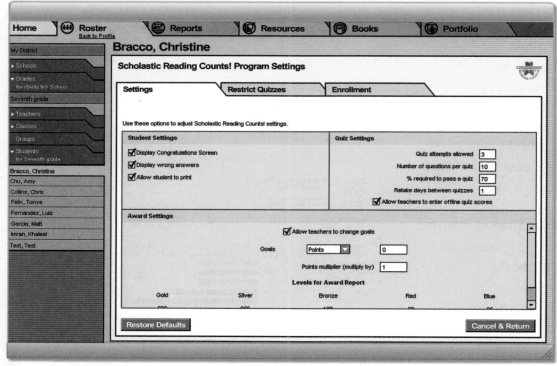

SAM Roster: *SRC!* **Settings**

Quiz settings can be adjusted for individual students or for an entire class or group. Reasons to adjust these settings include:

- Students whose IEP's mandate fewer questions or more time on tests may benefit from adjusting the total number of questions presented in each quiz.
- Provide students with an opportunity to access more complex texts with scaffolding and support by enabling the eReads settings in SAM.
- Throughout the year, as students reach higher levels of reading proficiency, you may wish to increase the percentage of correct answers required to pass a quiz.

Using the SAM Book Expert

Because of previous reading challenges, many students struggle to select appropriate books. Students may randomly select a book from the classroom library without regard to topic or level, just to meet reading requirements. Use the *Scholastic Reading Counts! (SRC!)* Quiz Manager in the SAM Book Expert to assist students with finding appropriate books to read.

Search for Books

1. Open the *SRC!* Quiz Manager in SAM Books.

2. Filter results by selecting books within an appropriate Lexile range. For independent reading, most students should read books 100L below to 50L above their current level.

3. Narrow results by genre, culture, grade level, theme, topic, and more.

4. Click **Search** to review results based on your search criteria.

5. Click on a book title from the Search results to learn more about the book, including a list of comprehension skills covered and a short summary of the book.

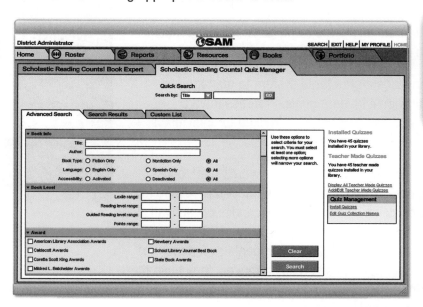

SAM Book Expert: *SRC!* **Quiz Manager**

Managing Search Results

Once you have found results that match your criteria, you can **View Custom List** to:

- Print a list of all books that match search criteria.
- Print a *SRC!* quiz and answer key.
- Print book labels for books.

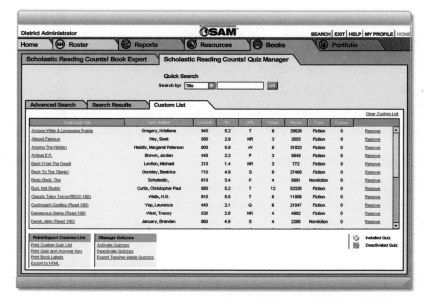

SAM Book Expert: *SRC!* **Quiz Search Results**

Using *SRC!* for Student Motivation

Establishing manageable goals and tracking progress toward reaching those goals facilitate student engagement in the classroom. For struggling readers who may have experienced frustration or failure with reading in the past, employing goals for independent reading is especially important.

SRC! provides a structured system to manage and track individual student goals. Progress toward achieving these goals can be tracked for individuals, groups, classes, or schools.

Establish an incentive system for words read, books read, quizzes passed, or points earned. Use results for groups or classes as part of an incentive or motivation system. Encourage students to review *SRC!* progress on the Student Dashboard. As students experience reading success and see results tracked, they build the confidence necessary to attempt new and more complex reading challenges.

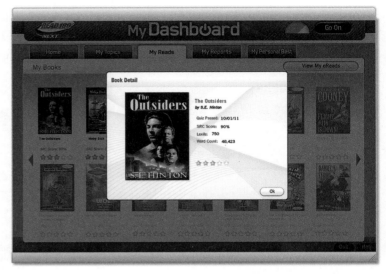

Student Dashboard: My Books

Motivation and Incentive Systems

There are a variety of ways to use *SRC!* to establish a classroom motivation system. Some possibilities include:

Words Read

- Highlight the top students each month.
- Compete for top group or class each grading period.
- Establish increasing goals of total words read each quarter for each student.
- Collaborate with other *READ 180* classrooms to attempt 1,000,000 words read by the end of the year.

Quizzes Passed / Points Earned

- Highlight the top students each grading period.
- Compete for top group or class each grading period.
- Establish increasing goals each grading period for each student.

Sample *Scholastic Reading Counts!* Certificate

Consider celebrating by inviting the principal or other administrator to read with students during the Modeled and Independent Reading rotation. Print customized certificates from the SAM Roster to recognize reading achievement.

Establishing Independent Reading Goals

Scholastic Reading Counts! can be used to establish and track annual student goals for independent reading. Goals can be set for books read or points earned when quizzes are passed. Specific goals depend on student reading level and book length.

Most *READ 180* students can be expected to read 8 to 10 pages in the Modeled and Independent Reading rotation each day. See the following chart for guidelines for establishing points or book goals for students.

For students who read below their grade level, refer to the level at which they are reading (their Lexile level). To build fluency, the below grade-level readers may need to read more books than what is recommended for their Lexile level. In these instances, refer to the goal at their readability levels, adjusting the goal up or down based on the ability of each student and the types of books the student will be reading.

Grade Level	Student's Ability	Lexile	Average Points Per Book	End of Year Goal (Points)	End of Year Goal (Books)
1	Emergent	BR	1	41	42
1	Beginning	BR–100L	1	38	38
1	Proficient	BR–200L	1	37	36
2	Basic	BR–250L	1	33	33
2	Proficient	BR–350L	2	50	30
2	Advanced	300L–450L	2	58	27
3	Basic	400L–550L	2	47	23
3	Proficient	500L–650L	3	65	22
3	Advanced	600L–750L	4	80	30
4	Basic	500L–650L	4	87	22
4	Proficient	600L–750L	5	100	20
4	Advanced	700L–850L	6	110	18
5	Basic	600L–750L	6	120	20
5	Proficient	700L–850L	7	128	18
5	Advanced	800L–950L	8	133	17
6	Basic	700L–850L	8	147	18
6	Proficient	900L–950L	10	167	17
6	Advanced	900L–1050L	12	180	15
7	Basic	750L–900L	10	167	17
7	Proficient	850L–1000L	12	180	15
7	Advanced	950L–1100L	14	187	13
8	Basic	800L–950L	11	165	15
8	Proficient	900L–1050L	14	187	13
8	Advanced	1000L–1150L	17	198	12
9	Basic	900L–1050L	14	187	13
9	Proficient	1000L–1150L	17	198	12
9	Advanced	1100L–1250L	21	210	10
HS	Basic	950L–1100L	21	140	7
HS	Proficient	1000L–1150L	26	173	7
HS	Advanced	1200L+	38	228	6

Other Independent Reading Assessments

Regular written accountability is also an integral component of daily progress monitoring of student participation and comprehension of readings completed independently. There are multiple ways to regularly monitor and assess student work completed in the Modeled and Independent Reading Rotation.

Daily Reading Logs

Daily reading logs help students maintain focus and synthesize information from daily reading. Incorporating daily reading logs into your assessment plan helps make students more accountable, especially when reading logs are checked daily during Small-Group Instruction. Have students rotate directly from Modeled and Independent Reading into Small-Group so that they can share their daily reading logs and receive immediate feedback.

Implementing and Assessing Daily Reading Logs

1. Download and make copies of the daily reading log (**SAM Keyword:** Reading Log).

2. Distribute blank reading logs during Whole-Group Instruction at the beginning of each week.

3. Have students pre-date reading logs for the week.

4. Alert students during the last 1–2 minutes of the rotation that they should complete their reading log or allow students to spend the first 1–2 minutes of Small-Group Instruction completing their reading logs while you assist the other groups in properly beginning rotations.

5. Quickly review daily reading logs at the beginning of Small-Group Instruction. Check for completion of work and total pages read and initial the log if expectations are met.

6. Complete a more thorough review of the reading log once a week or as students complete each book or eRead.

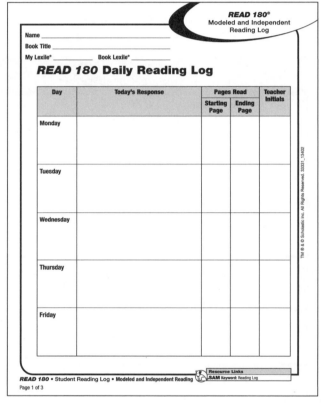

Daily Reading Log

Graphic Organizers and QuickWrites

The *Teaching Resources for Modeled and Independent Reading* provides additional resources to track student progress and comprehension during Modeled and Independent Reading. Graphic organizers and QuickWrites are available for all paperbacks, audiobooks, and eReads in the *READ 180* classroom library.

Graphic Organizers

Students can complete graphic organizers as they progress through their books or eReads. Schedule time to review their progress as they read their books and review the graphic organizer for accuracy before students take a *SRC!* quiz.

QuickWrites

Like graphic organizers, students can also complete QuickWrites as they progress through their books or eReads. Schedule time to review their progress as they read their book and review all of their QuickWrites responses for accuracy before they take a *Scholastic Reading Counts!* quiz.

Reading Conferences and Other Methods of Assessment

To monitor student progress and comprehension, you may wish to hold one-on-one student reading conferences. The *Teaching Resources for Modeled and Independent Reading* contains conference discussion starters and sample student responses for each book and eRead in the *READ 180* classroom library.

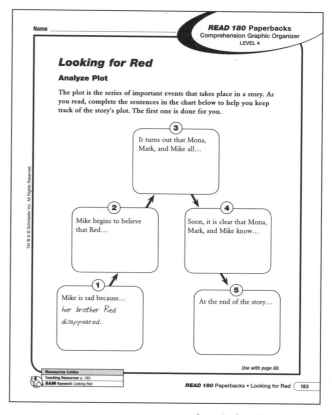

Sample Graphic Organizer

You may also wish to incorporate other methods of assessing students' independent reading, such as book talks, presentations, or assigning literary analysis as homework.

Structuring Modeled and Independent Reading Assessment

A strong Modeled and Independent Reading Rotation includes multiple measures of regular accountability and assessment, including:

1. Daily reading logs, assessed for completion daily and for content on a regular basis.
2. One or two additional measures of written accountability, such as graphic organizers or QuickWrites.
3. *Scholastic Reading Counts!* quiz, taken when students complete each text.

Incorporating these measures of continuous progress monitoring assessment ensures that students receive the support they need to achieve independent reading success.

Assessing *rBook* Writing

Students complete the writing process in each *rBook* Workshop. Rubrics to assess student writing are available for each *rBook* Workshop. Rubrics provide guidance in assessing student writing. As an assessment tool, rubrics offer guidelines to help ensure that all students are assessed on the same scale. They serve as a concrete reference to help determine student grades and explain these grades to students, families, and administrators.

Student Evaluation of *rBook* Writing

In each *rBook* Workshop, students are asked to brainstorm, draft, revise, and publish writing. Along the way, students are asked to assess a student model, evaluate their own writing, and discuss their peers' writing.

Student Self-Evaluation

After students have outlined and drafted their writing, they complete a self-assessment of their writing.

Self-assessments are included in the students' *rBooks* and are based on the themes and concepts addressed throughout the Workshop and the writing focus skills.

Rubrics included in the *rBook* are written in student-friendly language, enabling students to easily monitor their own writing and revise their writing based on their self-assessment.

Peer Evaluation

Once students have completed a self-assessment, they are asked to assess each other's writing.

Peer evaluation scaffolds are included in the *rBook*. Students use the feedback from the peer evaluation to continue to refine their writing. Sentence frames support students' structured academic discussions.

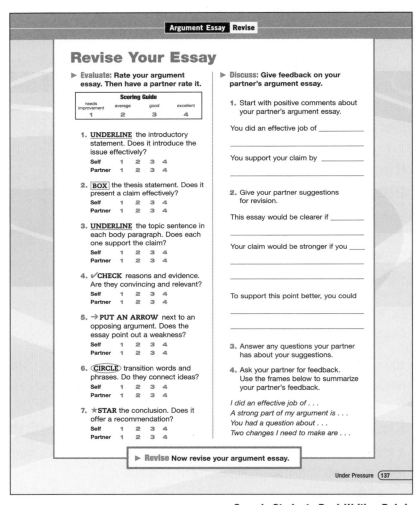

Sample Student *rBook* Writing Rubric

Teacher Evaluation of *rBook* Writing

Assess students' writing with a 4-point or 6-point rubric. Both 4-point and 6-point rubrics are available for each writing type taught in the *rBook*. These rubrics align directly with the skills taught and applied during the *rBook* Workshop. Rubrics for each writing type can be downloaded from SAM Resources. Student-friendly language enables you to conference with students about their individual writing results.

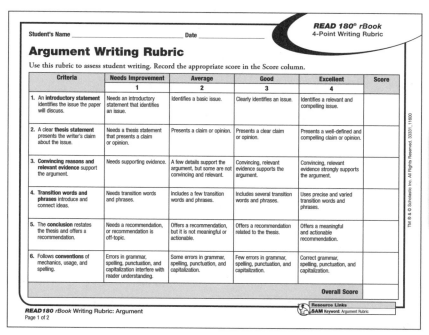

Sample 4-Point Writing Rubric

Access Rubrics

1. Link directly to the rubric associated with each Workshop writing type by clicking on the SAM Resource link on the *rBook Teacher's Edition* Writing CheckPoint page on the ITS.

2. Use SAM Keywords to download the appropriate rubric from SAM Resources.

Writing Type	SAM Keyword
Argument Writing	Argument Rubric
Narrative Writing	Narrative Rubric
Personal Narrative	Personal Narrative Rubric
Informational/Explanatory Writing	Informational Rubric
Informational Summary	Informational Summary Rubric
Research Paper	Research Paper Rubric
Literary Analysis	Literary Analysis Rubric
Opinion Writing	Argument Rubric

Score Writing and Share Results

1. Select whether to use a 4-point or 6-point rubric.

2. Download appropriate rubric and use criteria to assess each student's writing.

3. Use the scoring chart to assign a score for each criteria included in the rubric.

4. Determine an overall grade for the writing by averaging scores for each criteria or weighting criteria according to your own scale.

5. Share rubric assessment results with students to help them understand their writing strengths and challenges.

6. Provide time for writing revision during *rBook* Writing CheckPoints.

Assessing *rBook* Writing, continued

Other Writing Rubrics

In addition to the 4-point and 6-point rubrics available for each writing type taught in the *rBook,* there are also student rubrics and a 6+1 Traits rubric available. Download these rubrics from SAM Resources.

6+1 Traits Rubric

In her book, *6+1 Traits of Writing* (Scholastic, 2003), Ruth Culham presents strategies for assessing students' writing and focusing instruction. By consistently identifying and focusing on specific traits, students acquire a vocabulary to talk about their writing and apply a common framework for thinking about, revising, and evaluating their work.

The 6+1 Traits include the following traits that can be found in good writing of all genres:

1. **Ideas:** The meaning and development of the message
2. **Organization:** The structure of the writing
3. **Voice:** The way the writer brings the topic to life
4. **Word Choice:** The tone elicited by the specific vocabulary
5. **Sentence Fluency:** The way words and phrases flow
6. **Conventions:** The mechanical correctness of the writing
+1. **Presentation:** The overall appearance of the writing.

For classrooms or schools following Ruth Culham's *6+1 Traits of Writing,* rubrics to assess *READ 180* student writing are available in SAM Resources (**SAM Keyword:** 6+1).

Student Writing Rubrics

Blank rubrics for each writing type are available for student self-assessment or peer assessment of writing completed in the *rBook* or writing lessons from *Resources for Differentiated Instruction: Writing and Grammar Strategies.* Student rubrics can be downloaded from SAM Resources. Refer to the SAM Keyword List to locate the appropriate keyword (**SAM Keyword:** Keyword List).

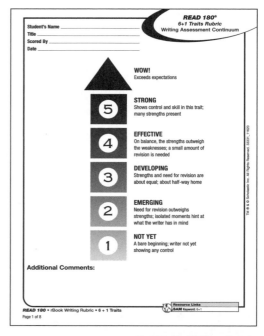

6+1 Traits Writing Rubric

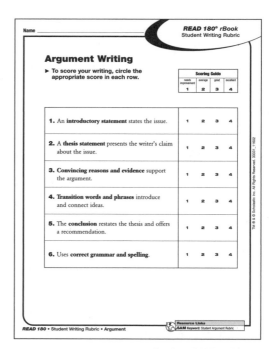

Student Writing Rubric

When to Use Rubrics

Select the most appropriate rubric to use based on school or district requirements, student reading level, assignment type, and time of year. Use the recommendations from the table below when determining when to use writing rubrics.

Rubric	What It Assesses	When to Use
4-Point or 6-Point *rBook* Writing Rubric	• Student response to *rBook* writing prompts • Student writing assigned from *Resources for Differentiated Instruction: Writing Strategies and Conventions*	• Use after students have assessed and revised their own work. • Share rubric results one-on-one with students during Small-Group Instruction.
Student 4-Point or 6-Point Writing Rubric		
6+1 Traits Writing Rubric		
rSkills Tests Writing Rubric	Student response to *rSkills Tests* Writing prompts	• Use after students have completed an *rSkills Test*. • Score results in SAM Digital Portfolio and print accompanying SAM reports to share results with students.

Using Rubric Results to Inform Instruction

Follow these steps to strengthen writing instruction by including rubric assessment results as part of the instructional process:

1. Determine the appropriate rubric to use.
2. Determine the appropriate time to use the rubric.
3. Use the rubric to assess student writing.
4. Determine individual, group, or class writing trends.
5. Reinforce writing instruction at *rBook* Writing CheckPoints, using information and trends identified with rubric assessment results.
6. Share rubric results with students.
7. Archive student writing and accompanying rubrics in student portfolios.

Assessing *rBook* Wrap-Up Project

Near the end of each *rBook* Workshop, students are asked to complete a Wrap-Up Project. Wrap-Up Projects are performance-based assessments that focus on important skills such as collaboration, supporting an argument, and synthesizing information. Each Workshop includes one of four project types: debate, proposal, presentation, or role-play.

rBook Wrap-Up Projects

Rubrics are available to assess each project type. As an assessment tool, rubrics offer guidelines to help ensure that all students are assessed on the same scale. They serve as a concrete reference to help determine student grades and explain them to others. Wrap-Up Project rubrics can be downloaded from SAM Resources.

Sample *rBook* Wrap-Up Project

Using Performance-Based Assessments

Use *rBook* Wrap-Up Projects to assess students' learning.

- Projects require students to synthesize data from multiple *rBook* readings.
- Students practice working independently, in pairs, and in groups.
- Projects help students reflect on and extend their Workshop learning.

Once students have completed their *rBook* Wrap-Up Project, use the accompanying rubric to assess their work.

rBook Wrap-Up Project Rubrics

Once students complete their project, assess their work with a 4-point rubric. These rubrics align directly with the skills taught and applied during the Wrap-Up Project. Rubrics for each project type can be downloaded from SAM Resources. Student-friendly language enables you to conference with students about their individual project results.

Access Rubrics

1. Link directly to the rubric associated with each Workshop project type by clicking on the SAM Resource link on the *rBook Teacher's Edition* Wrap-Up Project page on the ITS.

2. Use SAM Keywords to download the appropriate rubric from SAM Resources.

Project Type	SAM Keyword
Debate	Debate Rubric
Presentation	Presentation Rubric
Proposal	Proposal Rubric
Role-Play	Role-Play Rubric

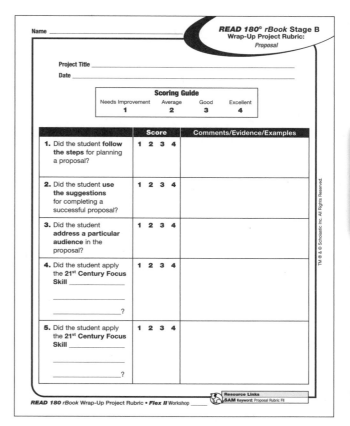

Wrap-Up Project Rubric

Score Wrap-Up Project and Share Results

1. Download appropriate rubric and use criteria to assess each student's project.

2. Assign a score for each criteria.

3. Determine an overall grade for the project by averaging scores for each criteria or weighting criteria according to your own scale.

4. Share rubric assessment results with students to help them understand their strengths and challenges.

5. Remind students to use feedback from the rubric when completing the same project type in subsequent *rBook* Workshops.

Assessing *rBook* Skills Instruction

Every day, students complete work in their *rBooks* during Whole-Group and Small-Group Instruction. It is important to regularly assess work and provide time to share feedback and allow time for students to revise their work.

rBook Workshop Rubric

Download a rubric to assess comprehensive student performance in each *rBook* Workshop (**SAM Keyword:** Workshop Rubric). The rubric will allow you to review each component of the Workshop to determine student ability to respond to each task.

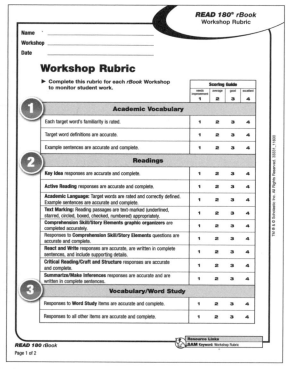
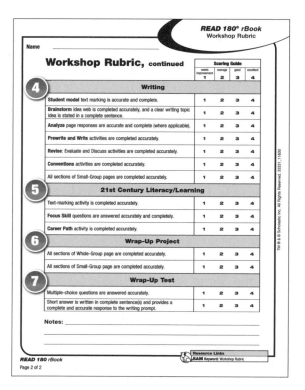

rBook Workshop Rubric

① **Academic Vocabulary**
Review target word activities.

② **Readings**
Review student work in each of the Workshop readings.

③ **Vocabulary and Word Study**
Assess student response to vocabulary instruction.

④ **Writing**
Assess completion of the writing process. The final draft of each writing can be assessed with a writing rubric.

⑤ **21st Century Literacy/Learning**
Review student work in the 21st Century Literacy/Learning activity.

⑥ **Wrap-Up Project**
Assess completion of the Wrap-Up Project. The project can also be assessed with a project rubric.

⑦ **Wrap-Up Test**
Assess student ability to apply Workshop skills in an assessment setting.

Completing an *rBook* Workshop Rubric

Complete each section of the Workshop Rubric as students complete that portion of the Workshop or wait until students have fully completed the Workshop before completing the rubric assessment.

Evaluate student *rBook* work based on completion, accuracy, and level of complexity of student response. Consider the student's current reading level, previous Workshop work, and other external factors when determining student scores.

Score each component of the *rBook* Workshop on a 1–4 scale:

rBook Workshop Scoring Guide		
Score	**Rating**	**Assign when . . .**
4	Excellent	Students fully and accurately complete the task.
3	Good	Students fully complete the task, but results may not be completely accurate.
2	Average	Students partially complete the task and results may be inaccurate.
1	Needs Improvement	Students do not complete the task.

Sharing Rubric Results With Students

Once you have assessed student *rBook* work with the Workshop Rubric, share the rubric results with students. Students may also use the rubric to complete a self-evaluation of their work, then compare their self-assessment results with your completed rubric.

Provide an opportunity for students to discuss their *rBook* progress, explain challenges, and celebrate successes. When possible, allow an opportunity for students to revise *rBook* work.

rBook Revision Tips

1. Circle one or two portions of the *rBook* Workshop for students to revise.
2. Allow students to revise *rBook* Workshop work during Whole-Group or Small-Group Instruction.
3. Have students complete *rBook* revision work on separate paper, and attach the paper to the original *rBook* work so that you and the student can review the revisions. In this way, students are afforded an opportunity to identify and correct mistakes.

Oral Fluency

Oral fluency is the ability to read connected text at a pace that allows comprehension of grade-level reading materials. Fluent readers decode text and recognize sight words automatically. This ability is critical to comprehension because it allows the reader to focus on meaning, rather than on decoding each word. Oral fluency assessment is one of multiple measures you can use to monitor your students' progress and inform instruction.

Oral Fluency Practice

Students must spend time reading aloud so you can gauge their progress with oral reading fluency. Regularly assess fluency levels to quickly identify students who may have a fluency problem that requires additional instructional support.

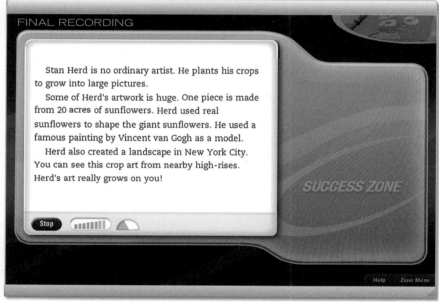

Success Zone: Final Recording

Final Fluency Recording

The **Final Recording** is the culminating activity in the Success Zone. It provides students with the opportunity to demonstrate mastery of the passage they have been focusing on during the current segment. Students read and make oral recordings of the passage multiple times during the Reading Zone. When students enter the Success Zone, they make a final oral recording of the passage, perform a self-assessment, re-record it if they choose, then save the recording. This activity provides students a sense of how their reading fluency has improved.

When students complete a recording, the Self Check button appears. As students listen to their recording, they may click words they missed to highlight them. Students may review their success at the end of the playback in the Self-Evaluation Student Report.

Assessing Oral Fluency Practice Results

Once students have completed an oral fluency recording in the Success Zone of the *READ 180* Software, you will receive a notice in your SAM Student Digital Portfolio that a recording is available for assessment.

Oral Fluency Results on SAM

To assess a student's oral fluency recording from SAM, follow these steps:

1. Click on the student's name in the SAM Student Digital Portfolio.

2. Click on the title of the current segment. This will bring up a copy of the passage so that you can follow along while you listen to the student's recording.

3. Click **Play** to listen to a student's recording.

4. Once you have listened to the recording, use the rubric in the SAM Student Digital Portfolio to assign a fluency score.

5. Click **Save**. Results can be printed and are also included in *READ 180* reports.

SAM Digital Portfolio: Oral Fluency Rubric

Oral Fluency and the Teacher Dashboard

You can set up notifications in the Teacher Dashboard to alert you when an oral fluency recording is ready to assess.

1. Log in to the Home Page of the Teacher Dashboard.

2. Click on **Notifications** next to your name.

3. Select **Segment Completion** in the Notifications Opt-In menu.

4. You will receive weekly e-mail notifications when new recordings are ready to grade.

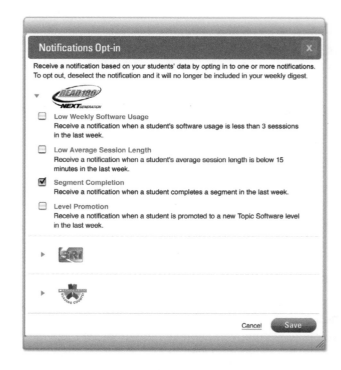

Teacher Dashboard: Notification Opt-In Menu

Oral Fluency Assessment

An Oral Fluency Assessment, or OFA, measures the number of words correct per minute (WCPM) that students read. You can compare your students' WCPM score with an overall average of students' WCPM scores at their grade level to see if their fluency levels are above, below, or on grade level. This assessment involves taking one-minute samples of students' oral reading. Reading passages should include fiction and nonfiction.

When to Administer an Oral Fluency Assessment

An Oral Fluency Assessment may be administered one-on-one, three times a year. You will find appropriate passages for administering OFA's in *Resources for Differentiated Instruction: Reading Skills and Strategies*.

How to Administer an Oral Fluency Assessment

Follow these steps to assess a student's oral fluency.

1. Print two copies of each passage—one for the student and one for you to record errors.

2. Before the timed reading begins, say to the student, *Today you are going to take an Oral Fluency Assessment. I'm going to give you a sheet of paper with a passage written on it. You may not know all the words in the passage, but try your best to read each of them. I will tell you how to read the words you do not know. I will time you for one minute.*

3. Hand your student a copy of the passage. Tell the student, *I will begin timing as soon as you begin reading. After one minute, I will say "Stop" so you will know to stop reading.* Begin timing as soon as the student starts reading.

4. As the student reads, follow along on your copy of the passage, marking words read incorrectly with an "X" and pronouncing words aloud that the student does not know.

5. After one minute, say *"Stop!" Make a vertical line after the last word the student read.*

Marking a Fluency Passage

Mark your copy of the passage as the student reads aloud. For a word to be considered correct, the student must read it correctly in context. For example, when reading the word *live* in the following sentence, the student must pronounce it with a long *i* sound: *There was a live audience during the show.*

The following table contains additional guidelines for marking fluency passages:

Count as Correct	Mark as Incorrect
• Words read correctly in context • Self-corrections made within three seconds • Repetitions	• Mispronunciations (e.g., ship for sheep) • Substitutions of any kind (e.g., dog for cat) • Omissions (words that are skipped or not read) • Words the student struggles to read for longer than three seconds

Interpreting Oral Fluency Data

After a student has read the passage aloud, follow these steps to calculate Words Read Correctly Per Minute (WCPM).

1. Count the total number of words read in each passage.

2. Count the total number of words read incorrectly in each passage, and subtract that number from the total number of words read. This will give you the Words Read Correctly Per Minute (WCPM). For each student you will need three WCPMs to produce a meaningful score.

3. Once you have three scores, take the median, or middle, score. For example, a student who scores 98, 101, and 104, has a median WCPM of 101.

4. Compare the student's median score to the Oral Reading Fluency Norms chart on **page 108** to determine whether the student is reading above, on, or below grade level.

5. Record the student's score.

Understanding Oral Reading Fluency Norms

The Oral Fluency Norms chart on **page 108** contains research-based oral fluency benchmarks that are good indicators of overall reading proficiency. Use these norms to measure students' fluency against standards for their grade and the time of year.

Follow these steps to determine whether a student's fluency is above, on, or below grade level:

1. Find the student's grade level on the Oral Reading Fluency Norms chart. Then look at the time of year during which testing took place.

2. Compare the student's median WCPM (the median score from the three passages read aloud) with the numbers shown for that grade level and time of year. Note where the student's WCPM falls in the Percentile column.

   - **90th Percentile:** Significantly above grade level
   - **75th Percentile:** Above grade level
   - **50th Percentile**: Grade level
   - **25th Percentile:** Below grade level
   - **10th Percentile:** Far below grade level

Using Results to Set Fluency Goals

Set a few measureable goals that can be achieved using intervention strategies: repeated readings, phrase-cueing texts, speed drills, and periodic monitoring. See *Resources for Differentiated Instruction: Reading Skills and Strategies* for more information.

Oral Reading Fluency Norms

This chart displays the norms for Oral Reading Fluency. The norms are updated at the fall, winter, and spring of each year. These norms are from the *2006 Hasbrouck & Tindal Oral Reading Fluency Data*.

Grade	Percentile	Fall WCPM*	Winter WCPM*	Spring WCPM*	Avg. Weekly Improvement**
1	90		81	111	1.9
	75		47	82	2.2
	50		23	53	1.9
	25		12	28	1.0
	10		6	15	0.6
2	90	106	125	142	1.1
	75	79	100	117	1.2
	50	51	72	89	1.2
	25	25	42	61	1.1
	10	11	18	31	0.6
3	90	128	146	162	1.1
	75	99	120	137	1.2
	50	71	92	107	1.1
	25	44	62	78	1.1
	10	21	36	48	0.8
4	90	145	166	180	1.1
	75	119	139	152	1.0
	50	94	112	123	0.9
	25	68	87	98	0.9
	10	45	61	72	0.8
5	90	166	182	194	0.9
	75	139	156	168	0.9
	50	110	127	139	0.9
	25	85	99	109	0.8
	10	61	74	83	0.7
6	90	177	195	204	0.8
	75	153	167	177	0.8
	50	127	140	150	0.7
	25	98	111	122	0.8
	10	68	82	93	0.8
7	90	180	192	202	0.7
	75	156	165	177	0.7
	50	128	136	150	0.7
	25	102	109	123	0.7
	10	79	88	98	0.6
8	90	185	199	199	0.4
	75	161	173	177	0.5
	50	133	146	151	0.6
	25	106	115	124	0.6
	10	77	84	97	0.6

* WCPM= Words Correct Per Minute
** Average words per week growth

Informal Assessments

Combining informal assessment with report data can offer a more complete picture of students' progress and achievements.

Using Anecdotal Information for Assessment

Through regular observation, you can target instruction to meet students' needs. Observe students at the beginning of an *rBook* Workshop to gather baseline information, during a Workshop to monitor progress and adjust pacing, and at the end of a Workshop to assess growth. Record your observations in daily participation or completion logs.

Using Developmental Checklists for Assessment

A developmental checklist or survey is a convenient way to note behaviors in each area of the *READ 180* Instructional Model. You may wish to create checklists for various rotations or create a more generic checklist that includes behaviors such as:

- Stays on task
- Participates in discussions
- Works well with peers during engagement routines

Compiling Student Portfolios

A portfolio is a collection of work that reflects a student's progress and achievements. You may wish to create separate folders or notebooks for each student in which to file writing samples, observation notes, completed activities from *rBook* CheckPoints and written responses completed during Modeled and Independent Reading.

Artifacts for Student Portfolios may include:

- *READ 180* Student Diagnostic Report
- *READ 180* Student Reading Report
- *rSkills Tests* Student Progress Report
- *SRI* Student Progress Report
- *Scholastic Reading Counts!* Student Reading Report
- *rSkills Tests* Summative Assessments
- *rBook* Writing
- Daily reading logs
- Modeled and Independent Reading QuickWrites and Graphic Organizers
- Oral Fluency Assessment Results

Grading in *READ 180*

When grading, consider a student's complete progress and performance in the *READ 180* classroom. Balance grades from each of the rotations—Whole-Group, Small-Group, Modeled and Independent Reading, and Instructional Software.

THE 90-MINUTE INSTRUCTIONAL MODEL

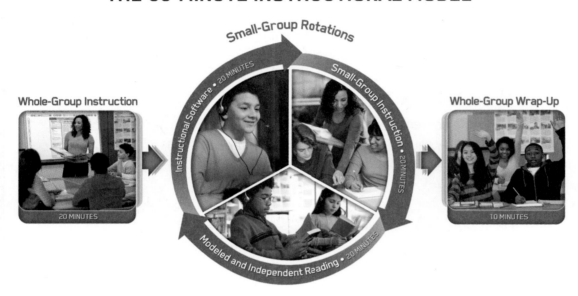

Setting Up a Grading System

When setting up your grade book for the year, consider how to balance grades and assignments from each of the rotations. When determining what data to use for grading, consider including SAM Report data as well as assignments and classroom artifacts not included in SAM, such as *rBook* work. Since students spend an equal amount of time in each rotation, you may wish to balance the assignment weights for each rotation as follows:

- **Whole-Group Instruction:** 25%
- **Small-Group Instruction:** 25%
- **Modeled and Independent Reading:** 25%
- **Instructional Software:** 25%

If you choose to assign homework, such as eReads articles and accompanying QuickWrites, you may wish to add that assignment type and adjust weighting accordingly.

Assigning Student Grades

Review the following list of grading options when establishing your gradebook for the school year. You may wish to include some or all of these assignment types when compiling grades for each student.

Whole-Group and Small-Group Instruction	
SAM Data	**Classroom Artifacts**
• *rSkills Tests* Grading Report • *rSkills Tests* Student Skills Report	• *rBook* Workshop Rubric • *rBook* Writing Rubric • *rBook* Wrap-Up Project • Resources for Differentiated Instruction (RDI) lessons • Participation in daily lessons • Do Now/Wrap-Up activities

Instructional Software	
SAM Data	**Classroom Artifacts**
• *READ 180* Grading Report • *READ 180* Participation Report • *READ 180* Student Reading Report • *READ 180* Student Diagnostic Report • *READ 180* Student Segment Status Report	• Daily software log • Daily focus/participation

Modeled and Independent Reading	
SAM Data	**Classroom Artifacts**
• *SRC!* Reading Progress Report • *SRC!* Student Reading Report • *SRC!* Student Quiz Success Report	• Daily reading logs • QuickWrites • Graphic organizers • Daily focus/participation • Projects or presentations

Conferencing With Students

Sharing progress data with students fosters student ownership and increases motivation. Schedule regular conferences with students. Use *READ 180*'s assessments and student reports to update students on their progress, set goals, and celebrate achievement.

When to Conference

In a *READ 180* classroom, the best opportunity for student conferencing is during rotations on pre-determined days.

Near the end of each marking period.

Visit the *READ 180* Community website to download projects associated with your current *rBook* Workshop. Pull students one at a time from Small-Group while the other students are working on the project.

When the daily schedule is shortened.

On days when the bell schedule is revised to allow for assemblies or meetings, your class may not have time to complete all rotations. If the class time is reduced enough to eliminate a rotation, consider moving students directly into rotations. Have students in the Small-Group rotation complete an independent activity while you conference one-on-one with students.

Determine which option best fits your classroom environment and communicate your conferencing plans to students. Establishing regular time within your schedule to conference with students creates a sense of stability and structure for students.

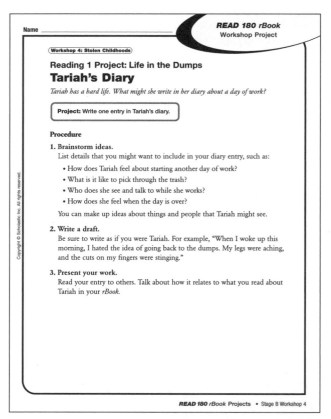

Sample *rBook* Workshop Project

How to Conference

1. Prepare all materials and information before the conference.
2. Time each conference so that all students have an opportunity to meet with you. Conferences typically range from 1–4 minutes per student.
3. On the day of student conferencing, remind students what to bring to the conference.
4. Begin by celebrating positive aspects of classroom performance.
5. Explain current progress—what is progressing well and areas of challenge. Review past goals and progress toward achieving the goal.
6. Allow students to use the progress information to articulate their own goals.
7. Have students write their goals in the *rBook* Student Logs or on conference logs.
8. Ensure that the student understands outcomes for the next conference and end on a positive note.

What to Prepare for a Student Conference

Consider the focus of your conference as you gather relevant information. During some conferences you may wish to complete a review of progress in each rotation, while at other times you may wish to have shorter conferences focusing on just one rotation. Topics and relevant materials for each rotation may include one or more of the following:

Whole-Group and Small-Group Instruction	Independent Reading	Instructional Software	*SRI* Results

• Student *rBook* and accompanying *rBook* rubrics
• *rSkills Tests* Reports: Student Skills, Student Test Printout, Student Progress
	• Daily reading logs
	• QuickWrite and Graphic Organizers
	• *SRC!* Reports: Student Reading, Student Quiz Success, Recommended Reading
		• *READ 180* Reports:
		  • Student Segment Status
		  • Student Reading
		  • Student Diagnostic
			• *SRI* Reports:
			  • Student Progress
			  • Read For Life
			  • Student Test Printout

What to Review at a Student Conference

Focus each conference on specific elements of student performance. Use current student results and benchmark data to help students understand their progress and articulate their goals for success. Conference on the same aspect of the classroom with all students or tailor the conferences to focus on the area where each student struggles most.

Whole-Group and Small-Group Instruction	Independent Reading	Instructional Software	*SRI* Results
• Participation in daily instruction • Completion and accuracy of *rBook* work • Translation of skills to *rSkills Tests*	• Book selection • Participation and amount read • *SRC!* Quiz success	• Daily participation • Software results: comprehension, vocabulary, spelling, fluency, and writing results • Software usage	• Current level • Expected gain • Grade-level proficiency range

Access student conferencing information and a blank conferencing log by downloading conferencing resources from SAM Resources (**SAM Keyword:** Conference Log).

Sharing Results With Families

Sharing progress data with students fosters student buy-in and increases motivation. Use *READ 180*'s assessments and student reports to schedule regular conferences with students. Update them on their progress, help them set goals, and celebrate achievement.

Introducing Your Classroom

Use an Open House or Back-To-School Night to introduce your classroom to families and establish a communication structure so that caregivers feel comfortable contacting you with questions or concerns.

During a classroom introduction, structure time to mirror the Instructional Model process students follow each day, allowing parents and caregivers to spend a little time in each rotational area.

- Use the section of the Implementation DVD that is relevant to students and their families.
- Allow parents to read a paperback or listen to an audiobook during Modeled and Independent Reading.
- Share current student *rBook* work, distribute Parent Letters from SAM, and distribute the Recommended Reading Report so that families can help their children select appropriate books at home.
- Offer an opportunity to have follow-up conversations on how to best meet student needs during the course of the school year and establish a structure for regular communication.
- Allow families to share additional information about their child's needs in a survey or during a one-on-one conversation with you.
- Share information about the Family Portal, where caregivers can go to learn more about the program, access research and results, view bilingual videos and tips, and download resources and activities to assist students at home.

Collaborating With Families

Families are a critical link in each student's reading progress. Maintain contact with families throughout the year, sharing achievements and concerns with parents as they happen.

- Send home letters introducing and providing classroom updates to the family.
- Schedule conferences to discuss any concerns about student progress.
- Share Recommended Reading Reports. Families can use the suggested book titles to find appropriate books at the library or bookstore.
- Invite families to visit the classroom during the year to read with students in the Modeled and Independent Reading Rotation. If parents have a connection to the current *rBook* Workshop topic, invite them to participate as a guest speaker.

What to Prepare for a Parent-Teacher Conference

Throughout the year, you may wish to hold conferences to speak with families one-on-one regarding their child's performance. Consider the focus of your conference as you gather relevant information. During some conferences you may wish to complete a review of progress in each rotation, while at other times you may wish to have shorter conferences focusing on just one aspect of student performance. Topics and relevant materials for each rotation may include one or more of the following:

Whole-Group and Small-Group Instruction	Modeled and Independent Reading	Instructional Software	*SRI* Results

• Student *rBook* and accompanying *rBook* rubrics
• *rSkills* Tests Reports: Student Skills, Student Test Printout, Student Progress
	• Daily reading logs
	• QuickWrite and Graphic Organizers
	• *SRC!* Reports: Student Reading, Student Quiz Success, Recommended Reading
		• *READ 180* Reports:
		  • Student Segment Status
		  • Student Reading
		  • Student Diagnostic
			• *SRI* Reports:
			  • Student Progress
			  • Read For Life
			  • Student Test Printout

How to Structure a Parent-Teacher Conference

Focus each conference on specific elements of student performance. Use current student results and benchmark data to help families understand their child's progress and ways they can help facilitate that progress.

1. Understand the conference goals prior to sitting down with families. What do you hope to communicate and what can families do to help their child at home? What questions or concerns might families have regarding their child's performance?

2. Gather relevant information. Determine which reports or student work best demonstrate the topics you wish to discuss with parents. Compile these items, remembering not to overwhelm families with too much information.

3. If the families requested the conference, begin the meeting by allowing the family to describe their questions and concerns while you listen. Repeat their concerns back to them to make sure you understood them clearly. Then address concerns one at a time.

4. When you begin sharing information about the student, begin by discussing the positive aspects of the student's performance. Be careful to share specific examples while avoiding using educational jargon without fully explaining the terms (e.g., *SRI*, rotations, *rBook*, etc.).

5. Work with family to craft a plan to support the student. Set goals and clearly communicate how caregivers can be involved in assisting the student with achieving those goals.

6. End the conference on a positive note and communicate how and when the family will receive updates.

Preparing Students for Assessments

READ 180 students may have had uncomfortable test-taking experiences and lack the strategies and confidence needed to experience success on formal reading assessments. Help students build confidence and improve performance by explicitly teaching test-taking strategies and tailoring assessments to meet individual student needs.

Incorporating Test-Taking Practice Into Instruction

Increase students' testing comfort level by incorporating test-taking strategies into instruction throughout the year. Begin by familiarizing students with testing procedures and terminology. For example, model how to read specific directions and question formats. Incorporating test-taking strategies into Whole- and Small-Group Instruction will help students build confidence and ease with taking tests.

- Integrate test preparation when a particular skill is taught so that students make the connection between what they learn and how it will be tested.
- Model and frequently remind students how to read and interpret directions for tasks throughout the day.
- Review results from previous tests to customize your teaching strategies.

You may wish to strategically incorporate lessons from *Test-Taking Strategies* into your instruction. The materials build students' familiarity with the most widely used types of tests and question/answer formats. Provide instruction from *Test-Taking Strategies* at the end of each *rBook* Workshop. If administering *rSkills Tests* during rotations, you can teach a Test-Taking Strategies lesson during Small-Group Instruction while students complete the *rSkills Test* on the computer during Instructional Software.

In addition, the Wrap-Up Test at the end of each *rBook* Workshop enables students to practice test-taking strategies as they answer comprehension, vocabulary, and critical reading multiple-choice questions related to materials and skills covered in the Workshop. The Wrap-Up Test can also familiarize students with appropriate strategies and terminology.

Building Confidence With Instruction and Practice

READ 180 develops the following skills and strategies to build student success:

- Developing rapid word recognition to increase fluency and comprehension
- Reading and analyzing texts from various genres and with different structures
- Building vocabulary—especially high-utility words used in content-area texts
- Using comprehension and self-monitoring strategies with challenging text
- Developing skill and fluency in several writing types

Tips for Administering Assessments

READ 180 offers a variety of assessment opportunities. In addition to daily assessment of students with the *READ 180* Topic Software, students demonstrate learning through the *Scholastic Reading Inventory, Scholastic Reading Counts!* quizzes, and *rSkills Tests.*

Scholastic Reading Inventory

The *SRI* test provides a non-threatening environment for testing. The following features are built into the *SRI* test:

- Questions are not timed. Students are not pressured to answer questions as quickly as possible to complete the test. In addition, students can exit the test if they become fatigued and resume the test the next day.
- Students are permitted to skip up to three questions per test and are not penalized for skipping questions.
- Students can take a practice test to ensure that they understand the testing procedures.
- Most districts establish "testing windows" that extend for multiple days. Maximize on these testing windows by guiding students to select a day within the testing window that feels most comfortable for them to take the test.

Scholastic Reading Counts!

Scholastic Reading Counts! quizzes are designed as short, motivational assessments of comprehension. Students can typically finish a quiz in one 20-minute rotation. You may wish to adjust the assessment environment to best meet the needs of your students:

- Adjust total questions per quiz. *Scholastic Reading Counts!* has a bank of 30 unique questions; the default setting for each quiz is 10 questions.
- Allow students to retake quizzes. If a student has an unsuccessful attempt at a quiz, conference with the student to review quiz results and check comprehension, then allow the student to attempt the quiz again.
- Allow students to use completed reading logs, graphic organizers, or QuickWrites during their quiz.
- For students who experience multiple unsuccessful quiz attempts, consider printing out a copy of a *Scholastic Reading Counts!* quiz and having the student complete the printed quiz while reading the book. Review responses and rationale with students prior to administering a quiz on the computer.

rSkills Tests

rSkills Tests are designed to be administered at the end of each *rBook* Workshop. Like the *SRI, rSkills Tests* are untimed so that students do not feel pressured to complete the test in one sitting.

- Consider administering Level a tests at the beginning of the year and moving to Level b tests, or consider assigning levels based on student reading level.
- Open response and writing prompts are optional. Consider which students may be hindered by being required to answer these types of questions.

Reports for Teachers

READ 180 Reports

rSkills Tests Reports

(Continued on next page)

Reports for Teachers (continued)

Scholastic Reading Inventory

Scholastic Reading Inventory Overview 189

CLASS/GROUP REPORTS

Individual Student Reports

Scholastic Reading Counts!

Scholastic Reading Counts! Overview 217

CLASS/GROUP REPORTS

Individual Student Reports

Meeting Teachers' Reporting Needs

As students participate in *READ 180,* the Scholastic Achievement Manager (SAM) gathers data about program usage and performance. Access this data through SAM reports that enable you to monitor progress and plan daily instruction.

SAM reports are available for the following components:
- *READ 180* Topic Software
- *rSkills Tests*
- *Scholastic Reading Inventory (SRI)*
- *Scholastic Reading Counts! (SRC!)*

Putting Reports Data to Work

SAM reports are designed for flexible use. You can specify a time period for data you wish to view, sort, save, and print. In addition, reports viewed onscreen contain links to accompanying instructional resources available through SAM. The *READ 180* Software Manual contains detailed instructions on how to adjust SAM settings and access SAM resources. You can also review aggregated SAM results in Data Snapshots on the Teacher Dashboard.

Each SAM report is linked to a specific instructional task. Data can be used to diagnose student needs, track progress, determine instructional pacing, and differentiate instruction. Each SAM report features an icon that identifies its main instructional purpose.

DIAGNOSTIC	INSTRUCTIONAL PLANNING	PROGRESS MONITORING	SCHOOL-TO-HOME	ACKNOWLEDGMENT
Diagnostic Reports identify skills individual students may be struggling with.	**Instructional Planning Reports** target instruction to meet student needs.	**Progress Monitoring Reports** monitor student achievement and progress.	**School-to-Home Reports** share progress information with families.	**Acknowledgment Reports** recognize student success.

Sharing Reports Data

SAM reports can be run for a class, a group, or an individual student, making it easy to share data with others. Schedule time to conference with students. Use student SAM report data to help students set goals and develop accountability for their reading progress.

Parent reports are available for each component of the *READ 180* program. These School-to-Home reports enable you to update parents and caregivers about their child's reading progress and involve them in their child's continued reading success. From time to time, you may also wish to review SAM classroom reports with your school administrators.

Purposeful Reporting

The following table describes specific purposes and examples of *READ 180, rSkills Tests, Scholastic Reading Inventory (SRI),* and *Scholastic Reading Counts!* reports available through the Scholastic Achievement Manager (SAM).

Report Type	Purpose	Reports
Acknowledgment ACKNOWLEDGMENT	• Student achievements and accomplishments • Establish incentive systems and track progress	***Scholastic Reading Counts!*** Award Report (p. 218) Reading Growth Acknowledgement (p. 229) Student Quiz Success Report (p. 236)
Diagnostic DIAGNOSTIC	• Identify skill strengths and weaknesses • Plan for differentiated instruction • Set and monitor reading goals	***READ 180*** Student Diagnostic Report (p. 156) ***rSkills Tests*** Student Skills Report (p. 184) Student Test Printout (p. 186) ***Scholastic Reading Inventory*** Student Test Printout (p. 214)
Instructional Planning INSTRUCTIONAL PLANNING	• Plan targeted, data-driven instruction to meet students' needs • Group students by skill needs • Set and monitor instructional goals	***READ 180*** Comprehension Skills Grouping Report (p. 142) Phonics & Word Study Grouping Report (p. 148) Spelling Skills Grouping Report (p. 154) ***rSkills Tests*** Grouping Report (p. 178) Summary Skills Report (p. 180) ***Scholastic Reading Inventory*** Intervention Grouping Report (p. 194) Student Roster (p. 203) Targeted Reading Report (p. 200) Recommended Reading Report (p. 204) Student Action Report (p. 206) ***Scholastic Reading Counts!*** Recommended Reading Report (p. 234)

Report Type	Purpose	Reports
Progress Monitoring PROGRESS MONITORING	• Monitor student participation in software programs • Track student progress and achievement • Share progress with students, families, and administrators • Set and monitor reading goals	***READ 180*** Completion Success Report (p. 138) Comprehension Skills Report (p. 140) Grading Report (p. 144) Participation Report (p. 146) Reading Progress Report (p. 150) Student Reading Report (p. 158) Student Segment Status Report (p. 162) ***rSkills Tests*** Grading Report (p. 174) Student Progress Report (p. 182) ***Scholastic Reading Inventory*** Growth Report (p. 190) Proficiency Report (p. 198) Incomplete Test Alert (p. 202) Student Progress Report (p. 208) College and Career Readiness Report (p. 212) ***Scholastic Reading Counts!*** Reading Progress Report (p. 230) Book Frequency and Rating Report (p. 224) Books Read Report (p. 220) Student Quiz Success Report (p. 236) Most Frequent Quizzes Report (p. 225) Points Report (p. 226) Quiz Alert (p. 228) Student Reading Report (p. 238)
School-to-Home SCHOOL-TO-HOME	• Introduce *READ 180* to families • Share progress updates • Facilitate discussions at parent-teacher conferences • Offer recommendations for family member involvement in student reading progress	***READ 180*** Student Word Zone Report (p. 166) Student Spelling Zone Report (p. 164) Parent Report I (p. 168) Parent Report II (p. 170) ***Scholastic Reading Inventory*** Parent Report I (p. 216) Parent Report II (p. 216) ***Scholastic Reading Counts!*** Parent Report I (p. 240) Parent Report II (p. 241) Parent Report III (p. 241)

Managing Reports in SAM

As students work on software, SAM stores the results of their work. This information is organized into a variety of reports that can be generated for each of the four software components—*READ 180, rSkills Tests, Scholastic Reading Inventory (SRI),* and *Scholastic Reading Counts! (SRC!).*

Select a Group for Reporting

1. Use the SmartBar on the left side of the reports screen to select whether to run a student, group, class, school, or district report.

2. Select the report you want to run.

3. If desired, click on the **Apply Demographic Filters** link to review results for certain populations of students. Applying demographic filters will re-create the report with only students falling into those demographic subgroups.

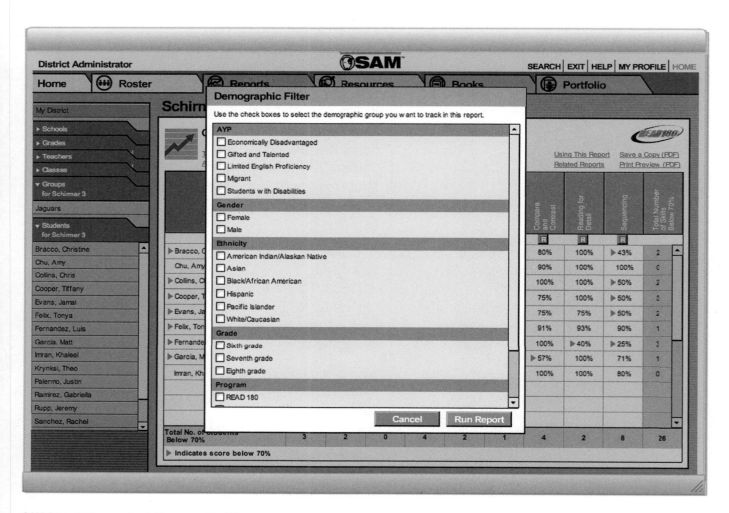

SAM Reports Screen: Apply Demographic Filters

Customize Time Period

1. Determine the time period settings you wish to apply to review results.

2. Select from a variety of preset time period setting options or choose to customize time period settings by selecting **Custom** in the Time Period Settings window.

3. Ensure that grading periods are set up in SAM so that the "Grading Period" setting will match this year's grading calendar.

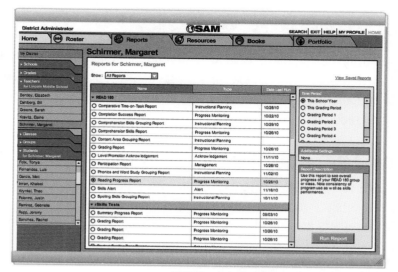

SAM Reports: Customize Report Time Period

View Related Resources

Some *READ 180* and *rSkills Tests* reports link to accompanying lesson plans and activities available on SAM. Reports with linked resources display an when the report is viewed on screen. Click on the R to link automatically to associated pages in SAM Resources.

Reports With Resource Links:

- *READ 180* Comprehension Skills
- *READ 180* Comprehension Skills Grouping
- *READ 180* Phonics and Word Study Grouping
- *READ 180* Spelling Skills Grouping
- *READ 180* Student Diagnostic
- *rSkills* Summary Skills
- *rSkills* Student Skills
- *rSkills* Grading
- *rSkills* Grouping

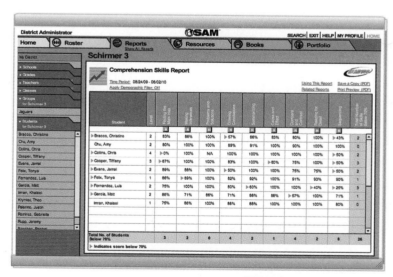

SAM Reports: Resource Links

Establishing a Reports Analysis Plan

READ 180 provides a comprehensive suite of reports for instructional planning, progress monitoring, and summative assessment. Establishing a data analysis plan fosters a seamless integration of using data and informing instruction. As part of your plan, consider creating a schedule for running and analyzing reports.

Purposeful Reporting

Certain reports are helpful at different points within the school year. Consider when it is most appropriate to analyze reports for monitoring student progress or making instructional decisions. Decide which reports are useful to share with students, families, and administrators.

As you print and analyze reports, archive the reports in your lesson plan book or create a data notebook to store your analyses. In this way you can refer back to previous data to more easily track progress and also keep a running record of student performance.

Establishing a Schedule for SAM Reports

Use your school calendar, your *rBook* Workshop pacing guides, and your testing calendar to establish a schedule for running and analyzing SAM reports. Then use the Teacher Dashboard to schedule reports.

Create a reports schedule:

1. Add *SRI* Reports first, planning to run them before, during, and after each *SRI* testing window.

2. Add reports used for grading next. Plan to run these reports near the end of each grading period.

3. Consider the pacing of your *rBook* Workshops. Plan to run grouping reports before each *rBook* CheckPoint. Run *rSkills Tests* reports at the end of each *rBook* Workshop.

4. Establish days to conference with students. Run reports for student conferencing prior to those conference days.

5. Finally, plan to run at least one report each week. When not running other reports planned above, alternate between progress monitoring with *READ 180* and *Scholastic Reading Counts!* reports.

Reports for Conferencing

To assist students with ownership of reading performance, monthly conferencing with students is recommended. Provide copies of SAM report data for students and conference about student progress. The following reports are best suited for student conferencing:

- *READ 180* Student Diagnostic, Student Reading, Student Segment Status
- *rSkills Tests* Student Skills, Student Progress, Student Test Printout
- *SRI* Student Progress, Read For Life, Student Test Printout
- *Scholastic Reading Counts!* Student Reading, Recommended Reading

Scheduling Class or Group Reports

Certain reports are most helpful at different points within the school year.
Review the chart below as you plan a schedule for running class or group reports.

Report	Beginning of Year	Every 4–6 Weeks	Four Times a Year	As Needed
READ 180 Reports				
Comparative Time-On-Task Report		●		
Completion Success Report			●	
Comprehension Skills Report		●		
Comprehension Skills Grouping Report		●		
Grading Report			●	
Participation Report		●		
Phonics and Word Study Grouping Report				●
Reading Progress Report		●		
Spelling Skills Grouping Report				●
rSkills Tests Reports				
Grading Report		●		
Grouping Report		●		
Summary Skills Report		●		
SRI Reports				
Growth Report			●	
Intervention Grouping Report	●		●	
Proficiency Report			●	
Targeted Reading Report	●		●	
Incomplete Test Alert	●		●	
Student Roster	●			
Scholastic Reading Counts! Reports				
Books Read Report		●		
Book Frequency and Rating Report				●
Most Frequent Quizzes Report				●
Points Report		●		
Quiz Alert		●		
Reading Growth Acknowledgment			●	
Reading Progress Report		●		

Managing Reports on the Teacher Dashboard

The Teacher Dashboard can simplify the reports analysis process. Review the aggregated SAM data on the Teacher Dashboard. Use the Teacher Dashboard Reports Scheduler to schedule SAM Reports to be sent to your email inbox.

Scheduling SAM Reports

Analyze SAM reports regularly. Use your school calendar, your testing calendar, and your *rBook* Workshop pacing guide to determine the most appropriate times to schedule each report.

In addition, review aggregated data on the Teacher Dashboard Home Page. These data snapshots provide an overview of student participation in each component of the software. Identify any areas of concern and schedule accompanying SAM reports to analyze.

Use the Report Scheduler to run the following reports:

- *READ 180* Grading Report
- *READ 180* Comprehension Skills Report
- *READ 180* Reading Progress Report
- *rSkills Tests* Grading Report
- *SRI* Growth Report
- *SRC!* Reading Progress Report

Launch the Report Scheduler

1. Log in to the Teacher Dashboard any time to schedule a SAM Report.

2. Review the Data Snapshots for each class. Review results to determine which reports to review.

3. From the Teacher Dashboard Home Page or Class Page, click **Schedule a Report** to launch the Report Scheduler.

Teacher Dashboard: Home Page

Using the Teacher Dashboard Report Scheduler

The Report Scheduler on the Teacher Dashboard contains many of the same features and functions as reports settings found in SAM. Use these settings to schedule a report.

Schedule a Report

1. **Who:** Select a class.
2. **What:** Select a program and a report.
3. **Time Period:** Select whether to run the report for the last two weeks, the grading period, or the school year. The selected time period is dependent on the date you schedule the report to be run.
4. **When:** Select the date to run the report.
5. **Confirm:** Review your selections. Click **DONE** to schedule the report.

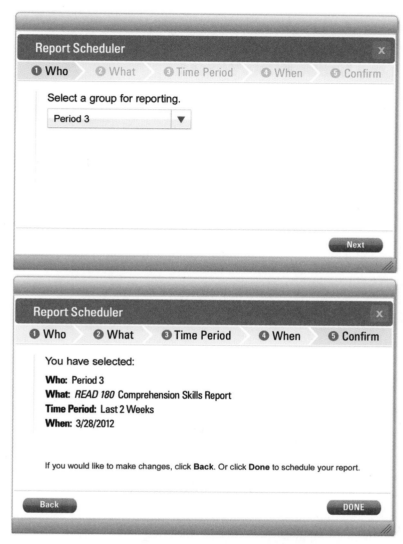

Teacher Dashboard: Report Scheduler

Review a Report

When the report is ready, you will receive an email notification. The report will be available in the Report Scheduler as a PDF. Use the report section of this guide to complete an analysis of student results. Use that analysis to make instructional decisions and redirect student focus where necessary.

Teacher Dashboard Notifications

The Teacher Dashboard simplifies the reports analysis process. Use the Teacher Dashboard to manage weekly notification digests. Review the notifications and use the information to determine which SAM reports to schedule for further analysis.

Launch the Notifications Wizard

Log in to the Teacher Dashboard any time to set or modify notifications settings. From the Teacher Dashboard Home Page, click **Notifications** to launch the Notifications Wizard.

You will receive a digest each week that lists any students who fit any notification alert criteria. All notifications will appear in one digest. You may change your Notifications options at any time.

Teacher Dashboard: Home Page

Manage Notifications

1. Click on the **Notifications** link on the Home Page of the Teacher Dashboard.

2. Place a check mark next to any notifications you wish to receive. Uncheck any you do not wish to receive.

3. Click **Save** to schedule the notifications.

4. A notification email will be sent to your inbox once a week and will contain information for all notifications you selected.

5. Return to this screen to adjust notifications options at any time.

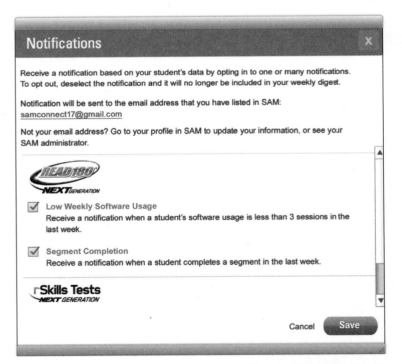

Teacher Dashboard: Notifications Wizard

Notifications Options

You can choose to receive one or more of the Notifications listed below. By default, the Teacher Dashboard will send weekly email alerts to inform you of any student performance results fitting specific criteria during the previous week. You may choose to opt out or change your Notifications settings at any time.

Receive This Notification	When	Follow-Up Reports
READ 180 Topic Software		
Low Weekly Software Usage	A student logged in for fewer than 3 sessions the previous week.	*READ 180* Participation Report *READ 180* Reading Progress Report
Segment Completion	A student completed a segment in the previous week.	*READ 180* Student Reading Report *READ 180* Student Segment Status Report
rSkills Tests		
Test Completion	A student completed an rSkills Test within the past week.	*rSkills Tests* Grading Report *rSkills Tests* Student Progress Report

Best Practice Reports

As students work on software, SAM stores the results of their work. This information is organized into a variety of reports that can be generated for each of the four software components— *READ 180*, *rSkills Tests*, *Scholastic Reading Inventory (SRI)*, and *Scholastic Reading Counts (SRC!)*.

Of the 64 available SAM reports, there are a few foundational reports to use regularly for progress monitoring and instructional decision-making. These Best Practice Reports include class/group reports and individual student reports that span all four components of the *READ 180* suite of software. Teachers new to *READ 180* may feel most comfortable focusing on these reports during their first year of teaching. Veteran *READ 180* teachers may use these reports as a foundation as they build and maintain a dynamic portfolio of student results.

Best Practice Class/Group Reports

Review the following class/group reports regularly to monitor student progress and determine where to target instruction.

Best Practice Report	Frequency	Use to Determine
Instructional Planning Reports		
SRI Intervention Grouping Report (p. 194)	**4 times a year** (after each *SRI* test)	*rBook* Groups and reading levels
READ 180 Comprehension Skills Grouping Report (p. 142)	**9 times a year** (before Reading CheckPoints)	*rBook* Reading CheckPoint groups
rSkills Tests Grouping Report (p. 178)	**9 times a year** (after *rSkills Tests*)	*rBook* End-of-Workshop CheckPoint Groups
SRC! Books Read Report (p. 220)	**Monthly**	Support needed for Modeled and Independent Reading
Progress Monitoring Reports		
SRI Growth Report (p. 190)	**4 times a year** (after each *SRI* test)	Student reading gains
READ 180 Reading Progress Report (p. 150)	**Monthly**	Student participation and progress in software
rSkills Tests Grading Report (p. 174)	**9 times a year** (after *rSkills Tests*)	Student results on *rSkills Tests*
SRC! Reading Progress Report (p. 230)	**Monthly**	Student participation and success in *SRC!* quizzes

Best Practice Individual Student Reports

To follow up on results of class or group reports, run and analyze the following Best Practice individual student reports. Regularly share results from these reports with students:

- *READ 180* Student Diagnostic Report (p. 156)
- *READ 180* Student Reading Report (p. 158)
- *rSkills Tests* Student Skills Report (p. 184)
- *rSkills Tests* Student Progress Report (p. 182)
- *SRI* Student Progress Report (p. 208)
- *SRI* Student Action Report (p. 206)
- *SRC!* Student Reading Report (p. 238)
- *SRC!* Recommended Reading Report (p. 234)

Best Practice Reports on the Teacher Dashboard

The Teacher Dashboard simplifies the report analysis process by allowing you to schedule reports from SAM. Once scheduled and run, these reports will be sent to your email inbox.

Best Practice Reports are highlighted in the Teacher Dashboard Report Scheduler. Regularly schedule and analyze these reports.

You can also identify reports as "Favorite" reports.

Teacher Dashboard: Reports Scheduler

READ 180 Reports Overview

Each time students log on to the *READ 180* Topic Software, the Scholastic Achievement Manager (SAM) captures information on their software use and progress in key skill areas. Access this information for individual students, groups, a class, or all students assigned to you through the *READ 180* Reports.

READ 180 Reports are flexible, allowing you to view and sort specific information to monitor progress through the *READ 180* Topic Software and target instruction to meet the specific needs of students during Small-Group Instruction.

Class/Group Reports

The following table summarizes how to use each *READ 180* class or group report.

If You Want to . . .	Run This Report
...track the amount of time students spend in each *READ 180* zone	Comparative Time-On-Task Report (p. 136)
...monitor overall software progress and Lexile growth	Completion Success Report (p. 138)
...review performance on specific comprehension skills	Comprehension Skills Report (p. 140)
...regroup students at Reading CheckPoints	Comprehension Skills Grouping Report (p. 142)
...assign grades based on software performance	Grading Report (p. 144)
...track how students are spending time in the Instructional Software rotation	Participation Report (p. 146)
...group students for phonics or fluency practice	Phonics and Word Study Grouping Report (p. 148)
...monitor software participation and progress	Reading Progress Report (p. 150)
...group students for decoding or spelling practice	Spelling Skills Grouping Report (p. 154)

Individual Student Reports

The following table summarizes how to use each individual student *READ 180* report.

If You Want to . . .	Run This Report
...view a student's progress in each software zone and target instruction	Student Diagnostic Report (p. 156)
...track a student's software and Scholastic Reading Counts! participation	Student Reading Report (p. 158)
...review a student's participation in the current software segment and track historical progress	Student Segment Status Report (p. 162)
...monitor a student's spelling progress	Student Spelling Zone Report (p. 164)
... monitor a student's word mastery progress	Student Word Zone Report (p. 166)
... introduce families to *READ 180*	Parent Report I (p. 168)
... update families on their child's *READ 180* participation	Parent Report II (p. 170)

Comparative Time-on-Task Report

Purpose

This report graphs and charts the total amount of time students spend in each *READ 180* Software zone.

Comparative Time-on-Task Report
CLASS: SCHIRMER 3

School: Lincoln Middle School
Teacher: Margaret Schirmer
Grade: 7

Time Period: 08/24/11 – 02/02/12 **1**

STUDENT	LEVEL	TIME SPENT ON READ 180 ACTIVITIES
Bracco, Christine	2	944 — 28% 13% 34% 7% 18%
Chu, Amy	2	736 — 27% 22% 34% 7% 11%
Collins, Chris	4	824 — 13% 36% 49% 2%
Cooper, Tiffany	3	1106 — 13% 21% 51% 9% 6%
Evans, Jamal	2	1067 — 27% 18% 40% 7% 8%
Felix, Tonya	1	863 — 24% 30% 38% 9%
Fernandez, Luis	2	583 — 21% 25% 42% 7% 5%
Garcia, Matt	2	1012 — 18% 15% 48% 11% 8%
Imran, Khaleel	2	545 — 32% 31% 19% 8% 11%
Kramer, Liz	4	588 — 16% 25% 53% 2% 3%
Krynski, Theo	4	814 — 14% 30% 38% 5% 12%
Palermo, Justin	1	379 — 36% 37% 18% 9%
Ramirez, Gabriella	3	585 — 32% 19% 38% 8% 3%
Rupp, Jeremy	3	815 — 19% 27% 45% 7% 2%
Sanchez, Rachel	3	1007 — 29% 14% 29% 16% 11%

MINUTES: 0 200 400 600 800 1,000 1,200 1,400 1,600 1,800 2,000

■ Reading Zone ■ Word Zone ■ Spelling Zone ■ Success Zone ■ Writing Zone

2 **3**

Using This Report

Purpose: The bars show the relative amounts of time students are spending in each of the READ 180 zones. Use this report to track how students are using the Software and their time.

Follow-Up: Encourage students to balance their time among the zones. Remind students to visit the Reading Zone each day.

How It Helps

I use the data from this report to remind students about balancing their time in each zone of the software.

Understand the Data

1 **Time Period**
Default time period setting of This School Year displays comprehensive participation results. For review of results for shorter periods of time, customize time period settings.

2 **Minutes**
Total time each student spent on the *READ 180* Software. Minutes are only calculated when a student is actively interacting with the software. Minutes are not calculated if the student has the software open on the computer but is working in a different program.

3 **Time Spent on *READ 180* Activities**
Percentage of time spent in each *READ 180* Software zone. **Page one** displays results graphically, listing total time spent in each zone as a percentage of overall time spent on the Software. **Page two** displays results in a chart with total time in minutes listed for each zone. Total time includes Writing Zone for students who have Writing Zone enabled.

Use the Data

Who: Teachers (Teacher, Class, or Group report)

When: Every one or two months

How: Apply the information in this report in the following ways:

Offer Support
Share the following tips with students who appear to spend too much time in one zone.

- Reading Zone: Click on Power Words for support
- Word Zone: Use the word window for support
- Spelling Zone: Listen to the word and how it is used in a sentence
- Writing Zone: Review the passage or Anchor Video for support in drafting your writing

Monitor Progress

- Encourage students to monitor their daily progress with the Student Dashboard. Tell students who are struggling with software usage to use information from the Student Dashboard to complete a daily software log (**SAM Keyword:** Software Log).
- Because students have varying reading challenges, the amount of time spent in each software zone may vary between students. For example, a student struggling with decoding challenges may spend more time in the Spelling Zone, while a student who struggles with comprehension may spend more time in the Reading Zone.

Review Related Reports
- *READ 180* Reading Progress Report (p. 150)
- *READ 180* Student Reading Report (p. 158)
- *READ 180* Student Segment Status Report (p. 162)

Data in Action

Balancing Time Among Zones Students often spend excessive time in the Spelling Zone because they enjoy the immediate corrective feedback. Explain the importance of balancing the time spent in each zone.

Completion Success Report

Purpose

This report displays software completion rates and *SRI* growth to review student response to *READ 180*.

Completion Success Report
CLASS: SCHIRMER 3

School: Lincoln Middle School
Teacher: Margaret Schirmer
Grade: 7

Time Period: 08/24/11 – 02/02/12 ①

STUDENT	CURRENT LEVEL ②	DATE STARTED READ 180 ③	AVG. SESSION LENGTH ④	SEGMENTS COMPLETED ⑤ CURRENT LEVEL	ALL DATES	TOTAL WORDS READ ⑥	LEXILE® ⑦	SRI GROWTH (LEXILE®) ⑧	LAST SRI TEST DATE ⑨
Bracco, Christine	2	09/16/11	17	10 out of 60	12	55,831	709	66	01/27/12
Chu, Amy	2	09/09/10	16	17 out of 60	48	105,245	834	391	01/26/12
▸ Collins, Chris	4	09/14/10	▸ 14	1 out of 60	10	16,815	868	84	01/26/12
Cooper, Tiffany	3	09/14/11	17	8 out of 60	8	105,771	781	(-99)	01/25/12
Evans, Jamal	2	09/14/11	15	14 out of 60	14	93,655	719	54	01/25/12
Felix, Tonya	1	09/11/11	16	20 out of 60	20	31,775	BR (10)	(-10)	01/25/12
▸ Fernandez, Luis	2	09/17/11	▸ 14	6 out of 60	6	21,097	242	42	01/25/12
Garcia, Matt	2	09/05/10	16	12 out of 60	26	43,503	550	N/A	09/01/11
▸ Imran, Khaleel	2	09/15/11	▸ 13	12 out of 60	12	289,267	719	9	01/25/12
▸ Kramer, Liz	4	09/14/11	▸ 12	1 out of 60	1	15,792	809	34	01/26/12
Krynski, Theo	4	09/08/10	14	5 out of 60	23	30,096	1120	136	01/25/12
Palermo, Justin	1	05/08/11	16	10 out of 60	23	24,537	438	38	01/27/12
▸ Ramirez, Gabriella	3	09/14/11	▸ 12	4 out of 60	2	15,715	743	82	01/28/12
Rupp, Jeremy	3	09/14/11	14	3 out of 60	3	17,793	727	36	01/27/12
Sanchez, Rachel	3	09/08/10	16	15 out of 60	43	251,855	792	9	01/25/12

▸ Indicates average participation is less than 15 minutes per day

Using This Report

Purpose: Multiple data points provide an excellent update of student progress through READ 180 segments. You can review and correlate time-on-task, content completion, and Lexile growth.

Follow-Up: Check to see if students who have completed content show positive Lexile growth. Review historical SRI data as part of any exit criteria.

How It Helps

I share this report with my administrators to help determine which students may be ready to exit the program.

Understand the Data

1 Time Period

Time period setting of All Dates displays results from initial date of student enrollment. Report will include results from all years of enrollment for students enrolled for more than one year.

2 Current Level

Student's current software level. *READ 180* level is initially determined by *SRI* results.

3 Date Started *READ 180*

Date a student began using *READ 180*. Students enrolled for more than one year with the same account will show initial date of enrollment.

4 Average Session Length

Average minutes spent on software each session (day). A low average session length may indicate infrequent software usage, logging off before the end of the rotation, or using other software during the rotation.

5 Segments Completed

Total number of Topic Software segments completed. Each topic contains 4 segments, for a total of 60 segments available at each software level. Current Level indicates the total number of segments completed at the student's current software level. All Dates indicates the total number of segments completed at all levels.

6 Total Words Read

Cumulative number of words a student has read in the *READ 180* passages, including repeated readings. Also includes words read from books or eReads articles when a student passes a *Scholastic Reading Counts!* quiz.

7 Lexile

Student's current Lexile score.

8 *SRI* Growth (Lexile)

Change in a student's Lexile score since beginning of the program. N/A indicates the student has only taken one *SRI* test.

9 Last *SRI* Test Date

Date most recent *SRI* test was completed.

Use the Data

Who: Teachers (Teacher, Class, or Group report)

When: At the end of each grading period

How: Apply the information in this report in the following ways:

Acknowledge Success

- Share with students the various measures of their reading progress—including Lexile growth, Topic Software segment completion, and the total number of words read.
- Ask students to track their software progress and reading growth in their *rBooks*. Use the Topic Software Log to celebrate progress.

Monitor Student Progress

- Use these and other data to make decisions about transitioning students from the *READ 180* program. See Exiting *READ 180* on **page 52** for more information about exit criteria.
- Review average daily use and segment completion to ensure that students are participating appropriately in the *READ 180* Topic Software. Reteach software usage procedures each grading period or after long breaks from school.

Review Related Reports

- *READ 180* Participation Report (p. 146)
- *READ 180* Student Reading Report (p. 158)
- *SRI* Student Progress Report (p. 208)

Data in Action

Topic Software Levels Each software level has 60 segments. When students move to a higher software level, all topics and segments will be available at the higher level. A new software level will take effect at the end of a segment or topic.

Comprehension Skills Report

Purpose

This report summarizes performance in each comprehension skill included in the *READ 180* Software.

PROGRESS MONITORING

Comprehension Skills Report
CLASS: SCHIRMER 3

School: Lincoln Middle School
Teacher: Margaret Schirmer
Grade: 7

Time Period: 08/24/11 – 02/02/12 **1**

STUDENT	LEVEL	CAUSE AND EFFECT	COMPARE AND CONTRAST	DRAWING CONCLUSIONS	FINDING THE MAIN IDEA	MAKING INFERENCES	PROBLEMS AND SOLUTIONS	READING FOR DETAIL	SEQUENCING	SUMMARIZING	TOTAL NUMBER OF SKILLS BELOW 70%
▶ Bracco, Christine	2	100%	100%	▶ 57%	83%	100%	100%	100%	▶ 43%	86%	2
Chu, Amy	2	100%	89%	89%	78%	100%	100%	100%	100%	100%	0
▶ Collins, Chris	4	100%	100%	100%	▶ 0%	100%	N/A	100%	▶ 50%	100%	2
▶ Cooper, Tiffany	3	▶ 50%	75%	80%	80%	100%	100%	100%	▶ 50%	100%	2
▶ Evans, Jamal	2	100%	75%	▶ 50%	86%	86%	100%	71%	▶ 57%	100%	2
▶ Felix, Tonya	1	100%	100%	80%	92%	▶ 60%	100%	92%	100%	91%	1
▶ Fernandez, Luis	2	100%	100%	80%	75%	100%	100%	▶ 50%	▶ 0%	▶ 50%	3
▶ Garcia, Matt	2	80%	▶ 40%	▶ 67%	83%	71%	83%	100%	80%	86%	2
Imran, Khaleel	2	100%	100%	80%	71%	86%	100%	100%	75%	86%	0
▶ Kramer, Liz	4	100%	100%	100%	100%	100%	N/A	▶ 0%	▶ 0%	▶ 0%	3
Krynski, Theo	4	100%	100%	100%	100%	100%	100%	100%	100%	75%	0
Palermo, Justin	1	100%	75%	80%	86%	80%	100%	100%	75%	100%	0
▶ Ramirez, Gabriella	3	100%	100%	100%	▶ 50%	100%	100%	▶ 67%	▶ 50%	100%	3
▶ Rupp, Jeremy	3	100%	▶ 0%	100%	75%	▶ 0%	100%	100%	N/A	▶ 50%	3
▶ Sanchez, Rachel	3	88%	▶ 50%	75%	86%	88%	100%	88%	88%	▶ 63%	2
TOTAL NO. OF STUDENTS BELOW 70%		1	3	3	2	2	0	3	7	4	25

2 (spans skill columns) **3** (Total Number of Skills Below 70% column) **4** (Total No. of Students Below 70% row)

▶ Indicates score below 70%

Using This Report

Purpose: Students whose names are marked with red flags have comprehension scores of less than 70%. Scan each row for problems with specific skills.

Follow-Up: Plan instructional time targeting specific comprehension skills for small groups. Identify skills for which a large number of students need additional support, and plan Whole-Group Instruction.

How It Helps

I consult this report to make any Reading CheckPoint grouping adjustments needed in the Teacher Dashboard Groupinator.

Understand the Data

1 Time Period
For comprehensive performance results, run for This School Year. Customize time period settings to review results for more specific time ranges. As students complete more comprehension questions throughout the year, the weight of each question will decrease.

2 Comprehension Skills
Percentage of Reading Zone Quick Check Comprehension questions answered correctly on the first try. N/A indicates that a student has not yet answered a question on that comprehension skill.

3 Total Number of Skills Below 70%
Number of skills on which a student scored below 70% on the Reading Zone Quick Check questions.

4 Total Number of Students Below 70%
Number of students scoring below 70% on a particular comprehension skill.

Use the Data

Who: Teachers (Teacher, Class, or Group report)

When: At *rBook* CheckPoints

How: Apply the information in this report in the following ways:

Prioritize Comprehension Instruction

- Provide additional comprehension practice and support during *rBook* instruction on skills where multiple students score below 70%.

- Review Groupinator results at *rBook* Reading CheckPoints. Use this report to make any necessary grouping adjustments. See Grouping at Reading CheckPoints on **page 44** for more information.

Monitor Progress

- Investigate low performance. Remind students to re-read Reading Zone passages each day. Emphasize that their first Quick Check question response is the answer that is recorded.

- Adjust software levels as necessary. For students scoring above 90% on all comprehension skills for multiple segments, review overall class performance to determine whether they might benefit from an increased software level.

Review Related Reports

- *READ 180* Comprehension Skills Grouping Report (p. 142)
- *READ 180* Student Diagnostic Report (p. 156)
- *READ 180* Student Reading Report (p. 158)

Data in Action

SAM Resources The SAM onscreen report includes small green "R's" above each comprehension skill. These are links to resources and materials to provide additional support for each comprehension skill. Click on the "R" to link directly to a list of SAM Resources that correspond with each skill.

Comprehension Skills Grouping Report

Best Practice Report

Purpose

This report places students into three groups based on comprehension results from the *READ 180* software.

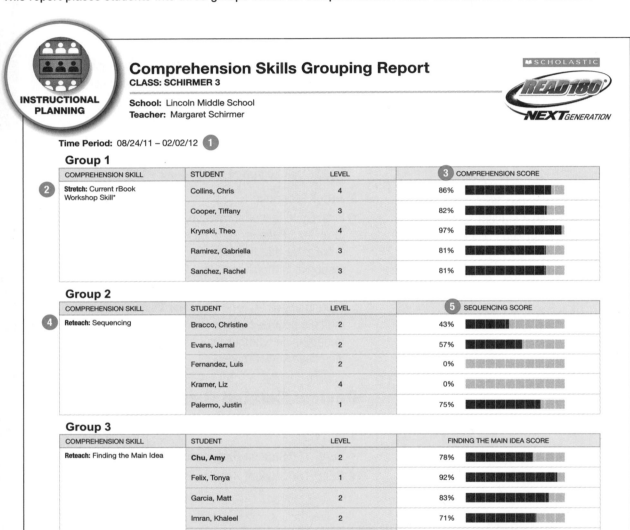

INSTRUCTIONAL PLANNING

Comprehension Skills Grouping Report
CLASS: SCHIRMER 3

School: Lincoln Middle School
Teacher: Margaret Schirmer

SCHOLASTIC
READ 180
*NEXT*GENERATION

Time Period: 08/24/11 – 02/02/12 ①

Group 1

COMPREHENSION SKILL	STUDENT	LEVEL	③ COMPREHENSION SCORE
② **Stretch:** Current rBook Workshop Skill*	Collins, Chris	4	86%
	Cooper, Tiffany	3	82%
	Krynski, Theo	4	97%
	Ramirez, Gabriella	3	81%
	Sanchez, Rachel	3	81%

Group 2

COMPREHENSION SKILL	STUDENT	LEVEL	⑤ SEQUENCING SCORE
④ **Reteach:** Sequencing	Bracco, Christine	2	43%
	Evans, Jamal	2	57%
	Fernandez, Luis	2	0%
	Kramer, Liz	4	0%
	Palermo, Justin	1	75%

Group 3

COMPREHENSION SKILL	STUDENT	LEVEL	FINDING THE MAIN IDEA SCORE
Reteach: Finding the Main Idea	Chu, Amy	2	78%
	Felix, Tonya	1	92%
	Garcia, Matt	2	83%
	Imran, Khaleel	2	71%
	Rupp, Jeremy	3	75%

⑥ | STUDENTS WITH NO DATA |
| No Data to Report |

⑦ * For rBook Literature Workshops, the Stretch skill is Making Inferences

Using This Report

Purpose: This report places students into Stretch or Reteach groups based on comprehension results in the software. Launch the Groupinator on the Teacher Dashboard for assistance in grouping and finding appropriate instructional resources.

Follow-Up: Use these results to group students for rBook Reading Check Points. Address specific Comprehension needs during Small-Group Instruction.

How It Helps

I use this report to group my students at rBook Reading CheckPoints. I access the data from the Groupinator, which links me directly to appropriate differentiated lessons for each group.

Understand the Data

1 Time Period

Run for This School Year for grouping results based on comprehensive performance in the *READ 180* Software. If customizing time period settings, consider that students need to complete at least one Software Topic to receive at least one question from each comprehension skill.

2 Comprehension Skill: Stretch

Students included in this group have high scores across all comprehension skills assessed in the Reading Zone.

3 Comprehension Score (Stretch)

Percentage of all Quick Check comprehension skill questions answered correctly on the first attempt. Score applies to Stretch groups only.

4 Comprehension Skill: Reteach

Students whose comprehension scores from the Reading Zone indicate that more instructional support is needed.

5 Skill Score (Reteach)

Percentage of Quick Check comprehension questions answered correctly from the comprehension skill assigned to the group. Score applies to Reteach groups only.

6 Students With No Data

Students who have not completed any Reading Zone Quick Check questions.

7 Literature Workshop

When teaching a literature workshop from the *rBook,* use Making Inferences lesson for the Stretch group.

Use the Data

Who: Teachers (Class report)

When: At *rBook* Reading CheckPoints

How: Apply the information from this report in the following ways:

Understand Performance Results

- The report is designed to create three equal groups and place students based on similar areas of need.
- Students are eligible to be placed in a Stretch group if they have performed well in all comprehension skill areas in the Reading Zone.
- Multiple Stretch groups may be created if two thirds or more of the class earns high overall comprehension scores.
- Students who are not placed in a Stretch group are placed in a Reteach group based on scores on specific comprehension skills. Students are grouped based on common skill areas of need.

Use Results for Instruction

- Access the results from Teacher Dashboard Groupinator to simplify the grouping and differentiating process.
- Use *Resources for Differentiated Instruction* lessons based on skill assigned to each group.
- If adjusting groups, use the *READ 180* Comprehension Skills Report to make regrouping decisions.

Review Related Reports

- *READ 180* Comprehension Skills Report (p. 140)
- *READ 180* Student Diagnostic Report (p. 156)
- *SRI* Intervention Grouping Report (p. 194)

Data in Action

Reading CheckPoint Groups SAM uses software level and comprehension scores to determine eligibility for a Stretch group. Students who have not earned strong overall comprehension scores are placed into Reteach groups. Groupinator results are linked to associated *Resources for Differentiated Instruction* lessons.

Grading Report

Purpose

This report shows information gathered from *READ 180* Software, *rSkills Tests*, and *Scholastic Reading Counts!*

PROGRESS MONITORING

Grading Report
CLASS: SCHIRMER 3

School: Lincoln Middle School
Teacher: Margaret Schirmer
Grade: 7

Time Period: 11/23/11 – 02/02/12 **1**

| STUDENT | LEVEL | READ 180 SOFTWARE PROGRESS | | | | | | | INDEPENDENT READING | TEACHER-DIRECTED INSTRUCTION |
		2 COMPREHENSION SCORE	**3** VOCABULARY SCORE	**4** WORD FLUENCY	**5** SPELLING SCORE	**6** CONTEXT PASSAGE	**7** FINAL FLUENCY RECORDING (OUT OF 6)	**8** RESPOND & WRITE SCORE (OUT OF 4)	**9** BOOK QUIZ AVERAGE (NO. OF BOOKS)	**10** RSKILLS TESTS OVERALL SCORE
Bracco, Christine	2	86%	85%	95%	97%	86%	2	2	78% (4)	60%
Chu, Amy	2	95%	95%	84%	98%	100%	N/A	3	84% (5)	89%
Collins, Chris	4	80%	80%	83%	98%	N/A	N/A	3	N/A	60%
Cooper, Tiffany	3	79%	74%	90%	97%	90%	N/A	2	43% (4)	N/A
Evans, Jamal	2	84%	91%	94%	97%	92%	5	1	70% (5)	74%
Felix, Tonya	1	88%	88%	90%	98%	100%	N/A	N/A	58% (4)	67%
Fernandez, Luis	2	86%	100%	92%	99%	95%	3	4	67% (3)	88%
Garcia, Matt	2	83%	87%	94%	99%	91%	3	4	39% (7)	58%
Imran, Khaleel	2	85%	97%	94%	97%	98%	5	N/A	88% (5)	100%
Kramer, Liz	4	60%	80%	93%	97%	N/A	N/A	3	N/A	64%
Krynski, Theo	4	100%	92%	88%	98%	96%	6	4	80% (3)	96%
Palermo, Justin	1	100%	67%	85%	100%	N/A	N/A	N/A	70% (1)	53%
Ramirez, Gabriella	3	67%	60%	87%	98%	96%	3	1	55% (4)	71%
Rupp, Jeremy	3	67%	45%	90%	97%	78%	4	2	N/A	57%
Sanchez, Rachel	3	79%	90%	92%	100%	89%	N/A	3	80% (4)	93%
AVERAGE	-	**83%**	**83%**	**92%**	**98%**	**92%**	-	-	**67%**	-

Using This Report

Purpose: This report shows information gathered during the Software and Modeled and Independent Reading small-group rotations to help you determine periodic student grades.

Follow-Up: Include student progress from all parts of the READ 180 Instructional Model in your grading assessment.

How It Helps

I use this report as a starting point when determining student grades. It contains useful summaries of software performance.

Understand the Data

1 Time Period

Default time period setting of This Grading Period displays student results during the current grading period. For best results, ensure grading periods are properly established in SAM.

2 Comprehension Score

Percentage of Reading Zone Quick Check comprehension questions answered correctly on the first try. Each segment contains ten comprehension questions.

3 Vocabulary Score

Percentage of Reading Zone Quick Check vocabulary questions answered correctly on the first try. Each segment contains five vocabulary questions.

4 Word Fluency

Percentage of words a student identified correctly in the Word Zone Speed Challenge activity. Challenge activities serve as a "post-test" for words assigned in each segment.

5 Spelling Score

Percentage of Spelling Zone study words spelled correctly in the Spelling Challenge activity.

6 Context Passage

Percentage of correct answers given on the first try in all Success Zone context passages.

7 Final Fluency Recording (out of 6)

Score entered in SAM Digital Portfolio for most recently completed Success Zone fluency recording.

8 Respond & Write Score (out of 4)

Score entered in SAM Portfolio for most recently published Respond & Write response.

9 Book Quiz Average (No. of Books)

Average score on all *Scholastic Reading Counts!* quizzes taken. Number in parentheses indicates total *SRC!* quizzes attempted during the selected time period.

10 *rSkills Tests* Overall Score

Average score for all *rSkills Tests* completed on the computer during the selected time period.

Use the Data

Who: Teachers (Teacher, Class, or Group report)

When: At the end of each grading period

How: Apply the information in this report in the following ways:

Determine Grades

- Use the data from this report as a starting point for assessing performance in the *READ 180* software, *rSkills Tests,* and *SRC!* quizzes.

- Include other factors when determining final student grades, such as *rBook* work, daily performance, and participation in daily activities. See Grading in *READ 180* on **page 110** for more information.

Review Software Usage

- Students with low scores in any of the *READ 180* software zones may be struggling with appropriate software usage. Review software usage tips with students each grading period.

- Students with low *SRC!* quiz averages may be struggling with comprehension of texts in the Modeled and Independent Reading Rotation or struggling with taking quizzes. Conference with students and review written work such as daily reading logs or graphic organizers to determine what support to provide.

Review Related Reports

- *READ 180* Reading Progress Report (p. 150)
- *rSkills Tests* Grading Report (p. 174)
- *SRC!* Reading Progress Report (p. 230)

Data in Action

Comparing Software Results Cross-reference results from "pretest" activities on the *READ 180* Reading Progress Report with results from the "post-test" activities on this report to monitor progress.

Participation Report

Purpose

This report displays student software participation to help find ways to maximize students' software usage.

MANAGEMENT

Participation Report
CLASS: SCHIRMER 3

School: Lincoln Middle School
Teacher: Margaret Schirmer
Grade: 7

Time Period: 08/24/11 – 02/02/12 ①

		② TOTAL USAGE			⑤ MEDIAN USAGE	⑥	⑦	⑧
STUDENT	LEVEL	TOTAL TIME (MIN.)	NO. OF SESSIONS	TOTAL SEGMENTS COMPLETED	SESSIONS PER WEEK	TIME PER SESSION (MIN.)	TIME PER WEEK (MIN.)	TIME PER SEGMENT (MIN.)
Bracco, Christine	2	944	50	10	3	17	50	80
Chu, Amy	2	736	43	17	3	16	40	34
▸ Collins, Chris	4	824	59	1	3	▸ 14	51	412
Cooper, Tiffany	3	1106	67	8	4	17	57	106
Evans, Jamal	2	1067	69	14	4	15	54	60
Felix, Tonya	1	863	59	20	3	16	36	33
▸ Fernandez, Luis	2	583	41	6	▸ 2	▸ 14	29	76
Garcia, Matt	2	1012	55	12	4	16	56	69
▸ Imran, Khaleel	2	545	44	12	3	▸ 13	30	39
▸ Kramer, Liz	4	588	52	1	3	▸ 12	40	285
▸ Krynski, Theo	4	814	54	5	3	▸ 14	37	125
▸ Palermo, Justin	1	379	22	10	▸ 2	16	35	34
▸ Ramirez, Gabriella	3	585	49	4	3	▸ 12	34	225
▸ Rupp, Jeremy	3	815	54	3	3	▸ 14	43	240
Sanchez, Rachel	3	1007	59	15	4	16	54	55

▸ Indicates average participation is less than 15 minutes a day or less than 3 sessions a week

Using This Report

Purpose: Students whose names are marked with red flags are using the Software less than three times a week or for sessions of less than 15 minutes.

Follow-Up: Observe the class and find ways to maximize students' Software access and usage.

How It Helps

I use this report to make sure my students are using the Topic Software at least twenty minutes a day so they get the full benefits of READ 180.

Understand the Data

1 Time Period

Default time period setting of This School Year displays comprehensive participation results. Customize time period settings to review results for shorter periods of time. For optimal results, run this report for a range of at least two weeks.

2 Total Time (Minutes)

Total minutes a student used the *READ 180* Topic Software during the selected time period.

3 Number of Sessions

Number of sessions a student logged on to *READ 180* during the selected time period. Each school day is considered a session, regardless of the number of times a student logs in that day.

4 Total Segments Completed

Total Topic Software segments a student has completed within the selected time period. Any segment completed at any level counts as a separate segment.

5 Sessions per Week

Median number of sessions a student logged on to *READ 180* each week. A red flag indicates usage less than three times a week.

6 Time per Session (Minutes)

Median number of minutes a student spent working on the software during each session. A red flag indicates software usage of less than 15 minutes per session.

7 Time per Week (Minutes)

Median number of minutes a student spent using the software each week.

8 Time per Segment (Minutes)

Median number of minutes a student spent completing each segment within the selected time period.

Use the Data

Who: Teachers (Teacher, Class, or Group report)

When: Monthly

How: Apply the information in this report in the following ways:

Monitor Software Use

- Check to see if students need support logging on and off the Software. Remind students to exit the program by returning to the Zone Menu and logging out. Improper logout may cause loss of session data.

- Encourage students to monitor their daily usage in the Student Dashboard. Require students who are struggling with software participation to use the Student Dashboard information to complete a daily software log (**SAM Keyword:** Software Log).

Conference With Students

- Follow up directly with students who are absent or are not reaching minimum participation benchmarks. Help students set and track goals for attendance and daily participation.

Review Related Reports

- *READ 180* Comparative Time-on-Task Report (p. 136)
- *READ 180* Completion Success Report (p. 138)
- *READ 180* Student Segment Status Report (p. 162)

Data in Action

Reviewing Report Data While most other *READ 180* reports track average student usage, the Participation Report tracks median software usage. The median result is not as heavily affected by one or two sessions with times outside the normal range.

Phonics and Word Study Grouping Report

Purpose

This report groups students based on common word recognition error patterns recorded in the Word Zone.

INSTRUCTIONAL PLANNING

Phonics and Word Study Grouping Report
CLASS: SCHIRMER 3

School: Lincoln Middle School
Teacher: Margaret Schirmer
Grade: 7

Time Period: 11/23/11 – 02/02/12 ①

② MOST COMMON ERROR TYPES	STUDENT	LEVEL	③ NUMBER OF ERRORS	④ RECENT EXAMPLES
Words with Phonograms	Chu, Amy	2	15	bride, sailed, wide, pave, crave
	Felix, Tonya	1	11	thinks, big, shines, next, six
	Fernandez, Luis	2	4	black, shares, nights, leave
	Imran, Khaleel	2	25	soon, wing, king, wind, face
	Krynski, Theo	4	9	steep, spin, plane, bare, gives
Inflectional Endings	Chu, Amy	2	13	killing, finished, soldiers, comics, days
	Collins, Chris	4	17	machines, wallets, laughing, detected, actresses
	Cooper, Tiffany	3	4	reasons, lawsuits, attracts
	Felix, Tonya	1	7	owns, brothers, started, worked, opened
	Krynski, Theo	4	6	descending, hair-raising, athletes, obstacles
	Ramirez, Gabriella	3	5	reading, rides, roaring
	Rupp, Jeremy	3	4	printers, prisoners, methods
Multi-Syllable Words	Chu, Amy	2	6	diary, fifteen, record, spirit, salsa
	Collins, Chris	4	22	clever, grocery, partly, simply, enterprise
	Cooper, Tiffany	3	4	irrelevant, supervise, incentive, irresponsible
	Fernandez, Luis	2	4	interest, pollution
	Kramer, Liz	4	4	popularity, exact, nifty
	Krynski, Theo	4	5	leisurely, snowboarder, pressure, skysurfer, skysurfers
	Rupp, Jeremy	3	4	process, watermarks, lapel, secret

Using This Report

Purpose: This report shows common word recognition errors among a group of students. Students are listed and grouped according to their specific error patterns.

Follow-Up: Work with the groups on one or more of the word elements during Small-Group Instruction time using Resources for Differentiated Instruction.

How It Helps

I use this report to determine whether phonics instruction is necessary. If so, this report helps me create appropriate groups and target instruction.

Understand the Data

1 Time Period

Default setting of This Grading Period displays results from recent software activity. For more comprehensive results, time period settings can be customized.

2 Most Common Error Types

Word patterns students identified incorrectly or slowly in the Word Zone Speed Challenge activity. Error types are ranked in order of the number of students who missed, or were slow to recognize, a word with that pattern. There are 31 possible error types.

3 Number of Errors

Total number of errors a student made of a particular type within the selected time period.

4 Recent Examples

Examples of words a student missed within the specified error type. Only the most recent errors are shown.

Use the Data

Who: Teachers (Teacher, Class, or Group report)

When: Run this report at *rBook* CheckPoints.

How: Apply the information in this report in the following ways:

Target Instruction

- Identify the error types challenging the greatest number of students. If a majority of students appear to be struggling with phonics, prioritize phonics as an instructional focus at *rBook* CheckPoints.
- If a student appears in four or five error categories, you may wish to work with the student one-on-one on basic phonemic awareness and decoding skills.

Focus on Software Usage

- Ensure that students are properly completing activities in the Word Zone. Review software instructions periodically with students.
- Review individual results on the *READ 180* Student Word Zone Report to identify specific lists of words students are practicing. Provide opportunities for additional practice or homework.

Review Related Reports

- *READ 180* Comprehension Skills Report (p. 140)
- *READ 180* Student Diagnostic Report (p. 156)
- *READ 180* Student Word Zone Report (p. 166)

Data in Action

Focus on Phonics Work with a small group of students using current error type examples to teach, review, and practice skills. Use SAM to print skill-based instructional resources such as lesson plans and practice pages.

Reading Progress Report | Best Practice Report

Purpose

This report provides an overview of student participation and performance in the *READ 180* Software.

PROGRESS MONITORING

Reading Progress Report
CLASS: SCHIRMER 3

School: Lincoln Middle School
Teacher: Margaret Schirmer
Grade: 7

Time Period: 08/24/11 – 02/02/12 **1**

SCHOLASTIC
READ180®
NEXTGENERATION

| | | CURRENT STATUS | | TIME-ON-TASK | | | | | CUMULATIVE PERFORMANCE | | | | |
| | | | | | | | | | | | | | |
STUDENT	LEVEL	LAST SRI SCORE (LEXILE®)	LATEST TOPIC SOFTWARE	SESSIONS	SEGMENTS	TIME (MIN.)	AVG. SESSION LENGTH	SESSIONS PER SEGMENT	WORDS READ	COMPREHENSION SCORE	VOCABULARY SCORE	WORD ZONE ASSESSMENT SCORE	SPELLING ZONE ASSESSMENT SCORE	RESPOND & WRITE SCORE (OUT OF 4)
Bracco, Christine	2	709	Beating the Odds	50	10	944	17	5	55,831	83%	91%	95%	90%	2
Chu, Amy	2	834	Scene Stealers	43	17	736	16	3	105,245	95%	94%	91%	90%	3
Collins, Chris	4	868	Extreme Sports	59	1	824	14	16	16,815	86%	94%	63%	47%	3
Cooper, Tiffany	3	781	Help Wanted	67	8	1106	17	9	105,771	82%	67%	89%	76%	2
Evans, Jamal	2	719	The Whole World Watched	69	14	1067	15	5	93,655	81%	96%	98%	91%	1
Felix, Tonya	1	BR (10)	You and the Law	59	20	863	16	3	31,775	90%	89%	88%	90%	N/A
Fernandez, Luis	2	242	Help Wanted	41	6	583	14	6	21,097	72%	87%	92%	84%	4
Garcia, Matt	2	550	Game On!	55	12	1012	16	5	43,503	77%	91%	97%	89%	4
Imran, Khaleel	2	719	Help Wanted	44	12	545	13	3	289,267	88%	98%	81%	86%	3
Kramer, Liz	4	809	The Big Giveback	52	1	588	12	21	15,792	67%	82%	82%	67%	3
Krynski, Theo	4	1120	Show Me the Money!	54	5	814	14	9	30,096	97%	93%	91%	88%	4
Palermo, Justin	1	438	Survive	22	10	379	16	3	24,537	87%	76%	88%	92%	N/A
Ramirez, Gabriella	3	743	Extreme Sports	49	4	585	12	14	15,715	81%	63%	92%	80%	1
Rupp, Jeremy	3	727	Show Me the Money!	54	3	815	14	13	17,793	79%	39%	86%	54%	2
Sanchez, Rachel	3	792	First Person	59	15	1007	16	4	251,855	81%	81%	99%	94%	3
AVERAGE	-	**718**	-	**52**	**9**	**803**	**15**	**8**	-	**83%**	**83%**	**89%**	**81%**	

2 **3** **4** **5** **6** **7** **8** **9** **10**

Using This Report

Purpose: This is an overview of students' overall progress in the READ 180 Software during the selected time period.

Follow-Up: Check regularly for Software usage patterns and correlations between time and performance data. Use other reports to "drill down" on individual student performance.

How It Helps

I use this report to ensure that my students are participating appropriately in the software each day.

Understand the Data

1 Time Period

Run for This School Year to review comprehensive performance results. Customize time period settings to analyze student progress within shorter time periods.

2 Sessions

Total sessions a student used the Topic Software. A session is one school day, regardless of how many times a student logs in that day.

3 Segments

Total segments a student completed at any level. Each software Topic includes 4 segments.

4 Time (Minutes)

Total number of minutes a student spent participating in software activities.

5 Average Session Length

Average minutes spent on software each session, updated each time a student logs in and out. Students should spend an average 15–19 minutes per session.

6 Sessions Per Segment

Average sessions it takes for a student to complete all zones in a software segment. Students should average 4–15 sessions per segment, depending on level and whether Writing Zone is enabled.

7 Words Read

Total cumulative words read in *READ 180*, regardless of time period settings. Total also includes total words read from *Scholastic Reading Counts!* quizzes passed.

8 Comprehension and Vocabulary Scores

Percentage of Reading Zone questions answered correctly on the *first attempt*.

9 Word and Spelling Zone Assessment Scores

Percentage of words student identified correctly in the Word Zone and Spelling Zone Assessments (the pre-test activities).

10 Respond & Write Score (Out of 4)

Score for most recent Writing Zone published response if graded in SAM Digital Portfolio.

Use the Data

Who: Teachers (Teacher, Class, or Group report)

When: Once or twice a month.

How: Apply the information from this report in the following ways:

Monitor Software Participation

- Help students track daily progress in the software. Have them review their Student Dashboard results and write down the total work completed in each zone daily on a software log. (**SAM Keyword:** Software Log)

- If multiple students' average session length is low, use a timer to ensure that each rotation is timed appropriately.

Review Performance Results

- If average zone scores are low, review software usage tips with students. Remind students that their first answers are recorded and that total amount of work assigned in Spelling and Word Zones depends on performance on Assessment activities.

- If students complete multiple segments in less than 4 sessions per segment and have earned 90% or better in each zone, you may wish to consider manually promoting the student to a new level.

Review Related Reports

- *READ 180* Grading Report (p. 144)
- *READ 180* Student Segment Status Report (p. 162)
- *READ 180* Student Reading Report (p. 158)

Data in Action

Software Performance Results Zone performance data may be affected if students do not properly log out of the software. Ensure that students exit the program each day by returning to the zone menu and choosing to close the software.

Analyze the Results | Reading Progress Report

Students should be able to complete each segment in one or two weeks with strong results in each zone.

DATA STORY

Student: Liz Kramer
Current Lexile: 809
Software Sessions: 52
Total Segments: 1

Identify students like Liz who struggle with software usage.

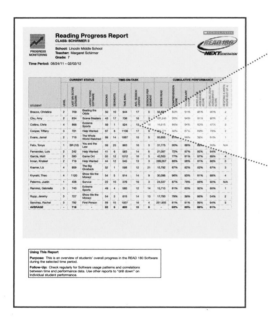

Reading Progress Report
CLASS: SCHIRMER 3

PROGRESS MONITORING

School: Lincoln Middle School
Teacher: Margaret Schirmer
Grade: 7

Time Period: 08/24/11 – 02/02/12

| STUDENT | CURRENT STATUS | | | TIME-ON-TASK | | | | CUMULATIVE PERFORMANCE | | | | | |
	LEVEL	LAST SRI SCORE (LEXILE®)	LATEST TOPIC SOFTWARE	SESSIONS	SEGMENTS	TIME (MIN.)	AVG. SESSION LENGTH	SESSIONS PER SEGMENT	WORDS READ	COMPREHENSION SCORE	VOCABULARY SCORE	WORD ZONE ASSESSMENT SCORE	SPELLING ZONE ASSESSMENT SCORE	RESPOND & WRITE SCORE (OUT OF 4)
Bracco, Christine	2	709	Beating the Odds	50	10	944	17	5	55,831	83%	91%	95%	90%	2
Chu, Amy	2	834	Scene Stealers	43	17	736	16	3	105,245	95%	94%	91%	90%	3
Collins, Chris	4	868	Extreme Sports	59	1	824	13	16	16,815	86%	94%	63%	47%	3
Cooper, Tiffany	3	781	Help Wanted	67	8	1106	17	9	105,771	82%	67%	89%	76%	2
Evans, Jamal	2	719	The Whole World Watched	69	14	1067	16	5	93,655	81%	96%	98%	91%	1
Felix, Tonya	1	BR (10)	You and the Law	59	20	863	16	3	31,775	90%	89%	88%	90%	N/A
Fernandez, Luis	2	242	Help Wanted	41	6	583	14	6	21,097	72%	87%	92%	84%	4
Garcia, Matt	2	580	Game On!	55	12	1012	16	5	43,503	77%	91%	97%	89%	4
Imran, Khaleel	2	719	Help Wanted	44	12	545	13	3	289,267	88%	98%	81%	86%	3
Kramer, Liz	4	809	The Big Giveback	52	1	588	12	21	15,792	67%	82%	82%	67%	3
Krynski, Theo	4	1120	Show Me the Money!	54	5	814	14	9	30,096	96%	93%	91%	88%	4
Palermo, Justin	1	438	Survive	22	10	379	16	3	24,537	87%	76%	88%	92%	N/A
Ramirez, Gabriella	3	743	Extreme Sports	49	4	585	12	14	15,715	81%	63%	92%	80%	1
Rupp, Jeremy	3	727	Show Me the Money!	54	3	815	14	13	17,793	79%	39%	86%	54%	2
Sanchez, Rachel	3	792	First Person	59	15	1007	16	4	251,855	81%	81%	99%	94%	3
AVERAGE	-	718	-	52	9	803	15	8	-	83%	83%	89%	81%	

🔍 **Enlargement: Reading Progress Report**

NEXT STEPS

Data Point	Data Analysis	NEXT STEPS
1 Liz is only working through her second segment, while the class average is 9 segments completed.	Liz has been in this class since the beginning of the year. She isn't progressing through segments as quickly as she should.	Review results on the *READ 180* Student Segment Status Report to determine the cause for low segment completion.
2 Liz is spending less than 15 minutes per day on the software.	Most of the class is maintaining appropriate session length. Liz is likely off-task during this rotation.	Have students track daily progress on a Software Log and review the log during Small-Group Instruction. (**SAM Keyword:** Software Log)
3 Liz's performance in each zone is not strong, even though she has a relatively high Lexile.	Liz has not been taking the Assessment and Quick Check questions seriously.	Review software tips and procedures with the class each grading period, especially after long breaks or if classwide performance is low.

Review Additional Data

Use the *READ 180* Student Segment Status Report to analyze segment performance and participation.

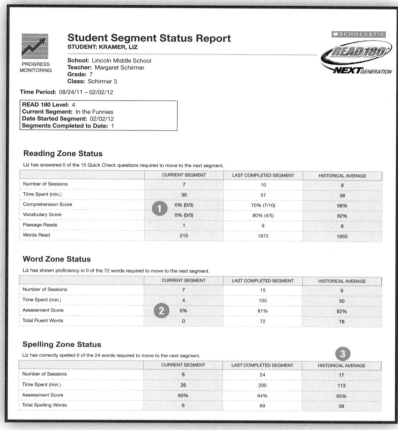

Enlargement: **Student Segment Status Report**

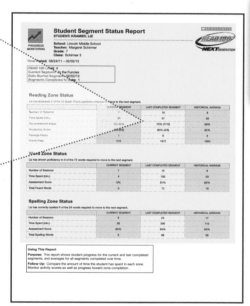

Data Point	Data Analysis	NEXT STEPS
① Liz spent 30 minutes in the Reading Zone but did not answer any questions.	Liz should answer three questions each day in the Reading Zone.	Have students write down how many Reading Zone questions they have left to answer each day. The number should decrease daily.
② Liz scored a 0% on her Word Zone Assessment.	Scoring a 0% on the Assessment "pre-test" means that Liz will have to review all of the words during her work in the Word Zone.	Remind students that their performance on the Assessment activity dictates how much work they will have to complete in the zone.
③ Liz's average time on the Spelling Zone is high, yet her average performance is low.	Students typically take longer in the Spelling Zone, but taking twice as much time as the Word Zone is too long for Liz.	When students are working in partners during Small-Group, go to the Instructional Software rotation to monitor student participation.

Spelling Skills Grouping Report

Purpose

This report groups students based on common spelling error patterns recorded in the Spelling Zone.

INSTRUCTIONAL PLANNING

Spelling Skills Grouping Report
CLASS: SCHIRMER 3

School: Lincoln Middle School
Teacher: Margaret Schirmer
Grade: 7

Time Period: 11/23/11 – 02/02/12

MOST COMMON ERROR TYPES	STUDENT	LEVEL	NUMBER OF ERRORS	RECENT EXAMPLES
Additions	Bracco, Christine	2	16	happened, decision, Arkansas, catch, entered
	Chu, Amy	2	10	stays, so, during, tigers, modern
	Cooper, Tiffany	3	45	extremely, surprise, develops, athletes, reviews
	Evans, Jamal	2	10	reaching, surprised, down, too, others
	Felix, Tonya	1	5	makes, brown, boards, dog's
	Fernandez, Luis	2	9	control, exactly, audience, remembers, environmental
	Garcia, Matt	2	8	thought, appears, needed, where, got
	Imran, Khaleel	1	12	know, spends, spent, right, speeds
	Kramer, Liz	4	8	accomplish, penalties, fortunately, risky, suggests
	Krynski, Theo	4	7	that's, process, imagine, equipment, done
	Ramirez, Gabriella	3	6	foamy, training, example, equipment
	Rupp, Jeremy	3	18	arrest, markings, options, technologies, nationally
Omissions	Bracco, Christine	2	8	happened, segregated, pollution, musician, addition
	Chu, Amy	2	8	they're, create, brake, athletes, quote
	Cooper, Tiffany	3	21	surprise, extremely, athletes, animals, triumphed
	Evans, Jamal	2	9	captured, opened, presidency, pile, levees
	Fernandez, Luis	2	9	comic, thinks, environmental, watch, though
	Garcia, Matt	2	8	appears, foresees, exciting, remembers, happened

How It Helps

It's helpful to know which spelling errors my students are making. That way, I can review spelling routines for the words my students are having difficulty with.

Using This Report

Purpose: This report shows common spelling errors among a group of students. Students are listed and grouped by specific error patterns. Use this report to plan Whole-Group, Small-Group, and individualized instruction.

Follow-Up: Work with the groups on one or more spelling elements during Small-Group Instruction time using Resources for Differentiated Instruction.

Understand the Data

1 **Time Period**
Default setting of This Grading Period will display results from recent software activity. For more comprehensive results, time period settings can be customized.

2 **Most Common Error Types**
General spelling errors students are making in the Spelling Clinic and Spelling Challenge activities.

3 **Number of Errors**
Number of times a student made a particular error type within the selected time period.

4 **Recent Examples**
Examples of words a student misspelled within a spelling error type. Only the most recent errors are shown.

Use the Data

Who: Teachers (Teacher, Class, or Group report)

When: Run this report at *rBook* CheckPoints.

How: Apply the information in this report in the following ways:

Target Instruction

- Identify the error types challenging the greatest number of students. If a majority of students appear to be struggling with spelling, prioritize spelling and phonics as an instructional focus during *rBook* CheckPoints.

- If a student appears in four or five error categories, you may wish to work with the student one-on-one on basic skills.

Focus on Software Usage

- Ensure that students are properly completing activities in the Spelling Zone. Review software instructions periodically with students.

- Review individual results on the *READ 180* Student Spelling Zone Report to identify specific lists of words students are practicing. Assign students additional practice with these words as homework.

Review Related Reports

- *READ 180* Comprehension Skills Report (p. 140)
- *READ 180* Student Diagnostic Report (p. 156)
- *READ 180* Student Spelling Zone Report (p. 164)

Data in Action

Focus on Spelling Work with a small group of students using examples of common error types to teach, review, and practice spelling.

Student Diagnostic Report | Best Practice Report

Purpose

This report details a student's skills performance in each of the *READ 180* Software zones.

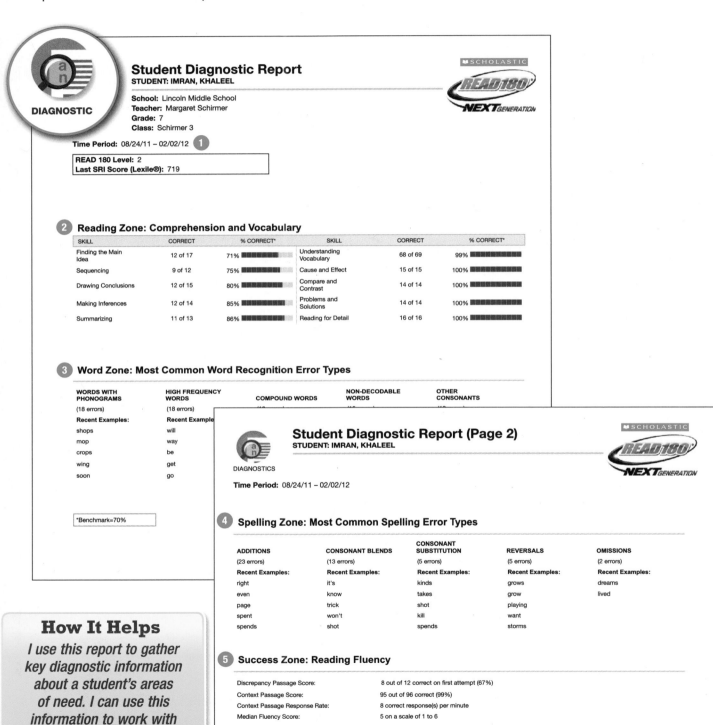

DIAGNOSTIC

Student Diagnostic Report
STUDENT: IMRAN, KHALEEL

School: Lincoln Middle School
Teacher: Margaret Schirmer
Grade: 7
Class: Schirmer 3

SCHOLASTIC
READ 180 NEXT GENERATION

Time Period: 08/24/11 – 02/02/12 ①

READ 180 Level: 2
Last SRI Score (Lexile®): 719

② **Reading Zone: Comprehension and Vocabulary**

SKILL	CORRECT	% CORRECT*	SKILL	CORRECT	% CORRECT*
Finding the Main Idea	12 of 17	71%	Understanding Vocabulary	68 of 69	99%
Sequencing	9 of 12	75%	Cause and Effect	15 of 15	100%
Drawing Conclusions	12 of 15	80%	Compare and Contrast	14 of 14	100%
Making Inferences	12 of 14	85%	Problems and Solutions	14 of 14	100%
Summarizing	11 of 13	86%	Reading for Detail	16 of 16	100%

③ **Word Zone: Most Common Word Recognition Error Types**

WORDS WITH PHONOGRAMS	HIGH FREQUENCY WORDS	COMPOUND WORDS	NON-DECODABLE WORDS	OTHER CONSONANTS
(18 errors)	(18 errors)			
Recent Examples:	**Recent Examples:**			
shops	will			
mop	way			
crops	be			
wing	get			
soon	go			

*Benchmark=70%

Student Diagnostic Report (Page 2)
STUDENT: IMRAN, KHALEEL

DIAGNOSTICS

SCHOLASTIC
READ 180 NEXT GENERATION

Time Period: 08/24/11 – 02/02/12

④ **Spelling Zone: Most Common Spelling Error Types**

ADDITIONS	CONSONANT BLENDS	CONSONANT SUBSTITUTION	REVERSALS	OMISSIONS
(23 errors)	(13 errors)	(5 errors)	(5 errors)	(2 errors)
Recent Examples:	**Recent Examples:**	**Recent Examples:**	**Recent Examples:**	**Recent Examples:**
right	it's	kinds	grows	dreams
even	know	takes	grow	lived
page	trick	shot	playing	
spent	won't	kill	want	
spends	shot	spends	storms	

⑤ **Success Zone: Reading Fluency**

Discrepancy Passage Score:	8 out of 12 correct on first attempt (67%)
Context Passage Score:	95 out of 96 correct (99%)
Context Passage Response Rate:	8 correct response(s) per minute
Median Fluency Score:	5 on a scale of 1 to 6

⑥ **Writing Zone: Respond & Write Results**

Median Teacher Rating:	3
Most Recent Respond & Write Segment:	Making Money
Most Recent Respond & Write Prompt:	Should the Treasury Department keep everything it does a secret? State your opinion. Then give two reasons to support it.

How It Helps

I use this report to gather key diagnostic information about a student's areas of need. I can use this information to work with students one-on-one.

Understand the Data

① Time Period
Default time period setting of This Grading Period displays recent software performance results. For more comprehensive data, time period settings can be customized.

② Comprehension and Vocabulary
Number and percentage of correct responses that the student gave on the first try on each Reading Zone Quick Check question. Skills are sorted by percentage of correct responses.

③ Most Common Word Recognition Error Types
Word patterns the student is not identifying quickly or correctly in the Word Zone Challenge activities. The five word patterns with the most errors are displayed, along with recent examples.

④ Most Common Spelling Error Types
Word patterns the student has the most difficulty spelling. The five spelling patterns with the most errors are displayed, along with recent examples.

⑤ Reading Fluency
Performance on Success Zone activities. Includes number of discrepancy passages identified correctly on the first try and percentage of context passage answers given correctly on the first try. Also includes a median fluency score (from 1 to 6), based on evaluation of all oral fluency recordings assessed during the selected time period. N/A indicates that a recording was not assessed in the SAM Digital Portfolio.

⑥ Respond and Write Results
Median Respond & Write score (from 1 to 4), based on evaluation of student's published Writing Zone response. N/A indicates that writing was not published or was not assessed in SAM Digital Portfolio during selected time period.

Use the Data

Who: Teachers, Students (Student report)

When: Every 6 to 8 weeks, to correspond with grading periods.

How: Apply the information in this report in the following ways:

Monitor Student Progress

- Look for error patterns in comprehension, vocabulary, phonics, spelling, or writing and focus instruction on these skills.
- Ensure that students are focusing appropriately in each zone. Review performance results from each section of this report to determine areas of challenge and follow up as necessary.

Conference With Students

- Share this report with students during one-on-one conferences. Help students use this data to track performance trends and set goals for improving reading comprehension, phonics, fluency, spelling, and/or writing performance.
- Remind students to take advantage of spelling, pronunciation, and decoding tips in the Reading Zone Word Window for words with which they are unfamiliar.

Review Related Reports

- *READ 180* Comprehension Skills Grouping Report (p. 142)
- *READ 180* Student Reading Report (p. 158)
- *rSkills Tests* Student Skills Report (p. 184)

> ## Data in Action
>
> **Reviewing Word and Spelling Zone Errors**
> Word Zone and Spelling Zone words appear on this report after students complete the challenge activities. These are words that students missed or answered slowly, even after practice during the current segment.

Student Reading Report | Best Practice Report

Purpose

This report tracks annual progress in the *READ 180* software and in *Scholastic Reading Counts!* Quizzes.

Student Reading Report
STUDENT: IMRAN, KHALEEL

School: Lincoln Middle School
Teacher: Margaret Schirmer
Grade: 7
Class: Schirmer 3

Time Period: 08/24/11 – 02/02/12 ①

READ 180 Level: 2
Current Topic Software: Help Wanted
Last SRI Score (Lexile®): 719

READ 180 Software Progress

② TOPIC SOFTWARE AND SEGMENT	③ LEVEL	④ DATE STARTED	⑤ DATE COMPLETED	⑥ NO. OF SESSIONS PER SEGMENT	⑦ COMPREHENSION AND VOCABULARY			⑧ WORDS MASTERED	
					COMP. SCORE	VOCAB. SCORE	CONTEXT PASSAGE SCORE	FLUENT	SPELLING
Help Wanted									
In the Funnies	2	02/05/12	In Progress	4	75%	87%	N/A	22	39
Jump Shot	2	01/26/12	02/05/12	8	75%	83%	100%	17	33
Show Me the Money									
Making Money	1	01/15/12	01/21/12	2	100%	100%	100%	26	44
Bogus Bill	1	01/11/12	01/12/12	2	100%	100%	100%	22	32
Fighting Forgery	1	01/04/12	01/08/12	2	100%	100%	100%	24	43
Mangled Money	1	12/03/11	12/16/11	4	75%	100%	88%	18	15
Disaster!									
Volcano!	1	11/23/11	12/02/11	3	80%	100%	100%	17	31
Avalanche!	1	11/12/11	11/23/11	5	75%	100%	100%	28	35
Earthquake!	1	11/05/11	11/12/11	5	80%	100%	100%	27	31
Flood!	1	10/29/11	11/05/11	3	100%	100%	100%	29	39
The Big Giveback									
Room to Read	1	10/20/11	10/27/11	5	100%	100%	100%	34	33
Hometown Hero	1	10/16/11	10/19/11	2	100%	100%	100%	38	39
Get Pumped!	1	09/22/11	10/15/11	8	100%	100%	100%	36	36
Tunes 4 the Troops	1	09/15/11	09/22/11	5	75%	100%	100%	35	33
TOTAL SEGMENTS COMPLETED: 13				N/A	88%	98%	99%	373	483

Student Reading Report (Page 2)
STUDENT: IMRAN, KHALEEL

Time Period: 08/24/11 – 02/02/12

Scholastic Reading Counts! Independent Reading Progress

ALL QUIZZES TAKEN	⑨ DATE	⑩ SCHOLASTIC READING COUNTS! SCORE	⑪ TOTAL WORDS READ
Adventures of Capt. Underpants	01/16/12	100%	5,360
New Moon	11/30/11	100%	133,409
Cyber Pranks (Read 180)	10/10/11	100%	1,890
Love Letters And Other Stories	11/01/11	100%	10,000
Homeless But College Bound (eReads)	11/06/11	90%	348
Disaster Reports Go Digital (eReads)	10/10/11	90%	379
Tunnel of Terror & Other …	09/23/11	90%	5,304
Twilight	12/11/11	80%	118,909
Oh Yuck! (Read 180)	09/03/11	80%	1,400
Classic Tales Terror (READ 180)	10/15/11	60%	N/A
Total Quizzes Taken: 10		89% (AVG)	276,999

How It Helps
I conference with students about their results and track their progress from segment to segment.

Understand the Data

① Time Period
Run for This School Year to review comprehensive performance.

② Topic Software and Segment
Chronologically lists each software Topic and segment student completed.

③ Level
Software level for each segment completed.

④ Date Started
Lists date student started each software segment at each level.

⑤ Date Completed
Lists date student completed each software segment at each level. In Progress indicates that the segment is not complete.

⑥ Number of Sessions Per Segment
Total sessions (days) it took for a student to complete a segment. Typically, students complete a segment within 4 to 15 sessions.

⑦ Comprehension and Vocabulary
Percentage of Reading Zone Quick Check questions answered correctly on the first try.

⑧ Words Mastered
Total words mastered in the Word Zone and Spelling Zone, including Study Words and words identified correctly in the Assessment activity.

⑨ SRC! Date
Date each SRC! quiz was taken.

⑩ SRC! Score
Percentage of questions answered correctly on each SRC! quiz attempt. SRC! results are sorted from highest score to lowest score.

⑪ SRC! Total Words Read
Total words read for each book. 0 indicates that a quiz was attempted but not passed.

Use the Data

Who: Teachers, Students, Caregivers (Student report)

When: Monthly, or in preparation for a conference.

How: Apply the information from this report in the following ways:

Monitor Participation

- Track progress throughout the year, noting improvement in scores and rate of completion.
- Provide additional support on appropriate software usage if results indicate a student is struggling to complete a segment or is performing below expectations in each zone.
- Review *Scholastic Reading Counts!* performance to ensure regular participation and quiz success.

Share Results

- Celebrate software progress — completed segments and topics and zone scores, as well as *Scholastic Reading Counts!* progress.
- Conference with students to determine cause for low scores or high number of sessions per segment. Reteach appropriate software usage procedures at the beginning of each grading period.
- Share results with caregivers at parent-teacher conferences.

Review Related Reports

- *READ 180* Student Diagnostic Report (p. 156)
- *READ 180* Student Segment Status Report (p. 162)
- *SRC!* Student Reading Report (p. 238)

Data in Action

Level Promotion During the course of the year, students may move up a level on the software. When this happens, students will have access to all 15 software topics at the new level. Use the Teacher Dashboard to schedule alerts to notify you when students are promoted to a new level.

Analyze the Results | Student Reading Report

The software's individualized support allows students to earn consistently strong results in each zone.

DATA STORY

Student: Khaleel Imran
Current Lexile: 719

Khaleel is ready for a new software level. Recognize achievement and provide appropriate challenge to keep students engaged.

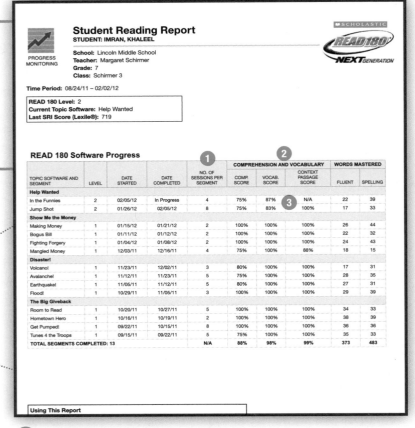

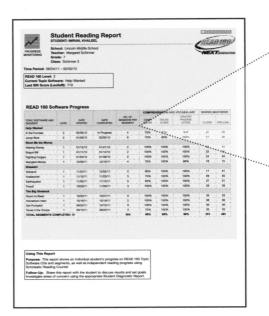

Student Reading Report
STUDENT: IMRAN, KHALEEL

PROGRESS MONITORING

School: Lincoln Middle School
Teacher: Margaret Schirmer
Grade: 7
Class: Schirmer 3

Time Period: 08/24/11 – 02/02/12

READ 180 Level: 2
Current Topic Software: Help Wanted
Last SRI Score (Lexile®): 719

READ 180 Software Progress

TOPIC SOFTWARE AND SEGMENT	LEVEL	DATE STARTED	DATE COMPLETED	NO. OF SESSIONS PER SEGMENT	COMPREHENSION AND VOCABULARY			WORDS MASTERED	
					COMP. SCORE	VOCAB. SCORE	CONTEXT PASSAGE SCORE	FLUENT	SPELLING
Help Wanted									
In the Funnies	2	02/05/12	In Progress	4	75%	87%	N/A	22	39
Jump Shot	2	01/26/12	02/05/12	8	75%	83%	100%	17	33
Show Me the Money									
Making Money	1	01/15/12	01/21/12	2	100%	100%	100%	26	44
Bogus Bill	1	01/11/12	01/12/12	2	100%	100%	100%	22	32
Fighting Forgery	1	01/04/12	01/08/12	2	100%	100%	100%	24	43
Mangled Money	1	12/03/11	12/16/11	4	75%	100%	88%	18	15
Disaster!									
Volcano!	1	11/23/11	12/02/11	3	80%	100%	100%	17	31
Avalanche!	1	11/12/11	11/23/11	5	75%	100%	100%	28	35
Earthquake!	1	11/05/11	11/12/11	5	80%	100%	100%	27	31
Flood!	1	10/29/11	11/05/11	3	100%	100%	100%	29	39
The Big Giveback									
Room to Read	1	10/20/11	10/27/11	5	100%	100%	100%	34	33
Hometown Hero	1	10/16/11	10/19/11	2	100%	100%	100%	38	39
Get Pumped!	1	09/22/11	10/15/11	8	100%	100%	100%	36	36
Tunes 4 the Troops	1	09/15/11	09/22/11	5	75%	100%	100%	35	33
TOTAL SEGMENTS COMPLETED: 13					N/A	88%	98%	99%	373	483

Using This Report

Enlargement: Student Reading Report

NEXT STEPS

	Data Point	Data Analysis	
1	Khaleel is completing Topic Software segments quickly.	Khaleel's quick software completion and current *SRI* score make him a candidate for a manual software level promotion.	Before adjusting software levels, ensure that students are earning high scores in all zones.
2	Khaleel's averages for comprehension and vocabulary are high.	High results confirm that Khaleel is ready for more challenge. Since he is Level 1, he must be manually promoted in SAM.	Level 1 students must be manually promoted. Access promotion features in the *READ 180* Settings in SAM Roster.
3	Khaleel seems to be earning appropriate scores and working at an appropriate pace in his new level.	After his promotion, monitor Khaleel's performance to ensure the software is at a comfortable level.	Celebrate changes in level with students. Encourage students to challenge themselves with related eReads articles.

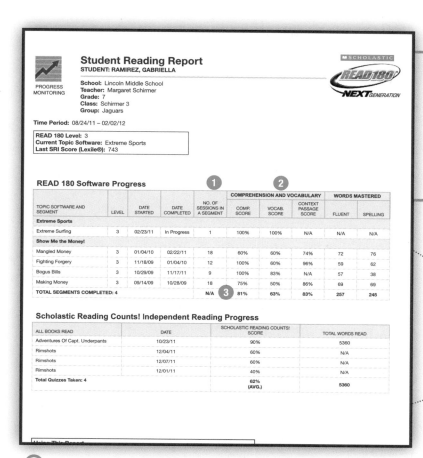

Student Reading Report
STUDENT: RAMIREZ, GABRIELLA

SCHOLASTIC READ 180 NEXT GENERATION

PROGRESS MONITORING

School: Lincoln Middle School
Teacher: Margaret Schirmer
Grade: 7
Class: Schirmer 3
Group: Jaguars

Time Period: 08/24/11 – 02/02/12

READ 180 Level: 3
Current Topic Software: Extreme Sports
Last SRI Score (Lexile®): 743

READ 180 Software Progress

| TOPIC SOFTWARE AND SEGMENT | LEVEL | DATE STARTED | DATE COMPLETED | NO. OF SESSIONS IN A SEGMENT | COMPREHENSION AND VOCABULARY | | | WORDS MASTERED | |
					COMP. SCORE	VOCAB. SCORE	CONTEXT PASSAGE SCORE	FLUENT	SPELLING
Extreme Sports									
Extreme Surfing	3	02/23/11	In Progress	1	100%	100%	N/A	N/A	N/A
Show Me the Money!									
Mangled Money	3	01/04/10	02/22/11	18	60%	60%	74%	72	76
Fighting Forgery	3	11/18/09	01/04/10	12	100%	60%	96%	59	62
Bogus Bills	3	10/29/09	11/17/11	9	100%	83%	N/A	57	38
Making Money	3	09/14/09	10/28/09	18	75%	50%	86%	69	69
TOTAL SEGMENTS COMPLETED: 4				N/A	81%	63%	83%	257	245

Scholastic Reading Counts! Independent Reading Progress

ALL BOOKS READ	DATE	SCHOLASTIC READING COUNTS! SCORE	TOTAL WORDS READ
Adventures Of Capt. Underpants	10/23/11	90%	5360
Rimshots	12/04/11	60%	N/A
Rimshots	12/07/11	60%	N/A
Rimshots	12/01/11	40%	N/A
Total Quizzes Taken: 4		62% (AVG.)	5360

Using This Report

🔍 **Enlargement: Student Reading Report**

Student: Gabriella Ramirez
Current Lexile: 743

Gabriella is struggling with software usage. Identify indicators of student challenges and provide appropriate support.

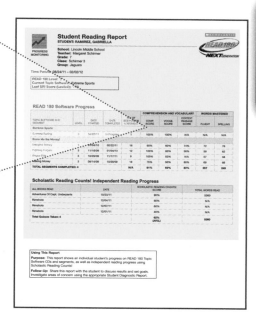

READ 180 Reports

Data Point	Data Analysis	**NEXT STEPS**
1 Gabriella is taking more than 15 sessions to complete a segment.	Determine whether large numbers of sessions per segment are due to low average minutes per day or struggles with zone activities.	Run the *READ 180* Student Segment Status Report to determine which zone(s) seem to be the most challenging.
2 Gabriella's vocabulary score is consistently low.	Since her comprehension score is appropriate, she may be forgetting to use her "Power Words" in the Reading Zone.	Remind students that clicking on the "Power Words" in the Reading Zone gives them clues for answering Vocabulary questions.
3 In her last completed segment, Gabriella's Reading Zone scores dropped significantly.	In the two previous segments, Gabriella's scores were improving, but they declined again recently.	Ask students to articulate the types of challenges they are having during conferences. Provide follow-up support as needed.

Student Segment Status Report

Purpose

This report shows a student's progress for the current segment, last segment, and historical average.

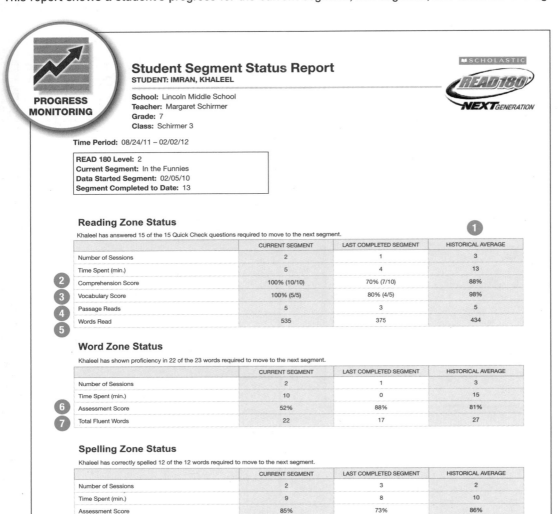

Student Segment Status Report
STUDENT: IMRAN, KHALEEL

School: Lincoln Middle School
Teacher: Margaret Schirmer
Grade: 7
Class: Schirmer 3

SCHOLASTIC READ 180 NEXT GENERATION

Time Period: 08/24/11 – 02/02/12

> **READ 180 Level:** 2
> **Current Segment:** In the Funnies
> **Data Started Segment:** 02/05/10
> **Segment Completed to Date:** 13

Reading Zone Status

Khaleel has answered 15 of the 15 Quick Check questions required to move to the next segment.

	CURRENT SEGMENT	LAST COMPLETED SEGMENT	HISTORICAL AVERAGE
Number of Sessions	2	1	3
Time Spent (min.)	5	4	13
Comprehension Score	100% (10/10)	70% (7/10)	88%
Vocabulary Score	100% (5/5)	80% (4/5)	98%
Passage Reads	5	3	5
Words Read	535	375	434

Word Zone Status

Khaleel has shown proficiency in 22 of the 23 words required to move to the next segment.

	CURRENT SEGMENT	LAST COMPLETED SEGMENT	HISTORICAL AVERAGE
Number of Sessions	2	1	3
Time Spent (min.)	10	0	15
Assessment Score	52%	88%	81%
Total Fluent Words	22	17	27

Spelling Zone Status

Khaleel has correctly spelled 12 of the 12 words required to move to the next segment.

	CURRENT SEGMENT	LAST COMPLETED SEGMENT	HISTORICAL AVERAGE
Number of Sessions	2	3	2
Time Spent (min.)	9	8	10
Assessment Score	85%	73%	86%
Total Spelling Words	39	33	35

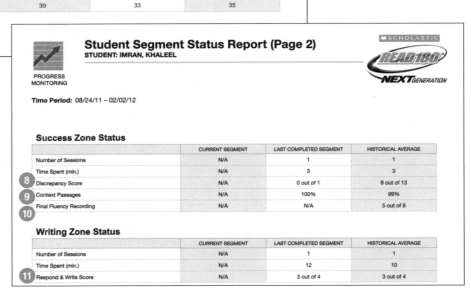

Student Segment Status Report (Page 2)
STUDENT: IMRAN, KHALEEL

PROGRESS MONITORING

SCHOLASTIC READ 180 NEXT GENERATION

Time Period: 08/24/11 – 02/02/12

Success Zone Status

	CURRENT SEGMENT	LAST COMPLETED SEGMENT	HISTORICAL AVERAGE
Number of Sessions	N/A	1	1
Time Spent (min.)	N/A	3	3
Discrepancy Score	N/A	0 out of 1	8 out of 13
Context Passages	N/A	100%	99%
Final Fluency Recording	N/A	N/A	5 out of 6

Writing Zone Status

	CURRENT SEGMENT	LAST COMPLETED SEGMENT	HISTORICAL AVERAGE
Number of Sessions	N/A	1	1
Time Spent (min.)	N/A	12	10
Respond & Write Score	N/A	3 out of 4	3 out of 4

How It Helps

I compare students' work in the current segment with past performance, helping me determine how my students are using their software time.

Understand the Data

1 Historical Average
Average results calculated across all segments completed during the year.

2 Comprehension Score
Percentage of Reading Zone Quick Check comprehension questions answered correctly on the first try. There are ten questions per segment.

3 Vocabulary Score
Percentage of Reading Zone Quick Check vocabulary questions answered correctly on the first try. There are five questions per segment.

4 Passage Reads
Number of times the student has read the entire Reading Zone passage using the Word, Phrase, Practice, or Record buttons.

5 Words Read
Total number of words read in the Reading Zone, including multiple reads.

6 Assessment Scores
Percentage of words the student identified correctly in the Word Zone and Spelling Zone Assessments ("pre-test" activities).

7 Total Words (Fluent and Spelling)
Number of words mastered, including words identified correctly in the Word Zone and Spelling Zone Assessments and Zone Challenges.

8 Discrepancy Score
Number of Success Zone Discrepancy Passages identified correctly on the first try.

9 Context Passages
Percentage of Success Zone context passage questions answered correctly on the first try.

10 Final Fluency Recording
Fluency score (from 1–6), based on Success Zone recording evaluations entered in SAM Digital Portfolio.

11 Respond & Write Score
Score on published response (from 1–4), based on Writing Zone evaluations entered in SAM Digital Portfolio.

Use the Data

Who: Teachers, Students (Student report)

When: Monthly, or when students complete a segment.

How: Monitor the following aspects of zone progress:

Reading Zone

- Ensure that students are completing Reading Zone questions each day. Remind students to begin each session in the Reading Zone. Students should not have work completed in Word or Spelling Zones and no work completed in the Reading Zone.

Word Zone and Spelling Zone

- The total number of words required to move to the next segment depends on the student's performance in the Assessment activity, which acts as a pre-test. Remind students to focus on the Assessment to reduce the amount of work needed to complete during the Word and Spelling Zones.

Success Zone

- For Final Fluency scores to appear on this report, a student's Success Zone recording must be assessed and a score entered in the SAM Digital Portfolio.

Writing Zone

- Students may publish their Respond & Write activities every segment or every other segment, depending on software settings.

Review Related Reports

- *READ 180* Student Reading Report (p. 158)
- *READ 180* Student Spelling Zone Report (p. 164)
- *READ 180* Student Word Zone Report (p. 166)

Data in Action

Historical Average The historical average column includes data from all segments completed during the school year, not just the current and previous segment displayed in the other two columns. Use the historical average data to establish usage trends and compare those trends against current segment performance.

Student Spelling Zone Report

Purpose

This report shows a student's progress working on and mastering words in the Spelling Zone.

SCHOOL-TO-HOME

Student Spelling Zone Report
STUDENT: IMRAN, KHALEEL

School: Lincoln Middle School
Teacher: Margaret Schirmer
Grade: 7
Class: Schirmer 3

Time Period: 08/24/11 – 02/02/12 **1**

2 **Spelling Zone Progress**

Percentage of Words Spelled Correctly in Assessments to Date: 88%
Total Words Mastered to Date: 373

Current Topic: Help Wanted

3 WORDS I SPELLED CORRECTLY

he	if	is	jump	keep	know	page	right	shot	speeds
spends	takes								

4 WORDS I LEARNED TO SPELL

dreams	his	on	photos	spells	spent	sports	spot

5 WORDS I AM STUDYING THIS WEEK

NO DATA TO REPORT

Using This Report

Purpose: This report shows a student's progress working on and mastering Study Words in the Spelling Zone.

Follow-Up: For additional practice, have the student use recent Study Words in QuickWrite responses. You may wish to share this report with the student and send it home with additional suggestions for practice activities.

How It Helps

This is a useful record of specific spelling words my students are studying and mastering as they use the READ 180 *Topic Software.*

Understand the Data

1 Time Period
This report is based on the most recent words the student has encountered.

2 Spelling Zone Progress
Spelling percentage and total spelling word data in the Spelling Zone since the student began *READ 180*.

3 Words I Spelled Correctly
Words the student spelled correctly in the Spelling Zone Assessment activity for the current topic. Up to 20 words may be listed.

4 Words I Learned to Spell
Words the student did not spell correctly in the Assessment activity for the current topic, but later mastered in the Spelling Clinic and Spelling Speed Challenge activity. Up to 50 words may be listed.

5 Words I Am Studying This Week
Words the student is currently learning to spell from the student's latest Spelling Zone session.

Use the Data

Who: Teachers

When: Monthly, or when a student begins a new software segment.

How: Apply the information in this report in the following ways:

Assign Additional Practice

- For homework assignments, you may wish to have students write original sentences using five of their already-known or newly-learned words.
- Ask students to incorporate these words into the writing they complete in the *rBook*.

Monitor Software Comfort Level
The total number of "Words I Knew" indicates performance on the initial assessment activity.

- Students who have few or no words on this list may need additional support in proper use of this zone.
- Students who have most of their words listed in this category may be ready for additional vocabulary challenge.

Review Related Reports

- *READ 180* Spelling Skills Grouping Report (p. 154)
- *READ 180* Student Segment Status Report (p. 162)
- *READ 180* Student Word Zone Report (p. 166)

Data in Action

Most Common Errors Students receive immediate corrective feedback for each spelling error they make, including specific additions, reversals, and omissions based on phonological and orthographic errors.

Student Word Zone Report

Purpose

This report shows a student's progress mastering words in the Word Zone.

SCHOOL-TO-HOME

Student Word Zone Report
STUDENT: IMRAN, KHALEEL

School: Lincoln Middle School
Teacher: Margaret Schirmer
Grade: 7
Class: Schirmer 3

Time Period: 08/24/11 – 06/02/12 **1**

2 **Word Zone Progress**

Percentage of Words Recognized in Assessments to Date: 83%
Total Words Mastered to Date: 483

Current Topic: Help Wanted

3 WORDS I KNEW

bull	buy	comic	eating	knows	looking	paid	photos	pull	push
puts	sees	speeds	spell	spent	sports	spot	two	use	while
white									

4 WORDS I LEARNED

deal	drawing	gets	lots	much	need	spends	strip	thinks	whirl
whisk	whiz								

5 WORDS I AM STUDYING THIS WEEK

ideas

Using This Report

Purpose: This report shows a student's progress working on and mastering words in the Word Zone.

Follow-Up: For additional practice, have the student use recent Study Words in QuickWrite responses. You may wish to share this report with the student and send it home with additional suggestions for practice activities.

How It Helps

I use this report to provide my students extra practice with their word study skills when they're away from the computer.

Understand the Data

1 **Time Period**
This report is based on the most recent words the student has encountered.

2 **Word Zone Progress**
Percentage of Words Recognized in Assessments To Date indicates total words a student identified quickly and correctly. Total words mastered to date includes words identified correctly in the Word Zone Assessment and Challenge activities.

3 **Words I Knew**
Words the student recognized correctly in the Word Zone Assessment activity for the current topic. Up to 21 words may be listed.

4 **Words I Learned**
Words the student did not recognize correctly in the Assessment activity for the current topic, but later mastered in the Speed Challenge. Up to 50 words may be listed in the order in which the student encountered them.

5 **Words I Am Studying This Week**
Study Word List from the student's latest Word Zone session.

Use the Data

Who: Teachers, students and parents (Student report)

When: Monthly, or when a student begins a new Software Topic.

How: Apply the information in this report in the following ways:

Assign Additional Practice

- For homework assignments, you may wish to have students write original sentences using five of their already-known or newly-learned words.
- Ask students to incorporate these words into the writing they complete in the *rBook*.

Monitor Software Comfort Level
The total number of "Words I Knew" indicates performance on the initial assessment activity.

- Students who have few or no words on this list may need additional support in proper use of this zone.
- Students who have most of their words listed in this category may be ready for additional vocabulary challenge.

Review Related Reports

- *READ 180* Phonics and Word Study Grouping Report (p. 148)
- *READ 180* Student Segment Status Report (p. 162)
- *READ 180* Student Spelling Zone Report (p. 164)

Data in Action

Tracking Word Mastery For a comprehensive picture of each student's word mastery, you may wish to print and file student Word Zone reports as students complete each Topic.

Parent Report I

Purpose

This report introduces parents and caregivers to *READ 180* and gives information about student placement.

SCHOOL-TO-HOME

STUDENT: IMRAN, KHALEEL

School: Lincoln Middle School
Teacher: Margaret Schirmer
Grade: 7
Class: Schirmer 3

① September 4, 2011

Dear Parent or Caregiver,

Khaleel has been enrolled in *READ 180*, an intensive reading program. *READ 180* will help Khaleel recognize and spell words correctly, read with fluency, and comprehend the text. The goal of this program is for Khaleel to read grade-level material independently, with confidence and fluency in all subjects.

This report shows you where Khaleel has been placed in the program. You will be receiving reports about how Khaleel is doing throughout the year.

ASSESSMENT	RESULTS
② **READ 180 Reading Level**	Level 2 of 4
③ **SRI* Test Score (Date)**	710 Lexiles® (08/31/11)
④ **SRI Performance Standard**	Basic

* *Scholastic Reading Inventory* (SRI) is a comprehension test that monitors students' reading levels and matches them to text.

⑤ Here are some things you could do at home to help Khaleel become a lifelong reader:

- **The Daily Read:** Make reading a daily activity by reading to, or with, your child for 20 minutes every day.
- **Fast and Fun Reads:** Use magazines, newspapers, comic books, recipes, TV schedules, travel guides, and road signs as reading opportunities, wherever you are and whatever you and your child are doing.
- **The Movie or the Book:** Rent videos or DVDs on a topic that your child is interested in. Find books on a similar topic.
- **Read and Ride:** Listen to books on tape or CD while traveling by car. Or bring a personal player with earphones for your child to listen to books while on a train or plane.
- **Read and Chat:** Talk about what your child is reading. Ask questions about the characters or what happens in the story.

Thank you for your support in making reading and the goals of *READ 180* important at home as well as in the classroom.

Sincerely,

_____

How It Helps

I send this report home at the beginning of the year and I also use it at parent-teacher conferences.

Understand the Data

1 **Time Period**
Time period setting of This School Year displays student's current performance results.

2 *READ 180* **Reading Level**
Student's current *READ 180* level, from 1–4. Initial level placement is determined by student's first *SRI* score.

3 *SRI* **Test Score and Date**
Most recent *SRI* test date and student score.

4 *SRI* **Performance Standard**
Most recent *SRI* test date and student score.

5 **Suggestions**
Activities parents and caregivers can complete at home to promote their child's reading success.

Use the Data

Who: Teachers, Students, Families (Student report)

When: At the beginning of the year.

How: Apply the information from this report in the following ways:

Offer Further Explanation

- Take time during Back-To-School Night or during parent-teacher conferences to review this information with parents or caregivers.
- Share the Recommended Reading Report or other introductory parent reports with families to help them understand the class and their child's progress and current performance.

Check In Periodically

- Contact parents from time to time to offer support and find out any home reading routines that they have found to be successful.

Review Related Reports

READ 180 Parent Report II (p. 170)
SRI Parent Report I (p. 216)
SRC! Parent Report I (p. 240)

Data in Action

Share Results With Families Remember that many parents and caregivers may be unfamiliar with educational terms. When reviewing student results, be sure to fully explain how the data corresponds to student reading achievement.

Parent Report II

Purpose

This report provides parents and caregivers an update on their child's *READ 180* participation and progress.

SCHOOL-TO-HOME

STUDENT: IMRAN, KHALEEL

School: Lincoln Middle School
Teacher: Margaret Schirmer
Grade: 7
Class: Schirmer 3

(1) February 2, 2012

Dear Parent or Caregiver,

Khaleel has been enrolled in *READ 180*, an intensive reading program. *READ 180* is helping Khaleel recognize and spell words correctly, read with fluency, and comprehend the text. The goal of this program is for Khaleel to read grade-level material confidently and fluently in all subjects. This report shows you how Khaleel is performing in the program this year.

READ 180 Progress

ASSESSMENT	RESULTS
READ 180 Reading Level	Level 2 of 4
(2) SRI* Test Score (Date)	719 Lexiles® (01/25/12)
(3) SRI Performance Standard	Basic
(4) Comprehension Score	88%
Vocabulary Score (5)	98%
(6) Number of Books Read	9
(7) Independent Reading Goal	20 Books
(8) Last Book Read	Adventures Of Capt. Underpants
TOTAL WORDS READ **(9)**	289,267

* *Scholastic Reading Inventory* (SRI) is a comprehension test that monitors students' reading levels and matches them to text.

(10) Here are some things you could do at home to help Khaleel become a lifelong reader:

- **The Daily Read:** Make reading a daily activity by reading to, or with, your child for 20 minutes every day.
- **Fast and Fun Reads:** Use magazines, newspapers, comic books, recipes, TV schedules, travel guides, and road signs as reading opportunities, wherever you are and whatever you and your child are doing.
- **The Movie or the Book:** Rent videos or DVDs on a topic that your child is interested in. Find books on a similar topic.
- **Read and Ride:** Listen to books on tape or CD while traveling by car. Or bring a personal player with earphones for your child to listen to books while on a train or plane.
- **Read and Chat:** Talk about what your child is reading. Ask questions about the characters or what happens in the story.

Thank you for your support in making reading and the goals of *READ 180* important at home as well as in the classroom.

Sincerely,

_____

How It Helps

I send this report home with report cards to update families on their child's progress.

Understand the Data

1 *SRI* Time Period
Time period setting of This School Year displays student's current performance results.

2 *SRI* Test Score and Date
Most recent *SRI* test date and score.

3 *SRI* Performance Standard
Lexile range for the student's current performance standard, based on student's grade level and current *SRI* results. Performance standards include Advanced, Proficient, Basic, and Below Basic.

4 Comprehension Score
Percentage of comprehension questions answered correctly on the first attempt in the *READ 180* Reading Zone.

5 Vocabulary Score
A Percentage of vocabulary questions answered correctly on the first attempt in the *READ 180* Reading Zone.

6 Number of Books Read
Total number of *Scholastic Reading Counts!* quizzes passed.

7 Independent Reading Goal
Annual books or points goal, if established in SAM Roster.

8 Last Book Read
Most recent book with passing score on *Scholastic Reading Counts!* quiz.

9 Total Words Read
Total number of words read in the *READ 180* Software and in each book where students have passed a *Scholastic Reading Counts!* quiz.

10 Suggestions
Activities parents and caregivers can do at home to promote their child's reading success.

Use the Data

Who: Teachers, Students, Families (Student report)

When: At the end of each grading period.

How: Apply the information from this report in the following ways:

Offer Further Explanation
- Take time during parent-teacher conferences to review this information with parents or caregivers.
- Share the Recommended Reading Report or other parent reports with families to help them understand the class.

Check In Periodically
- Contact parents from time to time to offer support and find out any home reading routines that they have found to be successful.

Review Related Reports

READ 180 Parent Report I (p. 168)
SRI Parent Report II (p. 216)
SRC! Parent Report II (p. 240)

Data in Action

Sharing Information With Families Parent Reports provide an overview of student participation and progress. They are useful conversation-starters for parent-teacher conferences.

rSkills Tests Reports Overview

Each time students complete an *rSkills Test* on the computer, the Scholastic Achievement Manager (SAM) captures their test results. The information in these reports will enable you to monitor your students' learning progress and how they are applying specific skills you teach in the *rBook* during Whole-Group and Small-Group Instruction. You can review results for individual students, groups, classes, or all students by using the *rSkills Tests* Reports.

rSkills Tests Reports

The following table summarizes how to use each *rSkills Test* report.

If You Want to ...	Run This Report
...review *rSkills Test* scores for one test	*rSkills Tests* Grading Report (p. 174)
...group students at *rBook* End-of-Workshop CheckPoints	*rSkills Tests* Grouping Report (p. 178)
...analyze overall performance on one *rSkills Test*	*rSkills Tests* Summary Skills Report (p. 180)
...monitor a student's *rSkills Test* results over time	*rSkills Tests* Student Progress Report (p. 182)
...analyze results for an individual student on one *rSkills Test*	*rSkills Tests* Student Skills Report (p. 184)
...review a student's answers on one *rSkills Test*	*rSkills Tests* Student Test Printout (p. 186)

Grading Report | Best Practice Report

Purpose

This report shows *rSkills Test* results for all students in a class or group, summarized by strand.

PROGRESS MONITORING

Grading Report
CLASS: SCHIRMER 3

School: Lincoln Middle School
Teacher: Margaret Schirmer
Grade: 7

READ 180 NEXTGENERATION

Time Period: 1/15/12 – 1/30/12 **①**

② **TEST 4 (Stage B)**
Average Test Score: 73%
Number of Students Tested: 14

③ **STUDENT(S) NOT TESTED**

Cooper, Tiffany

⑤ LEVEL a (Stage B)

STUDENT	TEST DATE	SUMMARIZE	SEQUENCE OF EVENTS	MULTIPLE-MEANING WORDS	USING A DICTIONARY	USING CORRECT VERB TENSE	USING COMMAS IN A SERIES	TEST SCORE
Bracco, Christine	1/25/12	83%	0%	50%	75%	50%	100%	60%
Evans, Jamal	1/25/12	67%	100%	100%	75%	50%	67%	88%
Felix, Tonya	1/25/12	33%	75%	75%	75%	75%	67%	64%
Fernandez, Luis	1/25/12	100%	75%	100%	75%	100%	67%	88%
Garcia, Matt	1/26/12	50%	50%	50%	100%	100%	0%	60%
Imran, Khaleel	1/25/12	100%	100%	100%	100%	100%	100%	100%
Palermo, Justin	1/26/12	50%	50%	75%	25%	50%	67%	52%
⑧ AVERAGE SKILL SCORE		**69%**	**64%**	**79%**	**75%**	**75%**	**65%**	**73%**

④ ⑥ ⑦

Writing

STUDENT	OPEN RESPONSE 1 (2-POINT RUBRIC)	OPEN RESPONSE 2 (4-POINT RUBRIC)	WRITING PROMPT	
			SCORE	RUBRIC VALUE
Bracco, Christine	1	2	5	6
Evans, Jamal	1	2	2	6
Felix, Tonya	2	4	4	6
Fernandez, Luis				
Garcia, Matt	2	3	4	6
Imran, Khaleel				
Palermo, Justin	2	3	3	6

⑨ ⑩

Using This Report

Purpose: This report shows students' results on one rSkills Test. Results from multiple choice and writing questions are included.

Follow-Up: Include student progress from all parts of the READ 180 Instructional Model in your grading assessment.

How It Helps

I use this report to monitor how well my class mastered the skills I taught during the current rBook Workshop.

Understand the Data

1 Time Period

Default time period setting of Last 15 Days displays results from any tests completed on the computer within the past two weeks. Each test level will appear on a separate page.

2 Test

Lists the *rSkills Test* results included in the report. Includes the test number, the average score for all students included in the report, and the total number of students who completed this test.

3 Student(s) Not Tested

Lists any students who did not complete the test.

4 Test Date

Date each student completed the test.

5 Test Level (Stage)

Lists whether the results displayed were from below grade-level tests (Level a) or grade-level tests (Level b). Each test level displays in a separate chart. Also includes *rBook* stage selected for test. Stages include A, B, C, FLEX, and FLEX II.

6 Test Skills

Percentage of multiple-choice questions each student answered correctly. Multiple choice strands include Comprehension, Vocabulary/Word Study, and Conventions.

7 Test Score

Percentage of 25 multiple-choice questions each student answered correctly.

8 Average Skill Score

Average score for all students for each of the multiple-choice skills.

9 Open Response

Score for open response questions, if assigned in *rSkills* Settings in SAM and score entered in SAM Student Digital Portfolio. Open Response 1 is worth 2 points; Open Response 2 is worth 4 points.

10 Writing

Score and rubric value for writing prompt, if assigned in *rSkills* Settings in SAM and score entered in SAM Student Digital Portfolio. Rubric can be set at 4-point rubric or 6-point rubric.

Use the Data

Who: Teachers (Teacher, Class, or Group report)

When: After each *rSkills* test, usually at the end of each *rBook* Workshop

How: Apply the information from this report in the following ways:

Target Instruction

- If the majority of students struggled with a particular skill, select an appropriate lesson to deliver to the entire class during Whole-Group Instruction at the End-of-Workshop CheckPoint.
- Use this report in conjunction with the *rSkills Tests* Grouping Report to adjust End-of-Workshop CheckPoint grouping decisions in the Teacher Dashboard Groupinator.
- If students are scoring well on the below grade-level tests (Level a), consider assigning a grade-level test (Level b) the next time students take an *rSkills Test*.

Review Results

- Review individual student results with the *rSkills Tests* Student Test Printout.
- Monitor test performance at each test level and overall results from one *rSkills Test* to the next. Print this report after each test and compare it with previous reports.
- Include *rSkills Test* results as a component of a student's overall grade. Refer to **page 110** for more information about assigning grades.

Review Related Reports

- *rSkills Tests* Grouping Report (p. 178)
- *rSkills Tests* Student Skills Report (p. 184)
- *rSkills Tests* Student Test Printout (p. 186)

Data in Action

***rSkills Test* Levels** Consider the level of the *rSkills Test* during analysis of the test results. Grade-level tests (Level b) have substantially longer and more complex passages.

Analyze the Results | Grading Report

DATA STORY

Student: Justin Palermo
rSkills Test: 4a
Lexile: 438

Justing struggled with his most recent rSkills Test. Identify causes and ways to provide additional support.

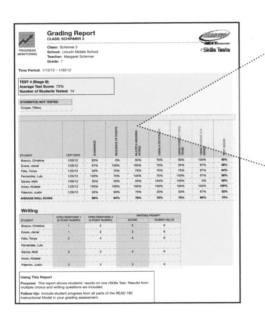

TEST 4 (Stage B)
Average Test Score: 73%
Number of Students Tested: 14

STUDENT(S) NOT TESTED
Cooper, Tiffany

STUDENT	TEST DATE	SUMMARIZE	SEQUENCE OF EVENTS	MULTIPLE-MEANING WORDS	USING A DICTIONARY	USING CORRECT VERB TENSE
Bracco, Christine	1/25/12	83%	0%	50%	75%	50%
Evans, Jamal	1/25/12	67%	100%	100%	75%	50%
Felix, Tonya	1/25/12	33%	75%	75%	75%	75%
Fernandez, Luis	1/25/12	100%	75%	100%	75%	100%
Garcia, Matt	1/26/12	50%	50%	50%	100%	100%
Imran, Khaleel	1/25/12	100%	100%	100%	100%	100%
Palermo, Justin	1/26/12	50%	50%	① 75%	② 25%	50%
AVERAGE SKILL SCORE		**69%**	**64%**	**79%**	**75%**	**75%**

Writing

STUDENT	OPEN RESPONSE 1 (2-POINT RUBRIC)	OPEN RESPONSE 2 (4-POINT RUBRIC)	WRITING PROMPT SCORE	WRITING PROMPT RUBRIC VALUE
Bracco, Christine	1	2	5	6
Evans, Jamal	1	2	2	6
Felix, Tonya	2	4	4	6
Fernandez, Luis				
Garcia, Matt	2	3	4	6
Imran, Khaleel				
Palermo, Justin	③ 2	3	3	6

Enlargement: Grading Report

Grading Report
CLASS: SCHIRMER 3

PROGRESS MONITORING

Class: Schirmer 3
School: Lincoln Middle School
Teacher: Margaret Schirmer
Grade: 7

rSkills Tests

Time Period: 1/15/12 – 1/30/12

TEST 4 (Stage B)
Average Test Score: 73%
Number of Students Tested: 14

STUDENT(S) NOT TESTED
Cooper, Tiffany

Using This Report

Purpose: This report shows students' results on one rSkills Test. Results from multiple choice and writing questions are included.

Follow-Up: Include student progress from all parts of the READ 180 Instructional Model in your grading assessment.

NEXT STEPS

Understand the Data	Use the Data	
① Justin's highest score was in Context Clues. He got three of four context clues questions correct on the test.	Comparison of results with Justin's *rBook* work also indicates that Justin did well on this skill.	Review the *rSkills Tests* Student Test Printout with students, discussing the thought process for answering each question.
② Justin's lowest score was in Compound Words.	Review of Justin's *rBook* Workshop work revealed that he also struggled with the skill during the Workshop.	Provide additional practice on skills where students earned low scores during the End-of-Workshop CheckPoint.
③ Justin struggled with the writing prompt. On a rubric scale of 6 points, Justin earned 3 points.	Review of the rubric indicated that Justin struggled with transitions, precise vocabulary, and summarizing information from a text.	Assess open response and writing prompt in the SAM Digital Portfolio. Enter scores and comments, then print results.

Review Additional Data

Review results from the *rSkills Tests* Student Test Printout.

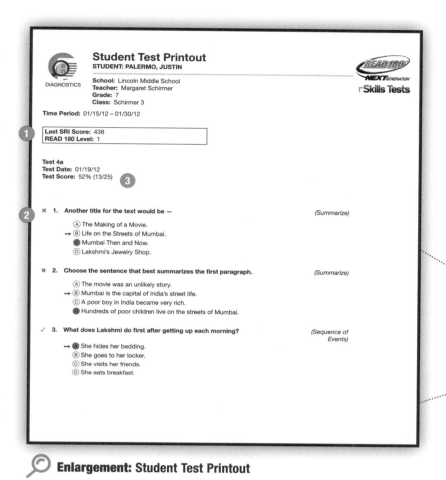

Enlargement: Student Test Printout

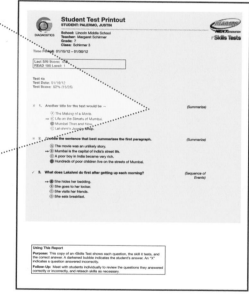

Student Test Printout
STUDENT: PALERMO, JUSTIN

School: Lincoln Middle School
Teacher: Margaret Schirmer
Grade: 7
Class: Schirmer 3

Time Period: 01/15/12 – 01/30/12

Last SRI Score: 438
READ 180 Level: 1

Test 4a
Test Date: 01/19/12
Test Score: 52% (13/25)

1. Another title for the text would be —   (Summarize)
   A The Making of a Movie.
   B Life on the Streets of Mumbai.
   C Mumbai Then and Now.
   D Lakshmi's Jewelry Shop.

2. Choose the sentence that best summarizes the first paragraph.   (Summarize)
   A The movie was an unlikely story.
   B Mumbai is the capital of India's street life.
   C A poor boy in India became very rich.
   D Hundreds of poor children live on the streets of Mumbai.

3. What does Lakshmi do first after getting up each morning?   (Sequence of Events)
   A She hides her bedding.
   B She goes to her locker.
   C She visits her friends.
   D She eats breakfast.

Using This Report
Purpose: This copy of an rSkills Test shows each question, the skill it tests, and the correct answer. A darkened bubble indicates the student's answer. An "X" indicates a question answered incorrectly.
Follow-Up: Meet with students individually to review the questions they answered correctly or incorrectly, and reteach skills as necessary.

rSkills Tests Reports

Data Point	Data Analysis	NEXT STEPS
1 Justin has a Lexile of 438 and is reading at Level 1.	Because Justin's reading level is 438, he was given the below grade-level *rSkills Test* for Workshop 4.	Review reading levels and current *rBook* Workshop performance when determining which test (Level a or Level b) to assign.
2 This is the first Summarize question that Justin missed on Test 4a.	The answer that Justin selected is plausible, indicating that he likely read the passage but struggled with selecting an appropriate summary.	Review specific test results with students during Small-Group Instruction. Discuss how and why they selected specific answers.
3 Justin's results from the open response and writing prompt are included in this printout.	Justin's biggest challenge was appropriately responding to the writing prompt.	Review rubric results. Based on your feedback, allow students an opportunity to revise their responses.

Grouping Report | Best Practice Report

Purpose

This report places students into three groups based on results from one *rSkills Test*.

Grouping Report
CLASS: SCHIRMER 3

School: Lincoln Middle School
Teacher: Margaret Schirmer
Grade: 7

Time Period: 01/15/12 – 01/30/12 **(1)**

Test 4 (Stage B) **(2)**
Number of Students Tested: 14 **(3)**

(4)

Group 1

(5) **(6)** **(7)**

STRAND AND SKILL	STUDENT	LEVEL	CORRECT/ TOTAL ITEMS	SKILL SCORE
Comprehension Sequence of Events	Bracco, Christine	a	0/4	0%
	Collins, Chris	b	2/4	50%
	Garcia, Matt	a	2/4	50%
	Palermo, Justin	a	2/4	50%
	Ramirez, Gabirella	b	2/4	50%

Group 2

STRAND AND SKILL	STUDENT	LEVEL	CORRECT/ TOTAL ITEMS	SKILL SCORE
Comprehension Sequence of Events	Felix, Tonya	a	3/4	75%
	Fernandez, Luis	a	3/4	75%
	Krynski, Theo	b	3/4	75%
	Rupp, Jeremy	b	2/4	50%
	Sanchez, Rachel	b	3/4	75%

Group 3

STRAND AND SKILL	STUDENT	LEVEL	CORRECT/ TOTAL ITEMS	SKILL SCORE
Vocabulary/Word Study Using Correct Verb Tense	Chu, Amy	b	3/4	75%
	Evans, Jamal	a	2/4	50%
	Imran, Khaleel *	a	4/4	100%
	Kramer, Liz	b	2/4	50%

(8) **Administer rSkills Test**
The following student(s) does not currently have a test score available for rSkills Test 4.

STUDENT NAME
Cooper, Tiffany

---

* This student earned a 100% on the rSkills Test. You may wish to allow the student to work on an rBook project during Small-Group Instruction. Visit the READ 180 Community website to download projects.

Using This Report

Purpose: This report groups students based on results from one rSkills Test. Three groups are created and an rBook workshop skill is assigned to each.

Follow-Up: Run this report after each rSkills Test. Use the groupings listed to complete the End-of-Workshop CheckPoint lesson.

How It Helps

I use this report to group my students at rBook End-of-Workshop CheckPoints. I access the data from the Teacher Dashboard Groupinator, which links me directly to appropriate differentiated lessons.

Understand the Data

1 Time Period

Run for the Past 15 Days to review grouping results from current *rSkills Test*. Customize time period settings to review previous test results.

2 Test (Stage)

rSkills Test completed within selected time period. Stage indicates *rBook* stage associated with results.

3 Number of Students Tested

Total students who completed the *rSkills Test* on the computer within the selected time period.

4 Strand and Skill

Students placed into three distinct groups based on *rSkills Test* results. Students grouped by one of three test strands: Comprehension, Vocabulary/Word Study, or Conventions. Groups are assigned specific skill to reteach based on *rSkills Test* results.

5 Level

Lists whether students took the below grade-level test (Level a) or the grade-level test (Level b). Students are grouped based on skill performance, not test level.

6 Correct/Total Items

Lists the total number of questions answered correctly and the total number of questions assigned for each skill used for grouping.

7 Skill Score

Percentage of questions each student answered correctly for the skill used for grouping.

8 Administer rSkills Test

Lists students who have not completed the selected *rSkills Test* on the computer.

Use the Data

Who: Teachers (Class report)

When: At *rBook* End-of-Workshop CheckPoints

How: Apply the information from this report in the following ways:

Understand Performance Results

- The report is designed to create three equal groups and place students based on similar areas of need.
- Students are placed into groups based on one of three multiple choice strands: Comprehension, Vocabulary/Word Study, and Conventions.
- Each group is assigned a skill to review based on common areas of need identified by *rSkills Test* results.

Use Results for Instruction

- Access the results from the Groupinator to simplify the grouping and differentiating process. Use *Resources for Differentiated Instruction* lessons based on skill assigned to each group.
- If adjusting groups, use the *rSkills Test* Grading Report for comprehensive data on test performance.
- Students with asterisks next to their names earned 100% on the *rSkills Test*. They are placed into a group to maintain three equal groups but should be assigned to complete an *rBook* Workshop Project while other students are reviewing *rBook* Workshop skills.

Review Related Reports

- *rSkills Test* Grading Report (p. 174)
- *rSkills Test* Summary Skills Report (p. 180)
- *rSkills Test* Student Skills Report (p. 184)

Data in Action

Assigning *rSkills Test* Levels Consider current reading level, performance in current *rBook* Workshop, previous *rSkills Test* results, and time of year when determining which *rSkills Test* level to assign each student.

Summary Skills Report

Purpose

This report displays results on one *rSkills Test* for a class or group, summarized by strand and skill.

Summary Skills Report
CLASS: SCHIRMER 3

School: Lincoln Middle School
Teacher: Margaret Schirmer
Grade: 7

Time Period: 01/15/12 – 01/30/12 ①

② **TEST 4b (Stage B)**
Average Test Score: 76% ③
④ **Number of Students Tested:** 7

⑤ SKILLS	⑥ SCORE RANGE	⑦ AVG. SCORE*	⑧ NO. OF ITEMS
Comprehension	**17% - 100%**	**63%**	**10**
Sequence of Events		64%	4
Summarize		61%	6
Vocabulary/Word Study	**25% - 100%**	**77%**	**8**
Multiple-Meaning Words		79%	4
Using a Dictionary		75%	4
Conventions	**50% - 100%**	**88%**	**7**
Using Correct Verb Tense		89%	4
Using Commas in a Series		86%	3

* Open-response scores are not included.

* Writing Prompt scores are not included.

Using This Report

Purpose: This report shows aggregated rSkills Test scores on one test for a class or group. The skill-by-skill score breakdown shows strengths and weaknesses.

Follow-Up: Target specific skills for Whole- and Small-Group Instruction that a majority of your students are having difficulty with.

How It Helps

I use this report to monitor how well my class mastered the skills I taught during each rBook Workshop.

Understand the Data

1 **Time Period**

Default time period setting of Last 15 Days displays results from tests completed in the past two weeks. Customize time period settings to view previous test results. Each test's results display on a separate page.

2 **Test**

Indicates which *rSkills Test* results are displayed in the report. Includes the test number, which corresponds to the *rBook* Workshop. Also includes the test level. Level a tests are below grade-level; Level b tests are grade-level.

3 **Average Test Score**

Average percentage of questions answered correctly for all students who completed the test.

4 **Number of Students Tested**

Total number of students who completed the test on the computer.

5 **Skills**

Specific Comprehension, Vocabulary/Word Study, and Conventions skills tested based on skills taught in the *rBook* Workshop.

6 **Score Range**

Minimum and maximum averages for each test strand: Comprehension, Vocabulary/Word Study and Conventions.

7 **Average Score**

Average percentage of questions answered correctly by test strand and skill. Score does not include open response and writing prompt.

8 **Number of Items**

Total questions for each test strand and skill. Each *rSkills Test* includes 25 multiple choice questions.

Use the Data

Who: Teachers

When: After each *rSkills Test,* usually every 4 to 6 weeks

How: You can use the information in this report in the following ways:

Target Skills

- Identify and prioritize skills requiring additional review. Skills or strands with a low average score or a low score range indicate that the majority of students may need further instruction at *rBook* End-of-Workshop CheckPoints.

- If students are scoring well on the below grade-level tests (Level a), consider assigning a grade-level test (Level b) at the end of the next *rBook* Workshop.

Track Results

- Monitor test performance at each test level, as well as overall results from one *rSkills Test* to the next. Print and archive this report to compare with results from other *rSkills Tests.*

Review Related Reports

- *rSkills Tests* Grouping Report (p. 178)
- *rSkills Tests* Grading Report (p. 174)
- *rSkills Tests* Student Skills Report (p. 184)

Data in Action

Test Levels Remember to take into account the level of the *rSkills Test* the student took. Students may have lower scores on grade-level tests because the passages are substantially longer and more difficult than those on below grade-level tests.

Student Progress Report

Purpose

This report graphs results for all *rSkills Tests* a student has taken and lists results by strand.

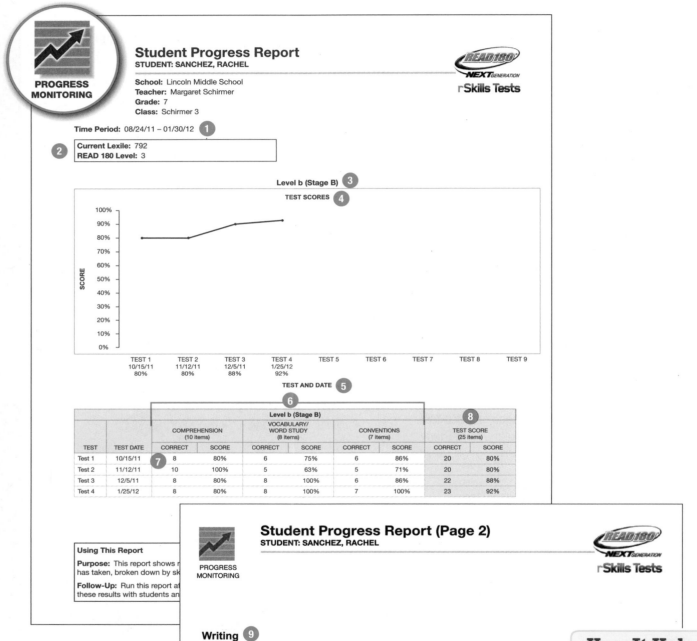

Student Progress Report
STUDENT: SANCHEZ, RACHEL

School: Lincoln Middle School
Teacher: Margaret Schirmer
Grade: 7
Class: Schirmer 3

Time Period: 08/24/11 – 01/30/12 ①

② **Current Lexile:** 792
READ 180 Level: 3

Level b (Stage B) ③

TEST SCORES ④

TEST	TEST DATE	COMPREHENSION (10 items)		VOCABULARY/ WORD STUDY (8 items)		CONVENTIONS (7 items)		TEST SCORE (25 items)	
		CORRECT	SCORE	CORRECT	SCORE	CORRECT	SCORE	CORRECT	SCORE
Test 1	10/15/11	8	80%	6	75%	6	86%	20	80%
Test 2	11/12/11	10	100%	5	63%	5	71%	20	80%
Test 3	12/5/11	8	80%	8	100%	6	86%	22	88%
Test 4	1/25/12	8	80%	8	100%	7	100%	23	92%

Graph x-axis: TEST 1 10/15/11 80%, TEST 2 11/12/11 80%, TEST 3 12/5/11 88%, TEST 4 1/25/12 92%, TEST 5, TEST 6, TEST 7, TEST 8, TEST 9 — **TEST AND DATE** ⑤

Using This Report

Purpose: This report shows ~~~ has taken, broken down by sk~~~

Follow-Up: Run this report a~~~ these results with students an~~~

Student Progress Report (Page 2)
STUDENT: SANCHEZ, RACHEL

Writing ⑨

TEST	OPEN RESPONSE 1 (2-POINT RUBRIC)	OPEN RESPONSE 2 (4-POINT RUBRIC)	WRITING PROMPT	
			SCORE	RUBRIC
Test 1				
Test 2	1	4	5	6
Test 3	2	2	4	6
Test 4	2	3	5	6

How It Helps

I share this report with students to give them a clear picture of their annual progress on rSkills Tests.

Understand the Data

1 Time Period
Default time period setting of This School Year displays results from all tests completed on the computer. Customize time period settings to compare results from specific tests.

2 Current Lexile and READ 180 Level
Current student *SRI* Score and *READ 180* software level regardless of time period settings.

3 Level (Stage)
rSkills Test level assigned. Level a is below grade-level; Level b is grade-level. Stage indicates which *rBook* corresponds with the test.

4 Test Scores
Graph of overall test scores for all *rSkills Tests* completed at one level. Includes test number, date, and score. Results from each level of the *rSkills Tests* will be graphed separately.

5 Test and Date
Date each test was completed on the computer. The date students complete a test may vary.

6 Strand Scores
Scores for each of the three multiple choice strands assessed on each *rSkills Test*: Comprehension, Vocabulary/Word Study, and Conventions.

7 Correct/Total
Number of correct answers and total questions in each multiple choice strand. There are 25 multiple choice questions on each *rSkills Test.*

8 Test Score
Number and percentage of total correct answers out of 25 multiple choice questions.

9 Writing
Scores for open response and writing prompts (if assigned in the *rSkills Tests* Settings) that have been entered into the SAM Digital Portfolio.

Use the Data

Who: Teachers, Students, Parents (Student report)
When: After each *rSkills Test,* usually every 4 to 6 weeks
How: Use this report in the following ways:

Track *rSkills Tests* results

• Print this report to share with students, discussing how results are graphed. Add this report to the student's portfolio.

• Support student motivation by helping students understand their reading progress. Guide students to track their own *rSkills Tests* results in their *rBook* Student Logs.

Encourage Growth

• Discuss performance trends with students. Assist them with setting and tracking goals based on current test results. Celebrate improvement in results.

• Conference with students whose results fall below 70%, using the *rSkills Tests* Student Test Printout to review student responses to specific test questions.

Review Related Reports

• *rSkills Tests* Student Skills Report (p. 184)
• *rSkills Tests* Student Test Printout (p. 186)
• *READ 180* Student Diagnostic Report (p. 156)

Data in Action

Critical Reading Skills Each *rSkills Test* includes optional Open Response questions that assess a student's ability to synthesize, analyze, or evaluate a text. Assign these test questions to students in the *rSkills Tests* Settings in the SAM Roster.

Student Skills Report

Purpose

This report shows *rSkills Tests* results for one student, summarized by each assessed strand and skill.

DIAGNOSTIC

Student Skills Report
STUDENT: SANCHEZ, RACHEL

School: Lincoln Middle School
Teacher: Margaret Schirmer
Grade: 7
Class: Schirmer 3
Group: Jaguars

Time Period: 01/15/12 – 02/02/12 **1**

2
SRI Score: 792
READ 180 Level: 3

3 TEST 4b (Stage B)
Test Date: 01/14/12 **4**
5 Test Score: 92% (23/25)

SKILLS **6**	CORRECT **7**	ITEMS **8**	SCORE **9**
Comprehension	**8**	**10**	**80%**
Summarize	5	6	
Sequence of Events	3	4	
Vocabulary/Word Study	**8**	**8**	**100%**
Multiple-Meaning Words	4	4	
Using a Dictionary	4	4	
Conventions	**7**	**7**	**100%**
Using Correct Verb Tense	4	4	
Using Commas in a Series	3	3	

WRITING **10**	SCORE	RUBRIC VALUE
Open Response 1 (Critical Reading: Analyze)	1	2
Open Response 2 (Critical Reading: Synthesize)	2	4
Writing Prompt (Informational Summary)	5	6

Using This Report

Purpose: This report shows an individualized student's results on one rSkills Test. It includes scores for each skill, along with the number of questions answered correctly for that skill.

Follow-Up: Share this report with your student. Encourage students to monitor their own progress as they master reading skills on the rSkills Test.

How It Helps

I share this report with each student, discussing reading progress and areas for continued focus during the upcoming rBook Workshop.

Understand the Data

1 **Time Period**
Default time period setting of Last 15 Days displays results from tests completed in the past two weeks. Customize time period settings to view previous test results. Each test's results display on a separate page.

2 ***SRI* Score and *READ 180* Level**
Current student Lexile and *READ 180* software level regardless of time period settings.

3 **Test**
Indicates whitch *rSkills Test* restuls are displayed in the report. Includes the test number, which corresponds to the *rBook* Workshop. Also includes the test level. Level a tests are below grade-level; Level b tests are grade-level.

4 **Test Date**
Date the test was completed on the computer.

5 **Test Score**
Percentage of questions answered correctly out of 25 multiple choice questions.

6 **Skills**
Specific comprehension, vocabulary/word study, and conventions skills tested, based on skills taught in the aligned *rBook* Workshop.

7 **Correct**
Number of items answered correctly for each test strand and skill.

8 **Items**
Total questions for each test strand and skill.

9 **Score**
Percentage of questions answered correctly in each test strand.

10 **Writing**
Scores for open response and writing prompts (if assigned in *rSkills Tests* Settings) that have been entered into the SAM Digital Portfolio.

Use the Data

Who: Teachers, Students (Student report)

When: After each *rSkills Test,* usually every 4 to 6 weeks

How: You can use the information in this report in the following ways:

Track *rSkills Tests* results

- Print this report and share with students. Add the report to the student's portfolio.

- Guide students to track their *rSkills Tests* results in the Student Log at the back of their *rBooks.* Assist them with setting and tracking goals based on test results.

Encourage Growth

- If a student consistently scores above the 70% benchmark on below grade-level tests, consider assigning a grade-level test to provide further challenge.

- Conference with students, comparing test results with *rBook* work. Examine trends in performance in comprehension, vocabulary, and writing. Help students make the connection between *rBook* work and *rSkills Tests* results.

Review Related Reports

- *rSkills Tests* Student Progress Report (p. 182)
- *rSkills Tests* Student Test Printout (p. 186)
- *READ 180* Student Diagnostic Report (p. 156)

Data in Action

Assigning *rSkills Tests* Levels Consider time of year, Lexile level, and recent *rBook* work when determining whether students should take the below grade-level test (Level a) or the grade-level tests (Level b).

Student Test Printout

Purpose

This *rSkills Test* printout includes student's responses to multiple choice and open response questions.

DIAGNOSTIC

Student Test Printout
STUDENT: PALERMO, JUSTIN

School: Lincoln Middle School
Teacher: Margaret Schirmer
Grade: 7
Class: Schirmer 3
Time Period: 01/15/12 – 01/30/12 **1**

2
SRI Score: 438
READ 180 Level: 1

Test 4a
3 **Test Date:** 01/19/12
4 **Test Score:** 52% (13/25)

5

6 ✖ 1. **Another title for the text would be —**   *(Summarize)*

    Ⓐ The Making of a Movie.
➜ Ⓑ Life on the Streets of Mumbai.
    Ⓒ Mumbai Then and Now.
    Ⓓ Lakshmi's Jewelry Shop.

✖ 2. **Choose the sentence that best summarizes the first paragraph.**   *(Summarize)*

    Ⓐ The movie was an unlikely story.
➜ Ⓑ Mumbai is the capital of India's street life.
    Ⓒ A poor boy in India became very rich.
    Ⓓ Hundreds of poor children live on the streets of Mumbai.

✓ 3. **What does Lakshmi do first after getting up each morning?**   *(Sequence of Events)*

➜ Ⓐ She hides her bedding.
    Ⓑ She goes to her locker.
    Ⓒ She visits her friends.
    Ⓓ She eats breakfast.

How It Helps

I use this printout to review specific rSkills Test questions and answers with each student, focusing on why students missed particular questions.

Using This Report

Purpose: This copy of an rSkills Test shows each question, the skill it tests, and the correct answer. A darkened bubble indicates the student's answer. An "X" indicates a question answered incorrectly.

Follow-Up: Meet with students individually to review the questions they answered correctly or incorrectly, and reteach skills as necessary.

Understand the Data

1 Time Period

Default time period setting of Last 15 Days displays results from the most recently completed test. To view results from previous tests, customize time period settings.

2 *SRI* Score and *READ 180* Level

Current student Lexile and *READ 180* software level regardless of time period settings.

3 Test Date

Date the test was completed on the computer. The date each student finishes a test may vary.

4 Test Score

Percentage and total correct answers out of 25 multiple choice questions. Also includes scores for open response and writing prompt questions if assigned in *rSkills Tests* Settings and scored in the SAM Student Digital Portfolio.

5 Skill

Specific skill assessed in each question.

6 Multiple Choice Questions

25 multiple choice questions that assess Comprehension, Vocabulary/Word Study, and Conventions. Correct answer indicated by arrow; student response highlighted.

Use the Data

Who: Teachers, Students (Student report)

When: After each *rSkills Test,* usually every 4 to 6 weeks.

How: You can use the information in this report in the following ways:

Review Results

- Students benefit from a detailed analysis of test performance. Conference one-on-one with students about their test results. Discuss questions answered incorrectly, encouraging students to explain their thinking process.

- Compare *rSkills Tests* results with scores on *rBook* Workshop work and results from *READ 180* Topic Software. Identify performance trends and provide additional support in areas where student appears to struggle.

Prepare for Upcoming Test

- Print this report to review results of a previous *rSkills Test* with students a few days prior to assigning a new test.

- Use previous test results to discuss test-taking strategies and best practices. Refer to Preparing Students for Assessments on **page 116** for more information.

Review Related Reports

- *rSkills Tests* Student Skills Report (p. 184)
- *rSkills Tests* Student Progress Report (p. 182)
- *READ 180* Student Diagnostic Report (p. 156)

Data in Action

Assessing Open Response and Writing
Once students have been assigned and have completed open response questions and the writing prompt, use the accompanying rubrics in SAM Digital Portfolio to assign a score and give feedback. The score and the feedback will appear on this report.

SRI Reports Overview

Each time students take the *Scholastic Reading Inventory (SRI),* the Scholastic Achievement Manager (SAM) captures and analyzes their test results. Using these reports will enable you to monitor growth and assess progress toward grade-level proficiency. You can review results for individual students, groups, classes, or all students by using the *SRI* Reports.

Class/Group Reports

The following table summarizes how to use each *SRI* class or group report.

If You Want to ...	Run This Report
...analyze growth between two *SRI* tests	*SRI* Growth Report (p. 190)
...group students for *rBook* instruction	*SRI* Intervention Grouping Report (p. 194)
...compare performance standards with grade-level performance	*SRI* Proficiency Report (p. 198)
...assist students with selecting readings at appropriate reading levels	*SRI* Targeted Reading Report (p. 200)
...identify students who may be struggling with *SRI*	*SRI* Incomplete Test Alert (p. 202)
...review student enrollment and login information	*SRI* Student Roster (p. 203)

Individual Student Reports

The following table summarizes how to use individual student *SRI* reports.

If You Want to ...	Run This Report
...view a list of recommended books based on interest and reading level	*SRI* Recommended Reading Report (p. 204)
...plan instruction based on *SRI* performance and reading ability	*SRI* Student Action Report (p. 206)
...review comprehensive student performance on *SRI*	*SRI* Student Progress Report (p. 208)
...compare student *SRI* performance with sample texts	*SRI* College and Career Readiness Report (p. 212)
...review an individual student's answers on an *SRI* test	*SRI* Student Test Printout (p. 214)
...introduce families to *SRI*	*SRI* Parent Report I (p. 216)
...update families on their child's *SRI* performance	*SRI* Parent Report II (p. 216)

Growth Report | Best Practice Report

Purpose

This report measures student Lexile growth between two *SRI* tests within a selected time period.

Growth Report
CLASS: Schirmer 3

School: Lincoln Middle School
Teacher: Margaret Schirmer
Grade: 7

Time Period: 08/24/11 – 02/02/12 ①

STUDENT	GRADE	FIRST TEST IN SELECTED TIME PERIOD ②		LAST TEST IN SELECTED TIME PERIOD ③ ④		GROWTH IN LEXILE® ⑤
		LEXILE®	DATE	LEXILE®	DATE	
Chu, Amy	7	443	09/01/11	834	01/26/12	391
Krynski, Theo	7	984	09/04/11	1120	01/25/12	136
Collins, Chris	7	784	09/04/11	868	01/26/12	84
Ramirez, Gabriella	7	661	09/02/11	743	01/28/12	82
Bracco, Christine	7	643	08/31/11	709	01/27/12	66
Evans, Jamal	7	665	08/31/11	719	01/25/12	54
Fernandez, Luis	7	200	08/31/11	242	01/25/12	42
Palermo, Justin	7	400	09/12/11	438	01/27/12	38
Rupp, Jeremy	7	691	09/02/11	727	01/27/12	36
Kramer, Liz	7	775	09/02/11	809	01/26/12	34
Sanchez, Rachel	7	783	09/02/11	792	01/25/12	9
Imran, Khaleel	7	710	08/31/11	719	01/25/12	9
Garcia, Matt	7	550	09/01/11	N/A	N/A	N/A
Felix, Tonya	7	⑥ BR (20)	09/01/11	BR (10)	01/25/12	(-10)
Cooper, Tiffany	7	880	09/02/11	781	01/25/12	(-99)

* Scale for bar chart is based on highest Lexile® growth within selected time period.

Using This Report

Purpose: To identify the growth each student is making, check the dates of the two tests for an individual student. On average, students are expected to grow approximately 75-100 Lexiles per year.

Follow-Up: Provide opportunities to challenge students who show significant progress. Provide appropriate levels of intervention and support to students who are showing little growth. If zero or negative Lexile growth is recorded, check to see if students' test experience is problematic in some way and retest accordingly.

How It Helps

I use this report to track my students' reading gains. I share these results with my school administrators.

Understand the Data

1 Time Period
Run for This School Year to review year-to-date reading progress from the first test administration to the most recent test. Customize time periods to review results between any two *SRI* test dates.

2 First Test in Selected Time Period
Lexile score and test date for the first *SRI* test administered within selected time period.

3 Last Test in Selected Time Period (Lexile)
Lexile score from most recent *SRI* test within selected time period. N/A indicates a second test was not completed within selected time period.

4 Last Test in Selected Time Period (Date)
Most recent *SRI* test date within selected time period. N/A indicates a second test was not completed within selected time period.

5 Growth in Lexile
Lexile increase from the first test to the last test within selected time period. Report is sorted by overall growth and graphs are scaled to student with largest growth. Declines in Lexile between two tests are indicated in parentheses.

6 BR
A Lexile score of "BR" indicates a Beginning Reader. Students who score BR have an *SRI* score of less than 100 Lexile points.

Use the Data

Who: Teachers, Administrators (Teacher, Class, or Group report)

When: After each *SRI* administration, usually 4 times per year

How: Apply the information from this report in the following ways:

Monitor Growth

- If students have taken the *SRI* more than twice, analyze the Growth Report for different testing administrations. For example, run the report to track growth between test 1 and test 3, test 1 and test 2, or test 2 and test 3.
- Celebrate growth. Discuss growth rates and progress toward goal. Print student reports to share during conferences. See Establishing *SRI* Growth Targets on **page 62** for more information.
- Share results with administrators. Print this report to keep your school administration updated on your students' reading progress.

Target Support

- Target additional support to students who are not showing strong gains or students whose current *SRI* scores are below grade level expectations.
- Review results for students whose scores declined. Analyze individual *SRI* Student Test Printouts and conference with students to determine the cause for the decline in score. Discuss appropriate interventions with your school administration.

Review Related Reports

- *SRI* Intervention Grouping Report (p. 194)
- *SRI* Targeted Reading Report (p. 200)
- *SRI* Student Progress Report (p. 208)

Data in Action

Expected Growth A student's expected annual growth depends on grade level and initial Lexile score. See **page 60** for more information about using *SRI* results for Progress Monitoring.

Analyze the Results | Growth Report

Establish individual growth expectations to help students strive for reading performance targets.

DATA STORY

Student: Tiffany Cooper
Current Lexile: 781
SRI Growth: -99

Identify students like Tiffany who struggle with SRI performance. Determine potential cause and appropriate follow-up support.

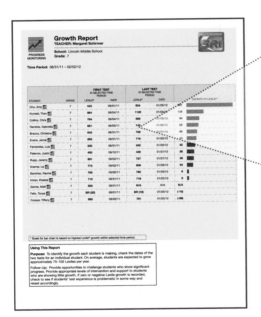

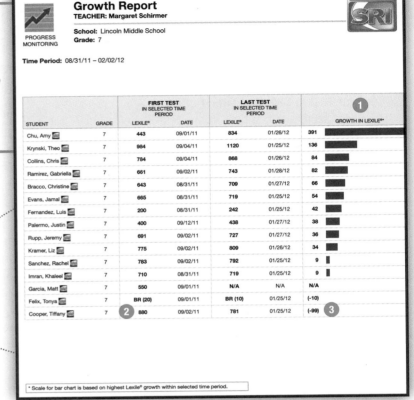

STUDENT	GRADE	FIRST TEST IN SELECTED TIME PERIOD		LAST TEST IN SELECTED TIME PERIOD		① GROWTH IN LEXILE*
		LEXILE®	DATE	LEXILE®	DATE	
Chu, Amy	7	443	09/01/11	834	01/26/12	391
Krynski, Theo	7	984	09/04/11	1120	01/25/12	136
Collins, Chris	7	784	09/04/11	868	01/26/12	84
Ramirez, Gabriella	7	661	09/02/11	743	01/28/12	82
Bracco, Christine	7	643	08/31/11	709	01/27/12	66
Evans, Jamal	7	665	08/31/11	719	01/25/12	54
Fernandez, Luis	7	200	08/31/11	242	01/25/12	42
Palermo, Justin	7	400	09/12/11	438	01/27/12	38
Rupp, Jeremy	7	691	09/02/11	727	01/27/12	36
Kramer, Liz	7	775	09/02/11	809	01/26/12	34
Sanchez, Rachel	7	783	09/02/11	792	01/25/12	9
Imran, Khaleel	7	710	08/31/11	719	01/25/12	9
Garcia, Matt	7	550	09/01/11	N/A	N/A	N/A
Felix, Tonya	7	BR (20)	09/01/11	BR (10)	01/25/12	(-10)
Cooper, Tiffany	7	② 880	09/02/11	781	01/25/12	(-99) ③

*Scale for bar chart is based on highest Lexile® growth within selected time period.

Enlargement: Growth Report

Data Point	Data Analysis	**NEXT STEPS**
① Most of the class made some growth between September and January test administrations.	Many students in the class are on target to reach grade level proficiency by the end of this school year.	Share current results and discuss exit criteria with school administration.
② Tiffany's fall Lexile score is an 880, and she is currently in 7th grade.	Tiffany's fall results indicate that she needs to make at least a 25 point Lexile gain to reach proficiency by the end of the year.	Use initial results and grade level to set realistic growth expectations for each student. See **page 62** for more information.
③ Tiffany's January test results indicate a large drop in score from her September results.	Small dips in score may occur as the *SRI* adapts to the student's reading level, but a drop of more than 60 points indicates a larger problem.	Review individual student performance on the *SRI* Test Printout and conference with student to determine cause for score decline.

Review Additional Data

Cross-reference the *SRI* Student Test Printout to analyze specific test results.

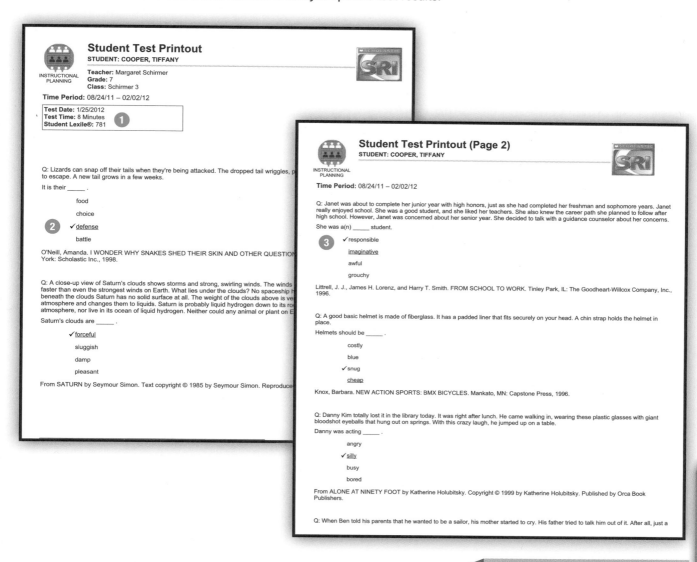

	Data Point	Data Analysis	**NEXT STEPS**
1	Tiffany only took 8 minutes to complete her test.	Although the total time it takes to complete a test varies by student, it should typically take about 20 minutes.	Discuss the nature of the test with students prior to beginning the test. Conference about previous results and goals for the current test.
2	Tiffany answered the first couple of questions correctly.	At first Tiffany's responses indicate that she is properly prepared for the test.	Ensure that all students are mentally and emotionally prepared for the test and that the environment is conducive for testing.
3	Tiffany began answering multiple questions incorrectly in a row, starting with the 4th question.	Tiffany's performance declined quickly. During a conference, Tiffany shared that another student began bothering her during the test.	When students' scores decline more than 60 points, you may wish to remove the score and allow the student to retest.

Intervention Grouping Report | Best Practice Report

Purpose

This report groups students based on *SRI* performance standards.

INSTRUCTIONAL PLANNING

Intervention Grouping Report
CLASS: SCHIRMER 3

School: Lincoln Middle School
Teacher: Margaret Schirmer
Grade: 7

Time Period: 08/24/11 – 02/02/12 ①

② PERFORMANCE STANDARD	STUDENT	GRADE	③ LEXILE®	④ DATE	⑤ PERCENTILE RANK	⑥ NCE	⑦ STANINE
Advanced	Krynski, Theo	7	1120	01/25/12	78	66	7
Proficient	Collins, Chris	7	868	01/26/12	36	42	4
Basic	Chu, Amy	7	834	01/26/12	32	40	4
Basic	Kramer, Liz	7	809	01/26/12	28	38	4
Basic	Sanchez, Rachel	7	792	01/25/12	26	36	4
Basic	Cooper, Tiffany	7	781	01/25/12	25	36	4
Basic	Ramirez, Gabriella	7	743	01/28/12	21	33	3
Basic	Rupp, Jeremy	7	727	01/27/12	19	32	3
Basic	Imran, Khaleel	7	719	01/25/12	19	32	3
Basic	Evans, Jamal	7	719	01/25/12	19	32	3
Basic	Bracco, Christine	7	709	01/27/12	17	30	3
Basic	Garcia, Matt	7	550	09/01/11	6	17	2
Below Basic	Palermo, Justin	7	438	01/25/12	1	1	1
Below Basic	Fernandez, Luis	7	242	01/25/12	1	1	1
Below Basic	Felix, Tonya	6	BR (10)	01/25/12	1	1	1

NORMATIVE DATA spans the Percentile Rank, NCE, and Stanine columns.

Using This Report

Purpose: This report groups students under the four SRI performance standards. The report is used to target for additional support students whose performance is Below Basic or Basic.

Follow-Up: Use the information on the report to set goals for students. Plan appropriate instructional support and intervention for students who are reading below grade level. Encourage students to read independently at their reading level.

How It Helps
I use this report to create initial rBook groups based on reading performance.

Understand the Data

1 **Time Period**

Run for This School Year to review current reading performance results. Customize time periods to review results from previous *SRI* tests.

2 **Performance Standard**

Student's reading level based on the four *SRI* performance standards: Advanced, Proficient, Basic, and Below Basic. Performance standard Lexile ranges vary by grade level.

3 **Lexile**

Students' Lexile score from the most recent *SRI* test within selected time period.

4 **Date**

Date of most recent completed *SRI* test within selected time period.

5 **Percentile Rank**

Percentage of students from a national sample who received lower scores than this student on a scale of 1 to 99. For example, a student who scores at the 65th percentile performed as well or better than 65 percent of the norm group.

6 **NCE (Normal Curve Equivalent)**

A comparison of student's rate of progress to the norm, based on a national sample. Students making exactly one year of progress earn a score of 0. Students progressing faster than the norm receive a score from 1 to 99, depending on the rate of increase.

7 **Stanine**

A standardized score that indicates a student's relative standing in a norm group. Stanines 1, 2, and 3 are below average; stanines 4, 5, and 6 are average; and stanines 7, 8, and 9 are above average.

Use the Data

Who: Teachers (Teacher, Class, or Group report)

When: After each *SRI* administration, usually 4 times per year.

How: You can use the information from this report in the following ways:

Establish Groups

- Regroup students based on new results. The Teacher Dashboard's Groupinator automatically creates new *rBook* groups each time students take an *SRI* test. Use the Groupinator to adjust groups.

Differentiate Instruction

- Students in lower performance standards may benefit from additional scaffolding. Use daily "Boost" activities to provide more support during *rBook* Small-Group instruction.
- Students in higher performance standards may benefit from more independent practice. Use daily "Stretch" activities to provide more challenge during *rBook* Small-Group instruction.

Review Related Reports

- *SRI* Targeted Reading Report (p. 200)
- *SRI* Student Action Report (p. 206)
- *SRI* Student Progress Report (p. 208)

Data in Action

Targeting Instruction Once you have determined which students would benefit from "Boost" or "Stretch" activities, access these daily differentiated instruction supports from the Teacher Dashboard Lesson Plan.

Analyze the Results | Intervention Grouping Report

Group students and offer appropriate Small-Group support based on current reading performance.

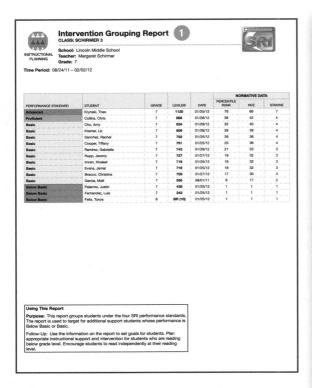

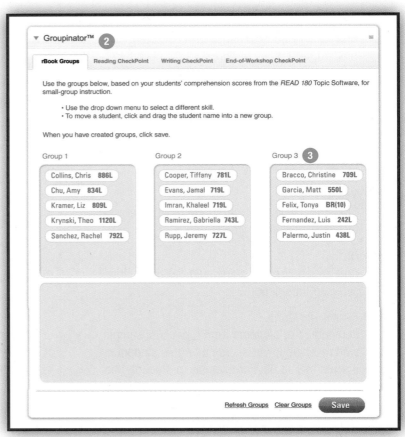

	NEXT STEPS
Data Point	**Data Analysis**	
① Results from the *SRI* Intervention Grouping Report are used to form groups for daily *rBook* instruction.	Data from this report is pulled to the Groupinator on the Teacher Dashboard for *rBook* Groups.	Access the Groupinator on the Class Page of the Teacher Dashboard to review *rBook* groups.
② The Groupinator uses the data from the *SRI* Intervention Grouping Report to create groups.	No matter how many performance standards exist in one class, the Groupinator will create three equal groups based on reading level.	Use the *SRI* Intervention Grouping Report and classroom performance results to make any necessary grouping adjustments.
③ *rBook* grouping recommendations on the Groupinator can be refreshed after each *SRI* testing window is closed.	As the year progresses, students' reading levels will change. Regroup students when new data indicates changes in student ability levels.	Click on **Refresh Groups** in the Groupinator to review *rBook* grouping recommendations based on current *SRI* performance.

Review Additional Data

Use Groupinator recommendations to determine appropriate differentiated instructional support during Small-Group Instruction.

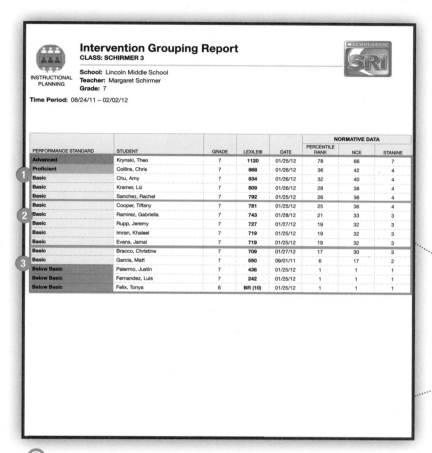

Enlargement: Intervention Grouping Report

Data Point	Data Analysis	**NEXT STEPS**
1 Group 1 includes five students who are reading at three different performance levels—Advanced, Proficient, and Basic.	Amy, Liz, and Rachel are reading at the Basic range. Consider their current classroom performance when finalizing groups.	Assign *rBook* Small-Group Stretch activities to groups with students whose reading levels are nearing grade-level proficiency.
2 Group 2 includes five students who are all reading at the Basic range.	There are students reading at the Basic range in all groups. If regrouping is necessary, focus on students at this range.	Teach the *rBook* Small-Group lesson as designed to groups with students whose reading levels are mainly in the Basic range.
3 Group 3 includes five students who are reading at two different performance levels—Basic and Below Basic.	Although Matt is reading at a Basic range, his Lexile indicates that he should stay grouped with students who need additional support.	Assign *rBook* Small-Group Boost activities to groups with students whose reading levels are mainly below the Basic range.

Proficiency Report

Purpose

This report shows *SRI* proficiency and compares current results to other students in the same grade.

PROGRESS MONITORING

Proficiency Report
CLASS: Schirmer 3

School: Lincoln Middle School
Teacher: Margaret Schirmer
Grade: 7

Time Period: 08/24/11 – 02/02/12　**1**

2　**Grade 7 Only**　**4**　**5**　**6**　**7**

3 PERFORMANCE STANDARD	MARGARET SCHIRMER			ALL GRADE 7	
	LEXILE® RANGE	STUDENTS	PERCENTAGE OF STUDENTS	STUDENTS	PERCENTAGE OF STUDENTS
Advanced	1101 and Above	1	7%	7	7%
Proficient	850 - 1100	1	7%	14	14%
Basic	550 - 849	10	67%	34	34%
Below Basic	BR - 549	3	20%	45	45%

BR = Beginning Reader

8　YEAR-END PROFICIENCY LEXILE® RANGE

GRADE 1	GRADE 2	GRADE 3	GRADE 4	GRADE 5	GRADE 6	GRADE 7	GRADE 8	GRADE 9	GRADE 10	GRADE 11	GRADE 12
100-400	300-600	500-800	600-900	700-1000	800-1050	850-1100	900-1150	1000-1200	1025-1250	1050-1300	1050-1300

Using This Report

Purpose: This report shows the current performance standards of a group or class, as compared to its corresponding grade.

Follow-Up: Compare the current performance standard breakdowns for the particular group or class to those of the grade as a whole. Use the information to set instructional goals, setting appropriate targets for the group or class.

How It Helps

I use this report to establish and track SRI proficiency goals for my class.

Understand the Data

1 **Time Period**

Default time period setting of This School Year displays results from the most recent *SRI* administration. Customize time period settings to review results from previous tests.

2 **Grade**

Results displayed by grade level. Classes with students in multiple grade levels will display results in separate charts for each grade level.

3 **Performance Standard**

Students grouped into four performance standards based on *SRI* test results and grade level: Advanced, Proficient, Basic, and Below Basic.

4 **Lexile Range**

Lexile range for students in each performance standard. Lexile ranges for each performance standard vary by grade level.

5 **Students**

Total number of students meeting each performance standard, based on most recent *SRI* results within selected time period.

6 **Percentage of Students**

Percentage of students meeting each performance standard, based on most recent *SRI* results within selected time period.

7 **All Grade**

Total students and percentage of students in each performance standard for each grade level. Students included took at least one *SRI* test. Results include all students in the grade level on the selected SAM server.

8 **Year-End Proficiency Lexile Range**

Expected year-end Lexile ranges for reading proficiency in each grade. Shaded area represents year-end proficiency range for grade levels from the selected group or class.

Use the Data

Who: Teachers (Teacher, Class, or Group report)

When: After each *SRI* administration, usually 4 times per year

How: Apply the information in this report in the following ways:

Establish and Track *SRI* Goals

- Consider scores in context by comparing your group or class *SRI* results to overall grade level results.
- Establish *SRI* growth goals based on performance standards and grade levels. For more information, see Establishing *SRI* Growth Targets on **page 62.**
- Track *SRI* results. Save a copy of this report after each *SRI* administration and compare your results from one administration to the next.

Share results

- Share results with administrators. Print this report to update your school administrators on your students' reading progress.
- Celebrate *SRI* growth with students. Recognize students who have made strong *SRI* gains, especially students who have moved to a higher performance standard.

Review Related Reports

- *SRI* Intervention Grouping Report (p. 194)
- *SRI* Targeted Reading Report (p. 200)
- *SRI* Student Action Report (p. 206)

Data in Action

Tracking Growths The total number of students in Basic and Below Basic should decrease throughout the year as students move to higher *SRI* Performance Standards.

Targeted Reading Report

Purpose

This report establishes reading ranges for text difficulty based on the student's Lexile measure.

INSTRUCTIONAL PLANNING

Targeted Reading Report
CLASS: Schirmer 3

School: Lincoln Middle School
Teacher: Margaret Schirmer
Grade: 7

Time Period: 08/24/11 – 02/02/12 **1**

| STUDENT | GRADE | **2** LEXILE® | **3** TEST DATE | **4** TEXT DIFFICULTY | | |
				5 EASY	**6** ON LEVEL	CHALLENGING **7**
Bracco, Christine	7	**709**	01/27/12	459-609	**609-759**	759-959
Chu, Amy	7	**834**	01/26/12	584-734	**734-884**	884-1084
Collins, Chris	7	**868**	01/26/12	618-768	**768-918**	918-1118
Cooper, Tiffany	7	**781**	01/25/12	531-681	**681-831**	831-1031
Evans, Jamal	7	**719**	01/25/12	469-619	**619-769**	769-969
Felix, Tonya	7	**BR (10)**	01/25/12	N/A	**BR**	BR-260
Fernandez, Luis	7	**242**	01/25/12	BR-142	**142-292**	292-492
Garcia, Matt	7	**550**	01/27/12	300-450	**450-600**	600-800
Imran, Khaleel	7	**719**	01/25/12	469-619	**619-769**	769-969
Kramer, Liz	7	**809**	01/26/12	559-709	**709-859**	859-1059
Krynski, Theo	7	**1120**	09/01/11	870-1020	**1020-1170**	1170-1370
Palermo, Justin	7	**438**	01/27/12	188-338	**338-488**	488-688
Ramirez, Gabriella	7	**743**	01/28/12	493-643	**643-793**	793-993
Rupp, Jeremy	7	**727**	01/27/12	477-627	**627-777**	777-977
Sanchez, Rachel	7	**792**	01/25/12	542-692	**692-842**	842-1042

BR = Beginning Reader

Using This Report

Purpose: This report establishes Lexile reading ranges for text difficulty – easy, average, and challenging – for each student based on the student's Lexile measure.

Follow-Up: Use the reading ranges to assign appropriately leveled text for different instructional purposes and to help students choose books at a comfortable level for independent reading.

How It Helps
I use this report to assign appropriately leveled texts at rBook Reading CheckPoints and guide book selection in Modeled and Independent Reading.

Understand the Data

1 Time Period
Default time period setting of This School Year displays results from most recent *SRI* administration. Customize time period settings to review results from previous tests.

2 Lexile
Each student's current *SRI* score, measured in Lexiles. BR indicates a Beginning Reader, a student with a Lexile below 100.

3 Test Date
Date most recent *SRI* test was completed within the selected time period.

4 Text Difficulty
Lexile ranges for text, based on the student's current Lexile score.

5 Easy
100L to 250L below the student's current Lexile score.

6 On Level
100L below to 50L above the student's current Lexile score.

7 Challenging
50L to 250L above the student's current Lexile score.

Use the Data

Who: Teachers (Teacher, Class, or Group report)

When: After each *SRI* administration, usually 4 times per year.

How: Apply the information in this report in the following ways:

Guide Independent Reading Choices

- Encourage reluctant readers to select *Easy* books for independent reading to boost confidence.
- Guide students to frequently select *On-Level* books, which are within their fluent and independent range.
- Suggest *Challenging* books when students are highly motivated and or have background knowledge about the topic.

Provide Appropriate Instructional Support

- Assign *rBook* Boost activities to provide more comprehension support when teaching *rBook* readings with Lexile measures falling within a student's *Challenging* range.
- Assign *rBook* Stretch activities to provide more independent practice with comprehension skills when teaching *rBook* readings with Lexile measures falling within a student's *Easy* range.
- Assign eReads in SAM Roster to encourage students to apply reading comprehension skills to more advanced texts.

Review Related Reports

- *SRI* Intervention Grouping Report (p. 194)
- *SRI* Recommended Reading Report (p. 204)
- *SRI* Student Action Report (p. 206)

Data in Action

Accelerating Reading Growths Review this report after each *SRI* test. As students' *SRI* scores increase, ensure that they are accessing more challenging texts during Modeled and Independent Reading and that they are being offered appropriate challenges during Small-Group Instruction.

Incomplete Test Alert

Purpose

This report lists students who did not complete or save the *SRI* test on their most recent attempt. It includes the date the test was attempted and the student's current grade level.

ALERT

Incomplete Test Alert
TEACHER: Margaret Schirmer

School: Lincoln Middle School
Grade: 7
Class: Schirmer 3

Time Period: 08/24/11 – 02/02/12

STUDENT	GRADE	ATTEMPTED TEST DATE
Rupp, Jeremy	7	11/09/11

Using This Report

Purpose: This report shows students who did not complete the SRI test on their latest test. It includes the student's grade and the date of the incomplete test.

Follow-Up: Plan each student's next SRI administration, and investigate why each student did not complete the test.

How It Helps

I review this report frequently during SRI *testing windows to ensure that all students complete an* SRI *test. I follow up with students listed on this report to ensure that they are not having trouble with the test.*

Student Roster

Purpose

This report lists students assigned to a selected group, class, or teacher. It includes each student's grade, ID, username, and password.

Student Roster
CLASS: SCHIRMER 3

School: Lincoln Middle School
Teacher: Margaret Schirmer
Grade: 7

Time Period: 08/24/11 – 02/02/12

STUDENT	GRADE	STUDENT ID	USERNAME	PASSWORD
Bracco, Christine	7	7299209	cbracco	pas5word
Chu, Amy	7	10135416	achu	pas5word
Collins, Chris	7	7805559	ccollins	pas5word
Cooper, Tiffany	7	7897663	tcooper	pas5word
Evans, Jamal	7	7813157	jevans	pas5word
Felix, Tonya	7	780555	tfelix	pas5word
Fernandez, Luis	7	7513484	lfernandez	pas5word
Garcia, Matt	7	10405447	mgarcia	pas5word
Imran, Khaleel	7	7793169	kimran	pas5word
Kramer, Liz	7	8084279	lkramer	pas5word
Krynksi, Theo	7	7162902	tkrynski	pas5word
Palermo, Justin	7	7471048	jpalermo	pas5word
Ramirez, Gabriella	7	7467053	gramirez	pas5word
Rupp, Jeremy	7	7793706	jrupp	pas5word
Sanchez, Rachel	7	10575041	rsanchez	pas5word

TOTAL STUDENTS = 15

How It Helps

This report is useful for classroom management. I keep a copy on hand in case students forget their passwords. It also helps me ensure that everyone in my READ 180 *class is enrolled in SRI.*

Using This Report

Purpose: The Student Roster lists the students assigned to a selected group, class, or teacher. It includes each student's grade, ID, username, and password.

Follow-Up: Review the roster to track which students are enrolled in SRI.

Recommended Reading Report

Purpose

This report provides an individualized list of books for each student, based on interests and *SRI* results.

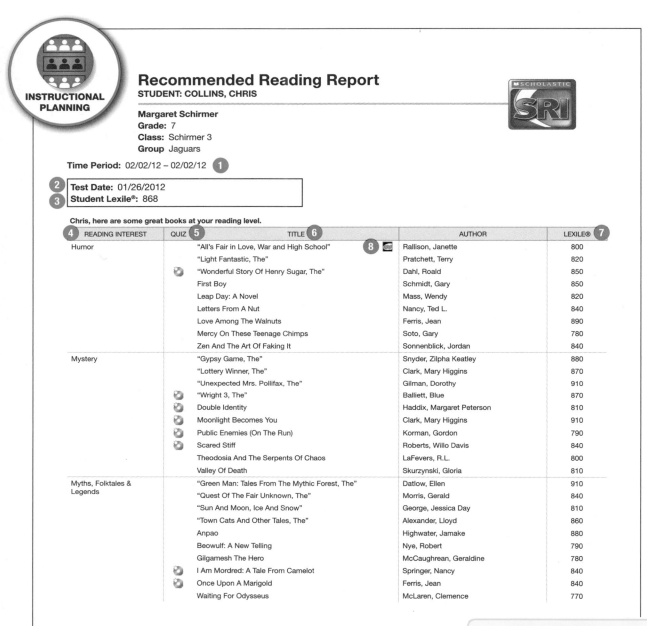

INSTRUCTIONAL PLANNING

Recommended Reading Report
STUDENT: COLLINS, CHRIS

SCHOLASTIC SRI

Margaret Schirmer
Grade: 7
Class: Schirmer 3
Group Jaguars

Time Period: 02/02/12 – 02/02/12 **①**

② **Test Date:** 01/26/2012
③ **Student Lexile®:** 868

Chris, here are some great books at your reading level.

④ READING INTEREST	QUIZ ⑤	TITLE ⑥	AUTHOR	LEXILE® ⑦
Humor		"All's Fair in Love, War and High School" ⑧ 📖	Rallison, Janette	800
		"Light Fantastic, The"	Pratchett, Terry	820
	🔵	"Wonderful Story Of Henry Sugar, The"	Dahl, Roald	850
		First Boy	Schmidt, Gary	850
		Leap Day: A Novel	Mass, Wendy	820
		Letters From A Nut	Nancy, Ted L.	840
		Love Among The Walnuts	Ferris, Jean	890
		Mercy On These Teenage Chimps	Soto, Gary	780
		Zen And The Art Of Faking It	Sonnenblick, Jordan	840
Mystery		"Gypsy Game, The"	Snyder, Zilpha Keatley	880
		"Lottery Winner, The"	Clark, Mary Higgins	870
		"Unexpected Mrs. Pollifax, The"	Gilman, Dorothy	910
	🔵	"Wright 3, The"	Balliett, Blue	870
	🔵	Double Identity	Haddix, Margaret Peterson	810
	🔵	Moonlight Becomes You	Clark, Mary Higgins	910
	🔵	Public Enemies (On The Run)	Korman, Gordon	790
	🔵	Scared Stiff	Roberts, Willo Davis	840
		Theodosia And The Serpents Of Chaos	LaFevers, R.L.	800
		Valley Of Death	Skurzynski, Gloria	810
Myths, Folktales & Legends		"Green Man: Tales From The Mythic Forest, The"	Datlow, Ellen	910
		"Quest Of The Fair Unknown, The"	Morris, Gerald	840
		"Sun And Moon, Ice And Snow"	George, Jessica Day	810
		"Town Cats And Other Tales, The"	Alexander, Lloyd	860
		Anpao	Highwater, Jamake	880
		Beowulf: A New Telling	Nye, Robert	790
		Gilgamesh The Hero	McCaughrean, Geraldine	780
	🔵	I Am Mordred: A Tale From Camelot	Springer, Nancy	840
	🔵	Once Upon A Marigold	Ferris, Jean	840
		Waiting For Odysseus	McLaren, Clemence	770

🔵 Scholastic Reading Counts! Installed Quiz	📖 READ 180 Title

Using This Report

Purpose: This report provides an individualized list of books for a student, based on his or her reading interest and SRI test results.

Follow-Up: Share the list with students, encouraging them to explore the recommended titles. Then, help students find and choose books.

How It Helps

I use this report to help students select books that match their interests and skill levels. I also share this report with caregivers so that they can help their children select appropriate books.

Understand the Data

1 Time Period
Time period setting is This School Year, which displays results from most recent *SRI* test.

2 Test Date
The student's most recent *SRI* test date.

3 Student Lexile
The student's current *SRI* test score.

4 Reading Interest
Topics of interest the student selected at the beginning of the *SRI* test. Students can select up to three topics of interest.

5 Quiz
Icon next to a book title indicates that *Scholastic Reading Counts!* quiz for that book has been installed and is available.

6 Title
Books related to the student's interests at the appropriate reading level.

7 Lexile
Lexile measure for each book.

8 *READ 180* Title
READ 180 icon next to a book title indicates that the book is available in the *READ 180* Paperback and Audiobook library.

Use the Data

Who: Teachers, Students, Parents (Student report)

When: After each *SRI* administration, usually 4 times a year.

How: You can apply the information in this report in the following ways:

Guide Independent Reading

- Print this report after each *SRI* test adminisration and use it to help students select books for independent reading.
- Use the SAM Book Expert to gather more information about the books listed in this report. See Using the SAM Book Expert on **page 91** for more information.

Share Results

- Share this report with school media specialists so that they can help students select appropriate books and can stock books based on student reading interest and level.
- Send this report home with students along with the *SRI* Parent Letter or with report cards to provide caregivers guidance in helping their children select books.

Review Related Reports

- *SRI* Student Action Report (p. 206)
- *SRI* College and Career Readiness Report (p. 212)
- *SRI* Parent Reports (p. 216)

Data in Action

Selecting Book Topics At the beginning of an *SRI* test, students choose book topics that interest them. Encourage students to select topics carefully so that their Recommended Reading Report reflects books that will truly interest them.

Student Action Report

Purpose

This report tracks a student's *SRI* history, provides reading ranges, and offers teaching recommendations.

INSTRUCTIONAL PLANNING

Student Action Report
STUDENT: COLLINS, CHRIS

Teacher: Margaret Schirmer
Grade: 7
Class: Schirmer 3

Time Period: 08/24/11 – 02/02/12 **1**

Chris's SRI Test History

Christine's Lexile(R) measure corresponds to the information indicated in the chart below:

TEST DATE	LEXILE® **2**	PERFORMANCE STANDARD **3**	TEST TYPE	NORMATIVE DATA		
				PERCENTILE RANK **4**	NCE **5**	STANINE **6**
09/04/11	784	Basic	SRI Computer Test	25	36	4
11/03/11	854	Proficient	SRI Computer Test	35	42	4
01/26/12	868	Proficient	SRI Computer Test	36	42	4

7 Targeted Reading Placement Chart

For a student with a Lexile(R) measure of **784**, use the Lexile(R) ranges indicated below to help guide book selection, according to your instructional purposes.

LEXILE® RANGE	INDEPENDENT READING	INSTRUCTIONAL READING
918-1118	The text is difficult for Chris.	Chris can build reading skill with direct instructional support.
768-918	Chris can read the text with a high level of engagement and with appropriate levels of challenge.	Chris has sufficient control over vocabulary and syntax to work on applying reading skills.
618-768	Chris can read these texts fluently but with little challenge.	Chris is unchallenged by vocabulary and syntax. This level can be used when teaching new or challenging content.

8 Recommendations for Chris

To help Chris grow as a reader, encourage Chris to:

- Read books within the target Lexile range (50 Lexiles above and 100 below Lexile measure).
- Use various word attack strategies (context clues, word families, reference materials) to determine the meaning of unknown words.
- Use reading strategies such as drawing conclusions, making and confirming predictions, and making inferences.
- Compare and contrast topics and themes presented across genres.
- Build vocabulary by reading and discussing at least 25 books per year (approximately 750,000 words).

Using This Report

Purpose: This report shows an individual student's SRI test history, a reading placement chart targeting appropriate Lexile ranges for different reading purposes, and teaching recommendations to help the student meet grade-level expectations.

Follow-Up: Review the student's performance and use the placement chart and recommendations for classroom or home assignments.

How It Helps

I use this report to help students select appropriate reading materials and help me determine what support to provide during Whole- and Small-Group Instruction.

Understand the Data

1 Time Period

Default time period setting of This School Year displays results from all *SRI* tests administered during the school year. Customize date ranges to track progress on selected tests within a school year or review progress over multiple years.

2 Lexile

Includes Lexile scores for all *SRI* tests taken within the selected time period.

3 Performance Standard

Student's reading level, based on the four *SRI* performance standards: Below Basic, Basic, Proficient, and Advanced. Lexile ranges for each performance standard vary by grade level.

4 Percentile Rank

Percentage of students from a national sample who received lower scores than this student. Percentiles range from 1 to 99.

5 Normal Curve Equivalent (NCE)

A comparison of the student's rate of progress to the norm, based on a national sample. Students who make exactly one year of growth are keeping pace with the norm and receive an NCE score of zero. Students progressing faster than the norm receive a score from 1–99, depending on the rate of increase.

6 Stanine

A standardized score ranging from 1 to 9. Stanines 1, 2, and 3 are below average; stanines 4, 5, and 6 are average; and stanines 7, 8, and 9 are above average.

7 Targeted Reading Placement Chart

Lexile ranges for independent and instructional reading based on the student's current Lexile.

8 Recommendations

Suggested teaching strategies customized to the student's grade, Lexile score, and *SRI* performance standard.

Use the Data

Who: Teachers, Students (Student report)

When: After each *SRI* administration, usually 4 times per year

How: You can use the information in this report in the following ways:

Review Test Results

- Establish *SRI* growth goals, then conference with students to explain results and track progress toward goal.
- Share results with support specialists at IEP meetings.

Provide Reading Support

- Filter results in the SAM Book Expert according to the Lexile ranges from this report to help students select independent reading materials at appropriate reading levels.
- Use the Instructional Reading column to determine whether the student would benefit from Boost or Stretch comprehension skills support during Small-Group Instruction. See the *rBook Teacher's Edition* on the Interactive Teaching System (ITS) for more information.

Review Related Reports

- *SRI* Targeted Reading Report (p. 200)
- *SRI* Recommended Reading Report (p. 204)
- *SRI* Student Progress Report (p. 208)

Data in Action

Boost and Stretch Assign Boost activities when *rBook* readings fall more than 50 Lexile points above the student's current reading level. Assign Stretch activities when *rBook* readings fall 100 Lexile points or more below student's current reading level.

Student Progress Report | Best Practice Report

Purpose

This report traces historical student progress on *SRI* tests in relation to year-end proficiency.

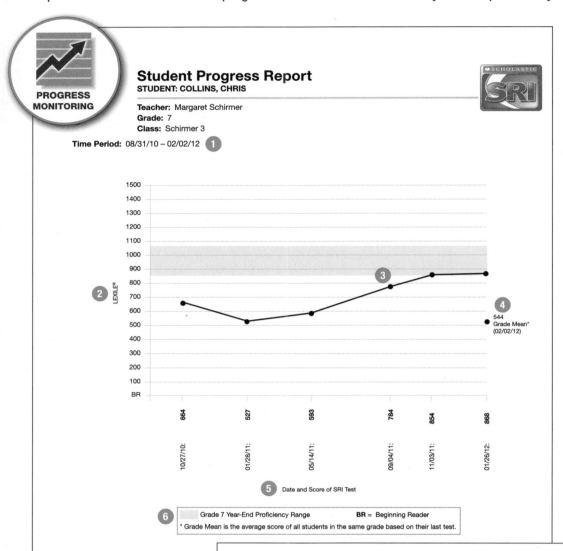

PROGRESS MONITORING

Student Progress Report
STUDENT: COLLINS, CHRIS

Teacher: Margaret Schirmer
Grade: 7
Class: Schirmer 3

Time Period: 08/31/10 – 02/02/12 ①

544 Grade Mean* (02/02/12) ④

Date	Score
10/27/10:	664
01/28/11:	527
05/14/11:	593
09/04/11:	784
11/03/11:	854
01/26/12:	868

⑤ Date and Score of SRI Test

⑥ Grade 7 Year-End Proficiency Range   BR = Beginning Reader
* Grade Mean is the average score of all students in the same grade based on their last test.

How It Helps

This graph helps me track each student's progress over time. I can share this report with the student, send it home to parents, or use it to point out particular successes to my principal.

Student Progress Report (Page 2)
STUDENT: COLLINS, CHRIS

Teacher: Margaret Schirmer
Grade: 7
Class: Schirmer 3

Time Period: 08/31/10 – 02/02/12

| | | | | | NORMATIVE DATA | | |
| | | | | ⑦ | ⑧ | ⑨ | ⑩ |
TEST DATE	TEST	LEXILE®	GRADE LEVEL	PERFORMANCE STANDARD	PERCENTILE RANK	NCE	STANINE
10/27/10	SRI Computer Test	664	Below	Basic	13	26	3
01/28/11	SRI Computer Test	527	Far Below	Below Basic	4	13	1
05/14/11	SRI Computer Test	593	Below	Basic	8	20	2
09/04/11	SRI Computer Test	784	Below	Basic	25	36	4
11/03/11	SRI Computer Test	854	On	Proficient	35	42	4
01/26/12	SRI Computer Test	868	On	Proficient	36	42	4

Understand the Data

1 **Time Period**
Default time period setting of This School Year displays comprehensive *SRI* results. Customize time period settings to target recent scores or review results for multiple years.

2 **Lexile**
Vertical axis shows Lexiles in increments of 100.

3 **Graph Entries**
Each dot represents a student's *SRI* test result on a particular date.

4 **Grade Mean**
Dot indicates the average score for all students in that particular grade, based on the latest *SRI* test results.

5 **Date and Score of *SRI* Test**
Horizontal axis displays date and score of all *SRI* tests completed within the selected time period.

6 **Year-End Proficiency Range**
Shaded area represents the year-end Lexile proficiency range for the student's current grade level.

7 **Performance Standard**
Student's reading level based on the four *SRI* performance standards. Performance standard Lexile ranges vary by grade level.

8 **Percentile Rank**
Percentage of students from a national sample who received lower scores than this student. For example, a student who scores at the 65th percentile performed as well as or better than 65 percent of the norm group.

9 **Normal Curve Equivalent (NCE)**
A comparison of student's rate of progress to the norm, based on a national sample. Students progressing faster than the norm would receive a score from 1 to 99, depending on the increase.

10 **Stanine**
A standardized score that indicates student's relative standing in a norm group. Stanines 1–3 are below average; stanines 4–6 are average; and stanines 7–9 are above average.

Use the Data

Who: Teachers, Students, Caregivers

When: After each *SRI* administration, usually 4 times a year

How: Apply the information in this report in the following ways:

Prepare for Upcoming Test

- Tell students that the *SRI* measures their reading level so that you can match them with books that they can read and enjoy.

- Prepare students for the *SRI* test by discussing previous test results. Remind them to use the Skip button if they are given a question they cannot answer. They can skip up to three questions.

- Explain to students that subsequent tests begin at their current Lexile level, so initial questions may seem more challenging.

- Help students set *SRI* growth goals and understand the year-end Lexile proficiency range. Refer to Establishing *SRI* Growth Targets on page 64 for more information about annual growth goals.

Review Test Results

- Use customizable certificates available in the SAM Roster to recognize growth.

- Conference with students whose scores dropped and plan appropriate intervention. Refer to the *SRI* Results section on **page 63** for more information.

- Share results with caregivers at parent-teacher conferences, highlighting reading achievement.

Review Related Reports

- *SRI* Recommended Reading Report (p. 204)
- *SRI* Student Action Report (p. 206)
- *SRI* College and Career Readiness Report (p. 212)

Data in Action

Test-Taking Strategies Remind students that the *SRI* will save their place, so they can exit out of the test if they begin to feel tired. They can resume the test the next day.

Analyze the Results | Student Progress Report

DATA STORY

Student: Chris Collins
Current Lexile: 868
Current Grade: 7

Recognize students like Chris who have made large gains in reading comprehension.

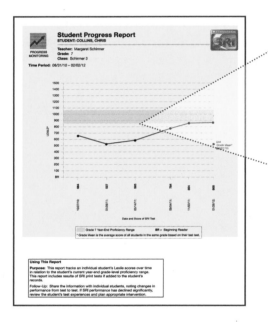

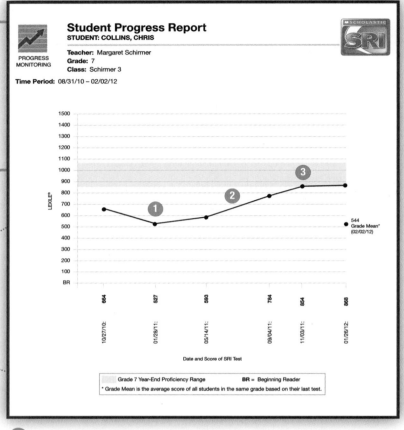

Student Progress Report
STUDENT: COLLINS, CHRIS

Teacher: Margaret Schirmer
Grade: 7
Class: Schirmer 3

PROGRESS MONITORING

Time Period: 08/31/10 – 02/02/12

544 Grade Mean* (02/02/12)

Date and Score of SRI Test

Grade 7 Year-End Proficiency Range   **BR** = Beginning Reader
* Grade Mean is the average score of all students in the same grade based on their last test.

Enlargement: Student Progress Report

Data Point	Data Analysis	NEXT STEPS
① Chris's data showed a slight decline from the first test to the second test.	Chris was not prepared for the challenging questions of the second test.	Remind students that their second *SRI* will seem harder since it starts at their current Lexile.
② Chris's overall *SRI* growth pattern is positive, with steady increases at each *SRI* administration.	Chris made over two years' growth during his first year in *READ 180*. He is on track for similar results this year.	Use this report to help students set and track *SRI* growth goals. Review Chris's *SRI* case study on **page 63.**
③ Chris's *SRI* graph has reached the blue 7th grade proficiency band.	Since Chris's Lexile score is higher and he is nearing proficiency, he may be ready to exit *READ 180*.	Speak with school administration to discuss exit criteria for students who have reached grade-level proficiency.

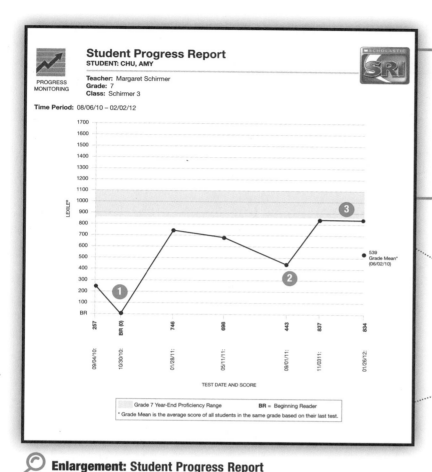

Enlargement: Student Progress Report

Student: Amy Chu
Current Lexile: 834
Current Grade: 7

Identify students like Amy whose results show decline and offer appropriate support.

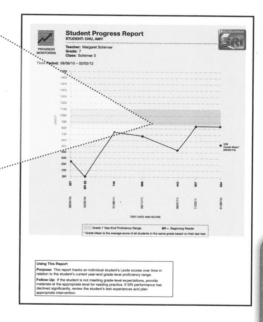

SRI Reports

Data Point	Data Analysis	NEXT STEPS
1 Amy had a large drop in score on her second *SRI test.*	Amy's Estimated Reading Level was not set for her first test, causing a problem with her first *SRI* test results.	Target all *READ 180* students for the first *SRI* test, setting their Estimated Reading Level to Below Grade Level or Far Below Grade Level.
2 Amy had another large drop in score in August of her second year.	Amy did not do much reading over the summer and also may be nervous about the new school year.	Tell students that they can wait a day or two to take the *SRI* test if they are feeling nervous or having a bad day.
3 Amy's results flatline in January.	Amy has reached grade-level proficiency. Once students have reached proficiency, overall gains may not be as large.	Discuss exit criteria and determine how best to support students once they have exited from *READ 180*.

College and Career Readiness Report

Purpose

This report tracks student *SRI* results in relation to narrative, functional, and informational texts.

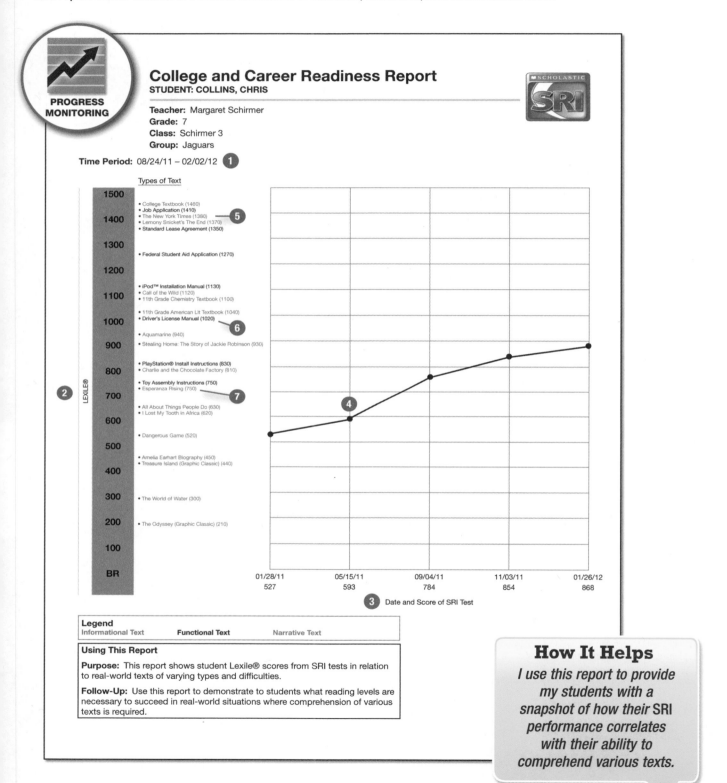

Legend

Informational Text	**Functional Text**	Narrative Text

Using This Report

Purpose: This report shows student Lexile® scores from SRI tests in relation to real-world texts of varying types and difficulties.

Follow-Up: Use this report to demonstrate to students what reading levels are necessary to succeed in real-world situations where comprehension of various texts is required.

How It Helps

I use this report to provide my students with a snapshot of how their SRI performance correlates with their ability to comprehend various texts.

Understand the Data

1 Time Period

Default time period setting is This School Year. Customize date ranges to track progress on selected tests within a school year or to review progress over multiple years.

2 Lexile

Vertical axis shows Lexiles in increments of 100.

3 Date and Score of *SRI* Test

Horizontal axis shows dates and scores for all *SRI* tests within selected time periods.

4 Graph Entries

Data points represent a student's *SRI* Lexile score on a particular date. Print tests with scores entered in SAM Roster also appear on this report.

5 Informational Text

Green indicates a text that conveys or explains different types of information such as reference materials and personal narratives.

6 Functional Text

Blue indicates a text that has practical application in everyday life, such as signs, directions, letters, and manuals.

7 Narrative Text

Red indicates a text that aims to entertain, to tell a story, or to provide a literary experience.

Use the Data

Who: Teachers, Students (Student report)

When: After each *SRI* administration, usually 4 times per year.

How: You can apply the information in this report in the following ways:

Prepare For Upcoming Test

- Discuss previous *SRI* test results with students during one-on-one conferences.
- Help students establish and track *SRI* growth goals. On average, one year's *SRI* growth is between 50 and 100 Lexile points, depending on a student's grade level and initial Lexile level. For more information see Establishing *SRI* Growth Targets on **page 62.**

Review Test Results

- Suggest texts that students can access to challenge comprehension and build fluency.
- Recognize achievement of students who made *SRI* gains.
- Use the *SRI* Student Test Printout to examine specific test results with students.
- Conference with families to help them understand the types of materials their children can read at home.

Review Related Reports

- *SRI* Recommended Reading Report (p. 204)
- *SRI* Student Test Printout (p. 214)
- *SRI* Parent Report II (p. 216)

Data in Action

Appropriate Growth Expectations Total *SRI* growth for the year depends on the student's grade level and initial Lexile. Review the *SRI* information in the assessment section to help students set individual growth goals.

Student Test Printout

Purpose

This report displays results of the student's *SRI* test, including passages, answers, and student responses.

INSTRUCTIONAL PLANNING

Student Test Printout
STUDENT: CHU, AMY

Teacher: Margaret Schirmer
Grade: 7
Class: Schirmer 3

Time Period: 08/24/11 – 02/02/12 ①

② **Test Date:** 1/26/2012
③ **Test Time:** 20 Minutes
④ **Student Lexile®:** 834

⑤ Q: We ran, and rested, and ran again. Rather than endure the extra effort of scaling the far side, we followed the valley to the west. In the darkness we stumbled and fell over the uneven ground, bruising ourselves. Behind us the light followed, relentlessly weaving to and fro. During one pause we saw that the Tripods had split up, one going up the other side of the valley and another marching to the east. But the third was coming our way and gaining on us.

The Tripods were _____ us.

✓ chasing
⑥ <u>carrying</u>
    calling
    cheating

⑦ Christopher, John. THE WHITE MOUNTAINS. 1967. Reprint, New York: Simon & Schuster Children's Publishing Division, 1988.

Q: Chavez kept trying to persuade the other workers to join together and demand a pay raise. But people were still too afraid of losing their jobs. Then he began teaching Mexican migrant workers how to speak English. If they knew English, they could take the steps to become American citizens.

Chavez wanted to _____ them.

    please
✓ help
    tease
    remove

Cedeno, Maria E. CESAR CHAVEZ: LABOR LEADER. Brookfield, CT: The Millbrook Press, 1993.

Using This Report

Purpose: This report provides a printout of the last SRI test the student has completed. It includes each passage and all four answer choices, with the student's answer choice and the correct answer choice both indicated. Each passage source is also listed.

Follow-Up: Review the printout of the test with the student, pointing out items the student answered incorrectly. Work through those items with students to help them understand why they came up with incorrect answers.

How It Helps

I use this report to review the test with students, discussing items answered incorrectly. We work together to understand why particular questions were missed.

Understand the Data

1 Time Period
Run for This School Year to display responses from the most recent test. Customize time period settings to review results from previous *SRI* tests.

2 Test Date
Student's most recent *SRI* test date within selected time period.

3 Test Time
The amount of time a student spent taking the test. The test is not timed, but most students complete the test in 20–30 minutes.

4 Student Lexile
Displays the student's current *SRI* score.

5 Passage
Displays each passage the student received.

6 Answer Choices
Each passage's multiple choice options are listed below the passage. Correct answers are indicated with a check mark; student responses are underlined.

7 Citation
Passages are selected from reading materials that students may encounter in daily life.

Use the Data

Who: Teachers, Students (Student report)

When: After each *SRI* testing session, usually 4 times a year.

How: You can apply the information in this report in the following ways:

Review Test Results

- Students benefit from a detailed analysis of their *SRI* performance. Conference one-on-one with students about their test results. Discuss answers that were marked incorrectly, helping students to identify why their choice was incorrect.

- For students whose *SRI* score declined, review results to identify the cause. Determine whether students spent an appropriate amount of time on the test or experienced test fatigue. See **page 63** for more information on tracking *SRI* test progress.

Prepare Students for an Upcoming *SRI* Test

- Review previous test results with students a few days prior to administering a new *SRI* test.

- Use previous test results to discuss test-taking strategies such as using skips, avoiding fatigue by exiting out of the test and resuming the next day, and best practices for answering multiple choice questions.

- Remind students to focus on each test question, since they are unable to go back to previous questions once they have moved to a new question.

Review Related Reports

- *SRI* Recommended Reading Report (p. 204)
- *SRI* Student Progress Report (p. 208)
- *SRI* Parent Reports (p. 216)

Data in Action

Skipping Questions Students are permitted to skip up to three questions per test and are not penalized for skipping these questions.

Parent Reports I and II

Purpose

These reports introduce *SRI* to parents or caregivers, provide their child's *SRI* test results, and offer suggestions for how parents can help their child build fundamental reading skills at home.

SCHOOL-TO-HOME

STUDENT: BRACCO, CHRISTINE

Teacher: Margaret Schirmer
Grade: 7
Class: Schirmer 3

February 2, 2012

Dear Parent or Caregiver,

Christine has just completed another *Scholastic Reading Inventory* (SRI) test, a classroom-based assessment designed to evaluate students' reading ability, monitor student reading progress, and match students to text. This letter is to inform you of Christine's latest results.

The results of Christine's SRI test are used in a number of ways. First, a student's score on the test is used to determine the student's reading ability compared to grade-level performance standards. These determinations can help tailor appropriate reading instruction. The results of subsequent SRI tests are then used to monitor progress over time. Student results are also used to match students to texts at their reading level, which helps to make reading rewarding, constructive, and enjoyable.

Christine's SRI Results

Test Date	Lexile® Test Results
January 27, 2012	709

Grade 7 End-of-Year Target Range: 850–1100 Lexiles®

Please continue to help support
will work best for you and Christi

· Set a goal for Christine to
  Christine's reading efforts.

· Help Christine find books 1
  identify books at the appro

· Continue to make connect
  likes animals, try to locate

· Spend time every day with
  advertisements, and food

· Share with Christine the ki
  about a magazine article th

Thank you for taking the time to
feel free to contact me.

Sincerely,

STUDENT: BRACCO, CHRISTINE

Teacher: Margaret Schirmer
Grade: 7
Class: Schirmer 3

SCHOOL-TO-HOME

September 4, 2011

Dear Parent or Caregiver,

This year Christine will be completing the *Scholastic Reading Inventory* (SRI), a classroom-based assessment designed to evaluate students' reading ability, monitor student reading progress, and match students to books at their reading level.

The SRI test involves reading a series of short passages taken from fiction and nonfiction books and articles. After each passage, the student is asked to complete a fill-in-the-blank sentence. The test is taken on a computer, and lasts about 20 minutes. Test results are reported using a readability measurement called the Lexile®. The Lexile score can be used to assess Christine's reading ability as well as to recommend books at an appropriate reading level.

Christine's SRI Results

Test Date	Lexile® Test Results
August 31, 2011	643

Grade 7 End-of-Year Target Range: 850–1100 Lexiles®

There are a number of things that you can do at home to help support Christine's reading progress. Here are some suggestions:

· Set a goal for Christine to read at least 20 minutes a day.

· Help Christine find books that are at an appropriate reading level. Please contact me about how to use the Lexile Framework to identify books at the appropriate reading range.

· Make connections between Christine's interests and books to read. For example, if Christine likes animals, try to locate books on animals, both fiction and nonfiction.

· Try to spend time every day with Christine looking through "nonbook" kinds of materials, such as websites, pieces of mail, advertisements, and food labels, to demonstrate how important a part reading plays in daily life.

· Consider sharing with Christine the kinds of things you are reading. Tell Christine about interesting things you read in the newspaper, or about a magazine article that taught you something new.

How It Helps

I send Parent Report I home after the first test to introduce parents to SRI. I send Parent Report II home after each subsequent test to update parents on their child's reading progress.

Scholastic Reading Counts! Reports Overview

Each time students take a *Scholastic Reading Counts!* quiz, the Scholastic Achievement Manager (SAM) captures their results. Using these reports will enable you to monitor independent reading, plan instruction, and match students with appropriate texts. You can access this data for individual students, groups, classes, or all of your students through the *SRC!* reports.

Class/Group Reports

The following table summarizes how to use each *SRC!* class or group report.

If You Want to ...	Run This Report
...acknowledge student's reading achievements	*SRC!* Award Report (p. 218)
...track how many quizzes students have passed	*SRC!* Books Read Report (p. 220)
...find out which books are most popular	*SRC!* Book Frequency and Rating Report (p. 224)
...see which quizzes students have taken most often	*SRC!* Most Frequent Quizzes Report (p. 225)
...track the total points earned for quizzes passed	*SRC!* Points Report (p. 226)
...identify students who may be struggling with quizzes	*SRC!* Quiz Alert (p. 228)
...acknowledge students who are successfully reading books above their current Lexile	*SRC!* Reading Growth Acknowledgment (p. 229)
... monitor student participation and progress	*SRC!* Reading Progress Report (p. 230)

Individual Student Reports

The following table summarizes how to use individual student *SRC!* reports.

If You Want to ...	Run This Report
...help student select appropriate books	*SRC!* Recommended Reading Report (p. 234)
...review results for quizzes passed	*SRC!* Student Quiz Success Report (p. 236)
...monitor quiz progress for an individual student	*SRC!* Student Reading Report (p. 238)
...introduce families to *Scholastic Reading Counts!*	*SRC!* Parent Report I (p. 240)
...provide updates about student progress in independent reading	*SRC!* Parent Report II and III (p. 241)

Award Report

Purpose

This report lists students who have passed the number of quizzes required to earn an award.

PROGRESS MONITORING

Award Report
CLASS: SCHIRMER 3

School: Lincoln Middle School
Teacher: Margaret Schirmer
Grade: 7

Time Period: 08/24/11 – 02/02/12

Gold Award (25 Books)

STUDENT	BOOKS READ
NO DATA TO REPORT	

Silver Award (15 Books)

STUDENT	BOOKS READ
Evans, Jamal	15

Bronze Award (10 Books)

STUDENT	BOOKS READ
Cooper, Tiffany	10

Red Award (5 Books)

STUDENT	BOOKS READ
Bracco, Christine	7
Chu, Amy	6
Felix, Tonya	6
Imran, Khaleel	9
Palermo, Justin	7
Sanchez, Rachel	9

Using This Report

Purpose: This report shows students who have earned the points required to qualify for an award. Use the report to monitor students' progress toward meeting their independent reading goals.

Follow-Up: Plan incentives and provide additional student motivation by displaying the report in the classroom.

How It Helps

I set up my award values at the beginning of the year and use this report to acknowledge students who have achieved awards at monthly reading celebrations.

Understand the Data

1 Time Period

Default time period of This School Year displays results for all quizzes passed during the school year. Customize time period settings to review results for specific periods of time.

2 Award Status

Lists students who have passed enough quizzes to earn Gold, Silver, Bronze, Red, and Blue awards. Award values can be managed in the SAM Roster.

3 Books or Points

Lists awards based on whether student goal is set as books read or points earned. Only *Scholastic Reading Counts!* quizzes with passing scores count toward award status.

Use the Data

Who: Teachers (Teacher, Class, or Group report)

When: Once or twice a month

How: Apply the information in the following ways:

Celebrate Reading Achievement

• Monitor student progress toward goal by printing this report and sharing results with the class once or twice a month. Create a chart or bulletin board to post award status and updates.

• Recognize reading achievement by customizing and printing *Scholastic Reading Counts!* certificates in the SAM Roster.

Share Results

• Print this report to update your school administration on your students' reading progress. Invite administrators to your classroom to congratulate students who have met or exceeded their goals.

• Encourage students to use the My Reads section of the Student Dashboard to track their own status. Celebrate students who are on track to meet or exceed their goals. Offer support to students who are struggling to meet their goals.

Review Related Reports

• *SRC!* Books Read Report (p. 220)
• *SRC!* Points Report (p. 226)
• *SRC!* Student Reading Report (p. 238)

Data in Action

Quiz Award Values The Awards Settings in the *Scholastic Reading Counts!* Settings section of the SAM Roster tab allows you to establish values for each award.

Books Read Report | Best Practice Report

Purpose

This report includes a table and bar graph to track total *Scholastic Reading Counts!* quizzes passed.

PROGRESS MONITORING

Books Read Report
CLASS: SCHIRMER 3

School: Lincoln Middle School
Teacher: Margaret Schirmer
Grade: 7

Time Period: 08/24/11 – 02/02/12 ①

STUDENT	② LEXILE®	③ AVG. BOOK LEXILE®	④ NUMBER OF QUIZZES PASSED		⑤ GOAL	⑥ TOTAL WORDS READ
Bracco, Christine	709	753	7		20	135,889
Chu, Amy	834	678	6		15	65,964
Collins, Chris	868	820	6		15	10,276
Cooper, Tiffany	781	735	10		17	83,026
Evans, Jamal	719	755	15		18	66,750
Felix, Tonya	BR (10)	375	6		30	17,093
Fernandez, Luis	242	690	2		30	9,664
Garcia, Matt	550	485	2		22	5,078
Imran, Khaleel	719	626	9		20	276,999
Kramer, Liz	809	750	2		18	10,888
Krynski, Theo	1120	730	4		13	8,550
Palermo, Justin	438	381	7		23	16,833
Ramirez, Gabriella	743	720	1		18	5,360
Rupp, Jeremy	727	N/A	0		18	0
Sanchez, Rachel	792	773	9		17	156,931
⑦ **TOTALS**	**700 (AVG)**	**638 (AVG)**	**86**		**294**	**869,301**

Using This Report

Purpose: This report consists of a table and bar graph that show the number of books read and related book information by teacher, grade, class, or group.

Follow-Up: Use the table and bar graph to share information with parents and to supplement student portfolios.

How It Helps

I use this report to track how many quizzes my students have passed and recognize their reading achievements.

Understand the Data

1 **Time Period**

Run for This School Year to review *Scholastic Reading Counts!* participation for the full year. Customize time period settings to analyze quarterly or monthly results.

2 **Lexile**

Student's *SRI* score from most recent test, regardless of time period settings.

3 **Average Book Lexile**

Average Lexile measure for all books with quizzes taken, including multiple quiz attempts and quizzes not passed.

4 **Number of Quizzes Passed**

Total *Scholastic Reading Counts!* quizzes passed within selected time period.

5 **Goal**

Goal for total book quizzes passed for the year, if books are established as the goal in SAM Roster.

6 **Total Words Read**

Total words read for each *Scholastic Reading Counts!* quiz passed.

7 **Totals**

Totals for the group or class, including quizzes passed, total books set as goal if established in SAM, total words read, as well as average book Lexile and average student Lexile.

Use the Data

Who: Teachers (Teacher, Class, or Group report)

When: Monthly or quarterly

How: Apply the information from this report in the following ways:

Establish and Track Goals

- Set class goals for books read and/or words read for each grading period. Post class goals and progress toward goal. Consider having groups or classes "compete" for the most words or books read.

- Set individual student goals for books read or quizzes passed each grading period. Refer to the Setting *Scholastic Reading Counts!* goals on **page 89** for more information. Help students track individual progress in their *rBook* Student Book Log or on a conferencing log (**SAM Keyword:** Conference Log).

Share Results

- Run this report once a month and update students and classes on overall performance.

- Share this report with school administration to demonstrate progress and participation in the independent reading rotation.

Review Related Reports

- *SRC!* Reading Progress Report (p. 230)
- *SRC!* Student Quiz Success Report (p. 236)
- *SRC!* Student Reading Report (p. 238)

Data in Action

Independent Reading Assessment Regular assessment of independent reading fosters on-task behavior. In addition to using *SRC!* quizzes, incorporate daily reading logs and other measures of written accountability, such as QuickWrites and Graphic Organizers.

Analyze Results | Books Read Report

Students who select books at appropriate interest and level should experience quiz success.

Student: Matt Garcia
Quizzes Passed: 2
Quizzes Taken: 13

Matt has not passed many quizzes. Identify the areas of challenge and offer support.

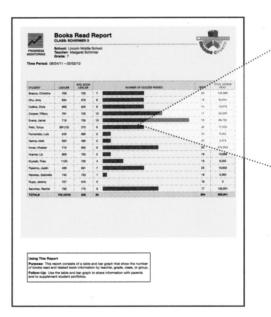

Enlargement: Books Read Report

Books Read Report
CLASS: SCHIRMER 3

PROGRESS MONITORING

School: Lincoln Middle School
Teacher: Margaret Schirmer
Grade: 7

Time Period: 08/24/11 – 02/02/12

STUDENT	LEXILE®	AVG. BOOK LEXILE®	NUMBER OF QUIZZES PASSED	GOAL	TOTAL WORDS READ
Bracco, Christine	709	753	7	20	135,889
Chu, Amy	834	678	6	15	65,964
Collins, Chris	868	820	6	15	10,276
Cooper, Tiffany	781	735	10	17	83,026
Evans, Jamal	719	755	15	18	66,750
Felix, Tonya	BR (10)	375	6	30	17,093
Fernandez, Luis	242	690	2	30	9,664
Garcia, Matt	550	485	2	22	5,078
Imran, Khaleel	719	626	9	20	276,999
Kramer, Liz	809	750	2	18	10,888
Krynski, Theo	1120	730	4	13	8,550
Palermo, Justin	438	381	7	23	16,833
Ramirez, Gabriella	743	720	1	18	5,360
Rupp, Jeremy	727	N/A	0	18	0
Sanchez, Rachel	792	773	9	17	156,931
TOTALS	**700 (AVG)**	**638**	**80**	**294**	**869,301**

Data Point	Data Analysis	**NEXT STEPS**
① Matt's goal for the year is 22 books.	Since it is nearly halfway through the year, Matt should be nearly halfway to his goal.	Set individual student quiz goals based on ability and reading level. Help students regularly monitor their quiz progress.
② Matt has passed 2 quizzes so far.	Matt is struggling with *Scholastic Reading Counts!* quizzes. He is either reading slowly or not passing quizzes.	Review the *SRC!* Student Reading Report to investigate specific quiz results.
③ The average Lexile for Matt's books is within 100 Lexile points of his current Lexile.	The quizzes Matt has passed are in his independent reading range. When reading books at appropriate levels, Matt can pass the accompanying quiz.	Ensure that students are reading books within their independent reading range. Review the *SRI* Targeted Reading Report for ranges.

Review Additional Data

Use the *Scholastic Reading Counts!* Student Reading Report to review specific quiz results for students who struggle.

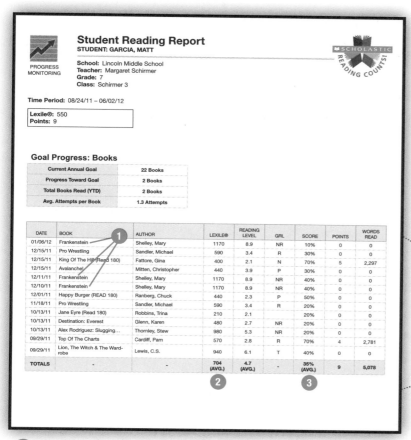

Student Reading Report
STUDENT: GARCIA, MATT

School: Lincoln Middle School
Teacher: Margaret Schirmer
Grade: 7
Class: Schirmer 3

Time Period: 08/24/11 – 06/02/12

Lexile®: 550
Points: 9

Goal Progress: Books

Current Annual Goal	22 Books
Progress Toward Goal	2 Books
Total Books Read (YTD)	2 Books
Avg. Attempts per Book	1.3 Attempts

DATE	BOOK	AUTHOR	LEXILE®	READING LEVEL	GRL	SCORE	POINTS	WORDS READ
01/06/12	Frankenstein	Shelley, Mary	1170	8.9	NR	10%	0	0
12/15/11	Pro Wrestling	Sandler, Michael	590	3.4	R	30%	0	0
12/15/11	King Of The Hill (Read 180)	Fattore, Gina	400	2.1	N	70%	5	2,297
12/15/11	Avalanche!	Mitten, Christopher	440	3.9	P	30%	0	0
12/11/11	Frankenstein	Shelley, Mary	1170	8.9	NR	40%	0	0
12/10/11	Frankenstein	Shelley, Mary	1170	8.9	NR	40%	0	0
12/01/11	Happy Burger (READ 180)	Ranberg, Chuck	440	2.3	P	50%	0	0
11/18/11	Pro Wrestling	Sandler, Michael	590	3.4	R	20%	0	0
10/13/11	Jane Eyre (Read 180)	Robbins, Trina	210	2.1		20%	0	0
10/13/11	Destination: Everest	Glenn, Karen	480	2.7	NR	20%	0	0
10/13/11	Alex Rodriguez: Slugging...	Thornley, Stew	980	5.3	NR	20%	0	0
09/29/11	Top Of The Charts	Cardiff, Pam	570	2.8	R	70%	4	2,781
09/29/11	Lion, The Witch & The Wardrobe	Lewis, C.S.	940	6.1	T	40%	0	0
TOTALS	-	-	**704 (AVG.)**	**4.7 (AVG.)**	-	**35% (AVG.)**	**9**	**5,078**

Enlargement: Student Reading Report

Student Reading Report
STUDENT: GARCIA, MATT

School: Lincoln Middle School
Teacher: Margaret Schirmer
Grade: 7
Class: Schirmer 3

Time Period: 08/24/11 – 06/02/12

Lexile®: 590
Points: 9

Goal Progress: Books

Current Annual Goal	22 Books
Progress Toward Goal	2 Books
Total Books Read (YTD)	2 Books
Avg. Attempts per Book	1.3 Attempts

Using This Report
Purpose: This report provides a comprehensive review of students' participation in the SRC! program.
Follow-Up: Review the data points on the report for indicators of low performance and intervene accordingly.

NEXT STEPS

	Data Point	Data Analysis	Next Steps
1	Matt has attempted a quiz on the same book three times.	His second attempt at a quiz was only one day after his first attempt.	If a student has an unsuccessful quiz attempt, provide additional support prior to allowing the student to take a quiz again.
2	Matt's average book Lexile is 704 and his current Lexile is 550.	Matt has been attempting to read books far above his current independent reading level.	Review student reading logs to ensure appropriate book selection. Use the Recommended Reading Report to help students select books.
3	Matt's average quiz score is 35%.	Matt has attempted 13 quizzes but has only passed 2.	Use the *Teaching Resources for Modeled and Independent Reading* to hold book conferences prior to the student attempting the quiz.

Book Frequency and Rating Report

Purpose

This report ranks books according to how students rated them during a selected time period. It includes the book Lexile, the point value for each book, and a summary of how many *Scholastic Reading Counts!* quizzes have been taken and passed.

INSTRUCTIONAL PLANNING

Book Frequency and Rating Report
SCHOOL: LINCOLN MIDDLE SCHOOL

Time Period: 08/24/11 – 02/02/12

AVG. STUDENT RATING	BOOK	AUTHOR	LEXILE®	POINTS	QUIZZES PASSED/ TAKEN
5.0	Behind The Bedroom Wall	Williams, Laura E.	660	6	1/3
5.0	BMX Racing	Gutman, Bill	770	3	1/1
5.0	Bone: Ghost Circles	Smith, Jeff	N/A	6	1/1
5.0	Bone: Out From Boneville	Smith, Jeff	360	4	1/1
5.0	Breaking Dawn	Meyer, Stephanie	690	40	2/2
5.0	Captain Underpants/Invasion Of	Pilkey, Dav	730	3	2/2
5.0	Captain Underpants/Perilous	Pilkey, Dav	640	3	1/1
5.0	Cat In the Hat, The	Seuss, Dr.	260	2	1/1
5.0	Charlie & The Chocolate …	Dahl, Roald	810	8	1/1
5.0	Eclipse	Meyer, Stephanie	670	33	2/2
5.0	Finding The Titanic (Read 180)	Ballard, Robert D.	540	3	1/3
5.0	Freak The Mighty	Philbrick, Rodman	1000	10	1/1
5.0	Friendship, The	Talyor, Mildred D.	750	3	1/1
5.0	New Moon	Meyer, Stephanie	690	29	4/4
5.0	Old Yeller	Gipson, Fred	910	8	1/2
5.0	Old Yeller (Anthology)	Gipson, Fred	880	2	1/1
5.0	Runaway Train	Campbell, Julia	420	3	1/1
5.0	Stealing Home: The Story Of…	Denenberg, Barry	930	6	3/3
5.0	Summer On Wheels	Soto, Gary	750	9	1/1
5.0	There's A Girl In-Hammerlock	Spinelli, Jerry	520	10	1/3
5.0	Twilight	Meyer, Stephanie	720	25	4/6
5.0	Watsons Go To Birmingham-1963	Curtis, Christopher Paul	1000	12	1/1
5.0	Winning Season: Emergency Quar	Wallace, Rich	720	6	1/1
5.0	Winning Season: The Roar Of…	Wallace, Rich	680	6	1/1
4.8	Money Hungry	Flake, Sharon G.	650	9	4/5
4.8	Quinceanera Means Sweet 15	Chambers, Veronica	630	12	4/4
4.7	Donner Party (Read 180)	Olson, Todd	330	5	2/3
4.5	Bone: Rock Jaw	Smith, Jeff	N/A	3	4/4

Using This Report

Purpose: This report ranks books according to how students rated them during a selected time period. It includes the Lexile level and point value for each book.

Follow-Up: Use the report to guide students' independent reading selections. Encourage students to choose other books on related themes or by the same authors as the most popular books.

How It Helps

I use this report to spark conversations between students about the books they have enjoyed. I also share this report with my media specialist so that we can ensure that these books are available in the library.

Most Frequent Quizzes Report

Purpose

This report provides information on how frequently specific *Scholastic Reading Counts!* quizzes have been taken. It includes the book or article title, Lexile, quiz success rate, and quiz results for individual students.

INSTRUCTIONAL PLANNING

Most Frequent Quizzes Report
CLASS: Schirmer 3

School: Lincoln Middle School
Teacher: Margaret Schirmer
Grade: 7

Time Period: 08/24/11 – 02/02/12

Adventures of Capt. Underpants

Lexile®	720
Points	3
Times Taken	6
Times Passed	6

STUDENT NAME	STUDENT LEXILE	DATE TAKEN	SCORE (%)
Cooper, Tiffany	781	10/08/11	90
Evans, Jamal	719	01/08/12	90
Imran, Khaleel	719	12/15/11	100
Kramer, Liz	809	12/01/12	100
Palermo, Justin	438	11/12/11	90
Ramirez, Gabriella	743	10/23/11	90
TOTALS	**754 (AVG.)**		**93% (AVG.)**

Oh Yuck! (READ 180)

Lexile®	990
Points	3
Times Taken	5
Times Passed	4

STUDENT NAME	STUDENT LEXILE	DATE TAKEN	SCORE (%)
Collins, Chris	868	10/29/11	50
Collins, Chris	868	11/02/11	90
Garcia, Matt	485	01/21/12	70
Imran, Khaleel	719	10/23/11	80
Krynski, Theo	1120	12/03/11	80
TOTALS	**894 (AVG.)**		**74% (AVG.)**

Using This Report

Purpose: This report provides information on quizzes student have taken most often. It includes the Lexile measure and point value for each book, overall quiz success rate, and quiz scores for individual students.

Follow-Up: Suggest related titles to students. Monitor student quiz scores and offer additional support to students who are having difficulty with the quizzes.

How It Helps

I use this report to track book popularity and suggest related book titles. I can also monitor student quiz results so that I can offer additional support as needed.

SRC! Reports

Points Report

Purpose

This report tracks points students have earned for passing *Scholastic Reading Counts!* quizzes.

PROGRESS MONITORING

Points Report
CLASS: SCHIRMER 3

School: Lincoln Middle School
Teacher: Margaret Schirmer
Grade: 7

Time Period: 08/24/11 – 02/02/12 **①**

STUDENT	LEXILE® **②**	AVG. BOOK LEXILE® **③**	POINTS EARNED **④**		POINTS AVAILABLE **⑤**	GOAL **⑥**	TOTAL WORDS READ **⑦**
Bracco, Christine	709	753	41		41	N/A	135,889
Chu, Amy	834	678	32		32	N/A	65,964
Collins, Chris	868	820	32		9	N/A	10,276
Cooper, Tiffany	781	735	26		26	N/A	83,026
Evans, Jamal	719	755	23		23	N/A	66,750
Felix, Tonya	BR (10)	375	24		24	N/A	17,093
Fernandez, Luis	242	690	7		7	N/A	9,664
Garcia, Matt	550	485	9		9	N/A	5,078
Imran, Khaleel	719	626	85		85	N/A	276,999
Kramer, Liz	809	750	6		6	N/A	10,888
Krynski, Theo	1120	730	15		15	N/A	8,550
Palermo, Justin	438	381	32		32	N/A	16,833
Ramirez, Gabriella	743	720	3		3	N/A	5,360
Rupp, Jeremy	727	N/A	0		0	N/A	0
Sanchez, Rachel	792	773	55		55	N/A	156,931
⑧ TOTALS	**700 (AVG)**	**638 (AVG)**	**352**		**329**	**0**	**869,301**

Using This Report

Purpose: This report tracks the number of points students have earned during a selected time period. It includes student Lexile scores, point goals, total number of words read, and average Lexile measure of books read.

Follow-Up: Congratulate students who have met or are nearing their goals. Provide support to students who are experiencing difficulty meeting their goals.

How It Helps

I use this report to motivate my students. By establishing annual point goals and tracking their progress, I can celebrate reading success with students.

Understand the Data

1 Time Period

Default time period of This School Year displays results for all quizzes passed during the school year. Customize time period settings to review results within shorter time frames.

2 Lexile

Student's most recent *SRI* score within the selected time period.

3 Average Book Lexile

Average Lexile for all books or eReads articles with quizzes passed.

4 Points Earned

Total number of points earned for *Scholastic Reading Counts!* quizzes passed.

5 Points Available

Total number of points that have not been "redeemed," if tracked in SAM Roster.

6 Goal

Reading goal for the year for each student, if points is selected as goal in SAM Roster.

7 Total Words Read

Words read for books and eReads articles when each *Scholastic Reading Counts!* quiz is passed.

8 Totals

Class or group totals for points established for points earned, points available, goal, and words read. Also includes class or group average student Lexile and average book Lexile for quizzes passed.

Use the Data

Who: Teachers (Teacher, Class, or Group report)

When: Once or twice a month

How: Apply the information in the following ways:

Monitor Quiz Progress

- Establish annual points goals for students in the *Scholastic Reading Counts!* Settings in the SAM Roster.
- Determine whether to establish the same goal for the entire class or assign individual goals based on student reading levels. For more information, see Establishing Modeled and Independent Reading Goals on **page 89**.
- Encourage students to track their own points status. Celebrate students who are on track to meet or exceed their goals. Offer support to students who are having trouble meeting their goals.

Share Results

- Print this report to update your school administration on your students' reading progress. Invite administrators to your classroom to congratulate students who have met their goals.
- Institute reading contests between groups, classes, or even with another *READ 180* classroom. Track total points read by the group or class throughout the year.

Review Related Reports

- *SRC!* Books Read Report (p. 220)
- *SRC!* Quiz Alert (p. 228)
- *SRC!* Student Reading Report (p. 238)

Data in Action

Redeeming Quiz Points The Points Recording Tool in the *Scholastic Reading Counts!* Grading section of the SAM Roster allows you to track when students have redeemed their points for class incentives.

Quiz Alert

Purpose

This report highlights a variety of challenges individual students may be experiencing with *Scholastic Reading Counts!* quizzes. A summary is provided in the top chart with details about each student's specific quiz challenge included in the charts below.

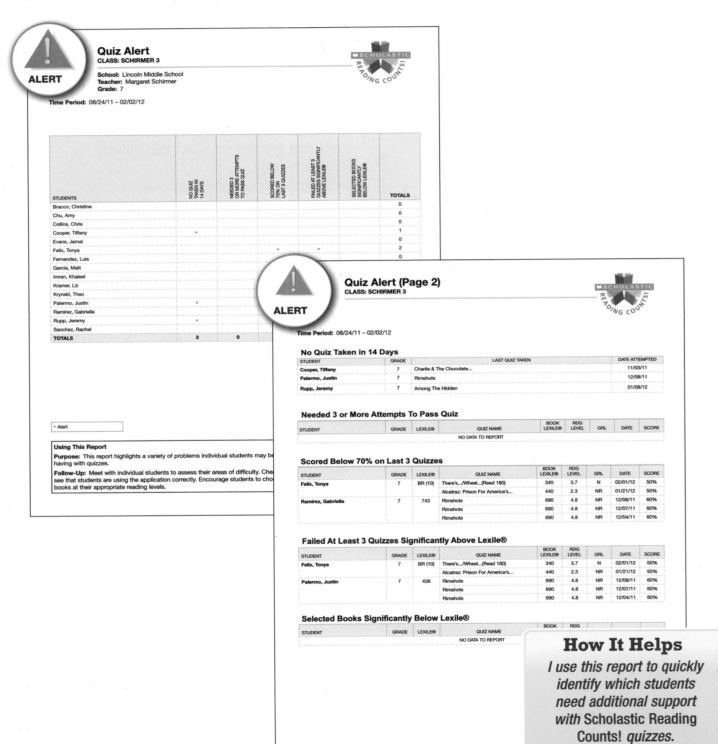

How It Helps

I use this report to quickly identify which students need additional support with Scholastic Reading Counts! *quizzes.*

Reading Growth Acknowledgment

Purpose

This report acknowledges students who have passed quizzes on books that have Lexile measures above the students' current Lexile scores. It lists the quiz passed, the score received, and the Lexile of the book.

Reading Growth Acknowledgment
CLASS: SCHIRMER 3

School: Lincoln Middle School
Teacher: Margaret Schirmer
Grade: 7

Time Period: 08/24/11 – 02/02/12

Reading Level Growth Acknowledgment

Student is able to pass quizzes at levels significantly above his or her Lexile® level.

STUDENT	GRADE	LEXILE®	QUIZ NAME	BOOK LEXILE®	RDG LEVEL	GRL	DATE	SCORE
Felix, Tonya	7	BR (10)	Alcatraz: Prison For America's	440	2.3	NR	02/05/12	90%
			UFOs: Fact Or Fiction?	440	2.8	O	12/03/11	80%
			King Of The Hill (Read 180)	400	2.1	N	11/17/11	90%
			Band, The	220	2.1	M	11/10/11	100%
			Frankenstein (Read 180)	300	2.1	NR	11/05/11	70%
			Still The Greatest/Rigoberta…	450	2.5	O	10/21/11	70%
Garcia, Matt	7	485	Captain Underpants/Attack Of	780	4.2	P	02/01/12	90%
			Hiroshima (Read 180)	660	4.3	S	01/21/12	80%
			Oh Yuck! (Read 180)	990	6.8	X	11/12/11	70%

Using This Report

Purpose: This report acknowledges students who have passed quizzes on books that have Lexile® measures above the student's current Lexile® score.

Follow-Up: Congratulate the student and offer encouragement for further success.

Reading Progress Report | Best Practice Report

Purpose

This report provides an overview of students' *Scholastic Reading Counts!* quiz participation and progress.

PROGRESS MONITORING

Reading Progress Report
CLASS: SCHIRMER 3

SCHOLASTIC READING COUNTS!

School: Lincoln Middle School
Teacher: Margaret Schirmer
Grade: 7

Time Period: 08/24/11 – 02/02/12 **1**

2 Year to Date Totals

Quizzes Taken	128
Quizzes Passed	86
Quiz Success Rate	64.3%
Points Earned	655
Words Read	869,301

STUDENT	GRADE	**3** LEXILE®	**4** QUIZZES PASSED/ TAKEN	**5** QUIZ SUCCESS RATE	**6** AVG. QUIZ SCORE	**7** BOOKS READ	**8** POINTS EARNED	**9** ANNUAL GOAL	**10** % OF GOAL ACHIEVED
Bracco, Christine	7	709	7/8	88%	84%	7	41	20(B)	47%
Chu, Amy	7	834	6/7	86%	86%	6	32	15(B)	40%
Collins, Chris	7	868	6/8	75%	▸ 62%	6	32	15(B)	40%
Cooper, Tiffany	7	781	10/12	83%	▸ 65%	10	26	17(B)	58%
Evans, Jamal	7	719	15/17	88%	▸ 49%	15	23	18(B)	83%
Felix, Tonya	7	BR (10)	6/13	46%	83%	6	24	30(B)	20%
Fernandez, Luis	7	242	2/3	67%	▸ 67%	2	7	30(B)	7%
Garcia, Matt	7	550	2/13	15%	▸ 35%	2	9	22(B)	9%
Imran, Khaleel	7	719	9/10	90%	89%	9	85	20(B)	45%
Kramer, Liz	7	809	2/5	40%	▸ 54%	2	6	18(B)	11%
Krynski, Theo	7	1120	4/4	100%	83%	4	15	13(B)	31%
Palermo, Justin	7	438	7/8	88%	76%	7	32	23(B)	30%
Ramirez, Gabriella	7	743	1/5	20%	▸ 62%	1	3	18(B)	6%
Rupp, Jeremy	7	727	0/0	N/A	N/A	0	0	18(B)	0%
Sanchez, Rachel	7	792	9/15	60%	73%	9	55	17(B)	53%
11 **TOTALS**	-	**700 (AVG.)**	**86/128**	**64% (AVG.)**	▸ **64% (AVG.)**	**86**	**352**	-	**31% (AVG.)**

(B)=Books   ▸ Indicates Score Below 70%

Using This Report

Purpose: This report provides an overview of students' progress in the program. In addition to tracking group quiz success rates, the report shows individual quiz performance and achievement.

Follow-Up: Use the information in the report to plan incentives and to help students monitor their progress. You may also use the report to guide instruction and create reading groups.

How It Helps

I use this report to monitor my students' independent reading progress and plan any necessary interventions.

Understand the Data

1 Time Period

Run for This School Year to review annual progress. Customize time period settings to review quarterly or monthly results.

2 Year to Date Totals

Cumulative quiz results for selected time period.

3 Lexile

Student's *SRI* score from the most recent test, regardless of time period settings.

4 Quizzes Passed/Taken

Ratio of total quizzes passed and total quiz attempts for each student.

5 Quiz Success Rate

Percentage of quizzes passed of all quizzes attempted during selected time period.

6 Average Quiz Score

Average score on all quizzes taken. Red arrows indicate quiz averages below 70%.

7 Books Read

Total *SRC!* quizzes passed for each student within selected time period.

8 Points Earned

Total points earned for each student within selected time period. Student must pass quiz to earn points.

9 Annual Goal

Reading goal for the year, measured in books (B) or points (P), if established in SAM Roster.

10 % of Goal Achieved

Percentage of goal student has achieved within selected time period.

11 Totals

Class or group total books read, quizzes taken, and points earned for passed quizzes within selected time period. Also includes class or group averages of student Lexile, quiz success rate, quiz score, and percent of goal achieved.

Use the Data

Who: Teachers (Teacher, Class, or Group report)

When: Once or twice a month

How: Apply the information from this report in the following ways:

Establish and Track Goals

- Use the SAM Roster to enter book goals or points earned for each student. Refer to Establishing Independent Reading Goals on **page 89** for more information about individualized goal-setting.

- Discuss individual student goals for books read or points earned each grading period during conferences. Help students track individual progress in their *rBook* Student Book Log or on a conferencing log (**SAM Keyword:** Conference Log).

Share Results

- Run this report once a month and update students on overall performance.

- Share this report with school administrators to demonstrate progress and participation in the independent reading rotation.

Review Related Reports

- *SRC!* Books Read Report (p. 220)
- *SRC!* Points Report (p. 226)
- *SRC!* Student Reading Report (p. 238)

Data in Action

***Scheduling Reading Counts!* Quizzes** To ensure regular use of *Scholastic Reading Counts!* quizzes, establish expectations for total pages read per day or quizzes passed per quarter. Help students determine when a book should be complete and write projected completion dates on a calendar.

Analyze Results | Reading Progress Report

With appropriate preparation and support, students should maintain strong quiz success rates and scores.

DATA STORY

Student: Rachel Sanchez
Quizzes Passed: 9
Quizzes Taken: 15

Rachel struggles to pass quizzes. Identify causes and ways to provide additional support.

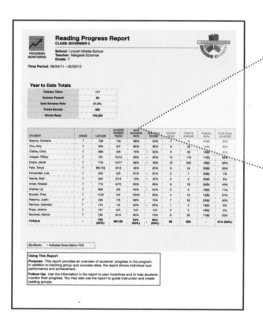

Reading Progress Report
CLASS: SCHIRMER 3

PROGRESS MONITORING

School: Lincoln Middle School
Teacher: Margaret Schirmer
Grade: 7

Time Period: 08/24/11 – 02/02/12

Year to Date Totals

Quizzes Taken	117
Quizzes Passed	60
Quiz Success Rate	51.3%
Points Earned	329
Words Read	743,252

STUDENT	GRADE	LEXILE®	QUIZZES PASSED/ TAKEN	QUIZ SUCCESS RATE	AVG. QUIZ SCORE	BOOKS READ	POINTS EARNED	ANNUAL GOAL	% OF GOAL ACHIEVED
Bracco, Christine	7	709	7/8	88%	84%	7	43	20(B)	35%
Chu, Amy	7	834	6/7	86%	86%	6	32	15(B)	40%
Collins, Chris	7	868	6/8	75%	▸ 62%	6	32	15(B)	40%
Cooper, Tiffany	7	781	10/12	83%	▸ 65%	10	118	17(B)	58%
Evans, Jamal	7	719	15/17	88%	▸ 49%	15	200	18(B)	83%
Felix, Tonya	7	BR (10)	6/13	46%	83%	6	24	30(B)	20%
Fernandez, Luis	7	242	2/3	67%	▸ 67%	2	7	30(B)	7%
Garcia, Matt	7	550	2/13	15%	▸ 35%	2	9	22(B)	9%
Imran, Khaleel	7	719	9/10	90%	89%	9	78	20(B)	45%
Kramer, Liz	7	809	2/5	40%	▸ 54%	2	6	18(B)	11%
Krynski, Theo	7	1120	4/4	100%	83%	4	15	13(B)	31%
Palermo, Justin	7	438	7/8	88%	76%	7	32	23(B)	30%
Ramirez, Gabriella	7	743	1/5	20%	62%	1	3	18(B)	6%
Rupp, Jeremy	7	727	0/0	N/A	N/A	0	0	18(B)	0%
Sanchez, Rachel	7	792	9/15	60%	73%	9	55	17(B)	53%
TOTALS	-	**700 (AVG.)**	**86/128**	**54% (AVG.)**	**64% (AVG.)**	**86**	**655**	-	**31% (AVG.)**

(B)=Books ▸ Indicates Score Below 70%

🔍 **Enlargement: Reading Progress Report**

Data Point	Data Analysis	**NEXT STEPS**
① Rachel has taken 15 quizzes but only passed 9.	Rachel is attempting quizzes but is not experiencing quiz success.	When students struggle to pass multiple quizzes, run and analyze the *SRC!* Student Reading Report to identify the cause.
② Rachel's quiz success rate is 60% while her average quiz score is 73%.	Rachel has passed 60% of the quizzes she attempted. Her average score on the quizzes she has taken is slightly higher at 73%.	Review student reading logs, graphic organizers, and QuickWrites prior to allowing students to take a quiz.
③ Rachel is 53% of the way to achieving her book goal.	It is halfway through the year, and Rachel is halfway to her goal.	Set individual goals based on student's initial Lexile. See the chart on **page 89** for guidance in determining appropriate goals.

Review Additional Data

Cross-reference the *Scholastic Reading Counts!* Student Reading Report to analyze specific performance results.

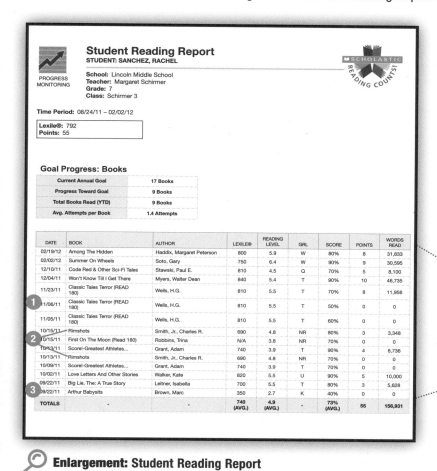

Enlargement: Student Reading Report

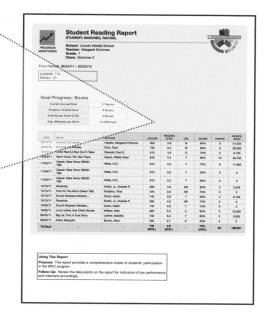

Data Point	Data Analysis	NEXT STEPS
① Rachel took a quiz on the same book three times.	Rachel made a second attempt at the same quiz only one day after her first attempt.	Students must wait at least 24 hours before retaking a quiz. Have students use this time to review their book and accompanying work.
② In another case, Rachel also took a quiz on the same book twice.	Rachel took a few days to review her book, then passed the quiz on her second attempt.	Before allowing a student to retake a quiz, review the book and previous quiz results with the student to provide additional support.
③ Rachel did not pass a quiz on a book that was well within her independent reading range.	Rachel took two quizzes on different books on the same day.	Promote quiz success by ensuring that students have read each book and completed all accompanying activities prior to taking a quiz.

SRC!
Reports

Recommended Reading Report

Purpose

This report provides an individualized reading list for students based on their interest choices.

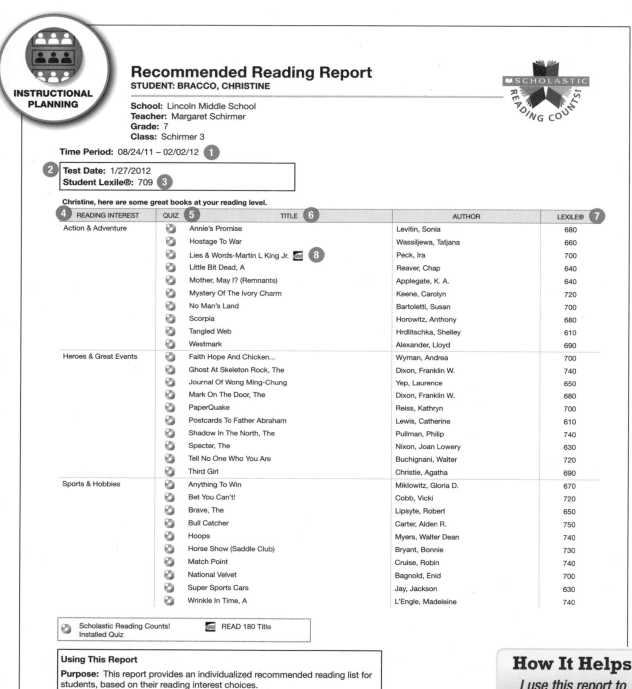

INSTRUCTIONAL PLANNING

Recommended Reading Report
STUDENT: BRACCO, CHRISTINE

SCHOLASTIC READING COUNTS!

School: Lincoln Middle School
Teacher: Margaret Schirmer
Grade: 7
Class: Schirmer 3

Time Period: 08/24/11 – 02/02/12 ①

②　**Test Date:** 1/27/2012
Student Lexile®: 709 ③

Christine, here are some great books at your reading level.

④ READING INTEREST	QUIZ ⑤	TITLE ⑥	AUTHOR	LEXILE® ⑦
Action & Adventure		Annie's Promise	Levitin, Sonia	680
		Hostage To War	Wassiljewa, Tatjana	660
		Lies & Words-Martin L King Jr. ⑧	Peck, Ira	700
		Little Bit Dead, A	Reaver, Chap	640
		Mother, May I? (Remnants)	Applegate, K. A.	640
		Mystery Of The Ivory Charm	Keene, Carolyn	720
		No Man's Land	Bartoletti, Susan	700
		Scorpia	Horowitz, Anthony	680
		Tangled Web	Hrdlitschka, Shelley	610
		Westmark	Alexander, Lloyd	690
Heroes & Great Events		Faith Hope And Chicken...	Wyman, Andrea	700
		Ghost At Skeleton Rock, The	Dixon, Franklin W.	740
		Journal Of Wong Ming-Chung	Yep, Laurence	650
		Mark On The Door, The	Dixon, Franklin W.	680
		PaperQuake	Reiss, Kathryn	700
		Postcards To Father Abraham	Lewis, Catherine	610
		Shadow In The North, The	Pullman, Philip	740
		Specter, The	Nixon, Joan Lowery	630
		Tell No One Who You Are	Buchignani, Walter	720
		Third Girl	Christie, Agatha	690
Sports & Hobbies		Anything To Win	Miklowitz, Gloria D.	670
		Bet You Can't!	Cobb, Vicki	720
		Brave, The	Lipsyte, Robert	650
		Bull Catcher	Carter, Alden R.	750
		Hoops	Myers, Walter Dean	740
		Horse Show (Saddle Club)	Bryant, Bonnie	730
		Match Point	Cruise, Robin	740
		National Velvet	Bagnold, Enid	700
		Super Sports Cars	Jay, Jackson	630
		Wrinkle In Time, A	L'Engle, Madeleine	740

	Scholastic Reading Counts! Installed Quiz		READ 180 Title

Using This Report

Purpose: This report provides an individualized recommended reading list for students, based on their reading interest choices.

Follow-Up: Help students acquire the titles recommended, and suggest other related titles for students' reading enjoyment.

How It Helps
I use this report to assist my students with selecting books that match their interest and skill levels.

Understand the Data

1 Time Period
Time period setting of This School Year displays results based on student's current Lexile score.

2 Test Date
Student's most recent *SRI* test date.

3 Student Lexile
Student's most recent *SRI* score. Book choices are filtered based on this score.

4 Reading Interest
Topics, or genres, the student selected at the beginning of the *SRI* test.

5 Quiz
Icon next to a book title indicates that a *Scholastic Reading Counts!* quiz has been installed and is available for the book.

6 Title
Books at appropriate reading levels and correlated to student interest.

7 Lexile
Lexile measure for each book.

8 *READ 180* Title
Icon next to a book title indicates that the book is available in the *READ 180* Paperback and Audiobook library.

Use the Data

Who: Teachers, Students, Parents (Student report)

When: After each *SRI* administration, usually 4 times a year

How: Apply information from this report in the following ways:

Guide Independent Reading

- Print this report after each *SRI* test and use it to help students select books for the Modeled and Independent Reading Rotation.
- Use the SAM Book Expert to share more information about books listed in this report with students.

Share Results

- Share this report with media specialists so that they can help students select appropriate books and can stock book titles based on student interest and reading level.
- Send this report home with students along with the *Scholastic Reading Counts!* parent letters or with report cards to provide caregivers with guidance in helping their children select appropriate books.

Review Related Reports

- *SRC!* Student Reading Report (p. 238)
- *SRC!* Parent Report I (p. 240)
- *SRC!* Parent Report II (p. 241)

Data in Action

Adjusting Report Settings The SRI Settings in the SAM Roster tab allows you to limit the books that appear on this report to display only book titles with installed *Scholastic Reading Counts!* quizzes.

Student Quiz Success Report

Purpose

This report provides data for each student on *Scholastic Reading Counts!* quizzes passed.

PROGRESS MONITORING

Student Quiz Success Report
STUDENT: BRACCO, CHRISTINE

SCHOLASTIC READING COUNTS!

School: Lincoln Middle School
Teacher: Margaret Schirmer
Grade: 7
Class: Schirmer 3

Time Period: 08/24/11 – 02/02/12 **1**

Lexile®: 709 **2**
Total Points: 41
Quizzes Passed: 7

3 DATE	**4** BOOK	**5** BOOK LEXILE®	AUTHOR	**6** SCORE	**7** POINTS	**8** WORDS READ
01/27/12	Score!-Greatest Athletes...	740	Grant, Adam	90%	4	8,736
01/12/12	Good Fight-Real (READ 180)	810	Olson, Tod	90%	3	6,883
12/04/11	Stargirl	610	Spinelli, Jerry	90%	16	60,580
11/03/11	Captain Underpants/Attack Of	780	Pilkey, Dav	100%	3	5,528
10/27/11	Adventures Of Capt. Underpants	720	Pilkey, Dav	100%	3	5,360
10/21/11	Disaster Reports Go Digital (eReads)	970	Smith, Jane	70%	2	379
10/01/11	Outsiders, The	750	Hinton, S.E.	90%	10	48,423
TOTALS	-	**753 (AVG.)**	-	**90% (AVG.)**	**41**	**135,889**

How It Helps

I share data from this report with my students so that they can celebrate their successes. I track words read for all of my students and post updates on our bulletin board.

Understand the Data

1 **Time Period**

Default time period setting of This School Year displays all quizzes passed during the year. Customize time period settings to review results for more targeted periods of time.

2 **Lexile**

Student's most recent *SRI* score within the selected time period.

3 **Date**

Date each *Scholastic Reading Counts!* quiz was passed for all books and eReads articles.

4 **Book**

Book or eReads article title for each quiz passed. Quizzes that were attempted but not passed are not included on this report.

5 **Book Lexile**

Lexile measure of each book or eReads article.

6 **Score**

Percentage of questions answered correctly.

7 **Points**

Each book and eReads article is assigned a set point value. Students earn points for each *Scholastic Reading Counts!* quiz passed.

8 **Words Read**

Total words read for all books and eReads articles when each *Scholastic Reading Counts!* quiz is passed.

Use the Data

Who: Teachers, Students, Parents (Student report)

When: Once or twice a month

How: Apply the information in the following ways:

Conference With Students

- Print this report each month and conference with students regarding their progress. Celebrate success and encourage continued reading growth.

- Establish goals for words read, pages read, or books read for each student. Have students use this report to track progress toward goal. See Establishing Goals for Modeled and Independent Reading on **page 93** for more information.

Share Results

- Add this report to student portfolios as a record of independent reading achievement.

- Print this report to share at conferences with parents or caregivers to provide more detail on students' reading progress.

Review Related Reports

- *SRC!* Reading Progress Report (p. 230)
- *SRC!* Student Reading Report (p. 238)
- *SRC!* Parent Report II (p. 241)

Data in Action

Reading Achievement Many students enrolled in *READ 180* have experienced failure in reading in the past. Use this report to help students overcome feelings of reading frustration. Build confidence and self-esteem by regularly celebrating quiz success.

Student Reading Report

Purpose

This report summarizes each student's *Scholastic Reading Counts!* quiz participation.

PROGRESS MONITORING

Student Reading Report
STUDENT: BRACCO, CHRISTINE

School: Lincoln Middle School
Teacher: Margaret Schirmer
Grade: 7
Class: Schirmer 3

Time Period: 08/24/11 – 02/02/12

| Lexile®: 709 |
| Points: 41 |

 Goal Progress: Books

Current Annual Goal	20 Books
Progress Toward Goal	7 Books
Total Books Read (YTD)	7 Books
Avg. Attempts per Book	1.0 Attempt

DATE	BOOK	AUTHOR	BOOK LEXILE®	READING LEVEL	GRL	SCORE	POINTS	WORDS READ
01/27/12	Score!-Greatest Athletes...	Grant, Adam	740	3.9	T	90%	4	8,736
01/21/12	Tornadoes (Natural Disaters)	Thompson, Luke	980	6.8	U	40%	0	0
01/12/12	Good Fight-Real (READ 180)	Olson, Tod	810	5.5	NR	90%	3	6,883
12/04/11	Stargirl	Spinelli, Jerry	590	6.1		90%	16	60,580
11/03/11	Captain Underpants/Attack Of	Pilkey, Dav	780	4.2	P	100%	3	5,528
10/27/11	Adventures Of Capt. Under-pants	Pilkey, Dav	720	3.5	P	100%	3	5,360
10/21/11	Disaster Reports Go Digital (eReads)	Smith, Jane	970	6.8	NR	70%	2	379
10/01/11	Outsiders, The	Hinton, S.E.	750	5.1	Z	90%	10	48,423
TOTALS	-	-	**793 (AVG.)**	**5.2 (AVG.)**	-	**84% (AVG.)**	**41**	**135,889**

(column header markers: 3 DATE, 4 BOOK/AUTHOR, 5 BOOK LEXILE®, 6 READING LEVEL, 7 GRL, 8 SCORE, 9 POINTS, 10 WORDS READ)

Using This Report

Purpose: This report provides a comprehensive review of students' participation in the SRC! program.

Follow-Up: Review the data points on the report for indicators of low performance and intervene accordingly.

How It Helps

I share this report with my students so that they can monitor their own quiz progress. We discuss any challenges they are experiencing, then they track their progress in their rBooks.

Understand the Data

1 **Time Period**

Default time period setting of This School Year displays all quizzes passed during the year. Customize time period settings to review results for more targeted periods of time.

2 **Goal Progress**

Student's annual goal, if established in SAM. Also includes progress toward goal, listed as points or books, depending on SAM settings.

3 **Date**

Date of each *Scholastic Reading Counts!* quiz attempt. Each book or eReads article quiz can be attempted up to three times.

4 **Book**

Book or eReads article title for each quiz attempt. Books with multiple quiz attempts will be listed multiple times.

5 **Book Lexile**

Lexile measure of each book or eReads article.

6 **Reading Level**

Grade- and month-based reading level of the book or eReads article (e.g., 4.2 indicates the second month of fourth grade).

7 **Guided Reading Level (GRL)**

Complexity of the book, based on length, plot, vocabulary, and other features. There are 18 levels for Grades K–4, ranging from A through R.

8 **Score**

Percentage of questions answered correctly.

9 **Points**

Each book and eReads article is assigned a set point value. Students earn points for each *Scholastic Reading Counts!* quiz passed. A score of 0 indicates a quiz attempted but not passed.

10 **Words Read**

Total words read for all books and eReads articles when each *Scholastic Reading Counts!* quiz is passed.

Use the Data

Who: Teachers, Students, Parents (Student report)

When: Once or twice a month

How: You can use the information in this report in the following ways:

Conference With Students

- Print this report each month to conference with students regarding progress. Discuss and address challenges a student might be having with comprehension or taking quizzes.
- Establish goals for words read, books read, or quizzes passed for each student. Help students track progress toward goal with this report. See Establishing Goals for Modeled and Independent Reading on **page 89** for more information.

Share Results

- Add this report to student portfolios as a record of independent reading achievement.
- Print this report to share at conferences with parents or caregivers to provide more detail on students' reading progress.

Review Related Reports

- *SRC!* Reading Progress Report (p. 230)
- *SRC!* Student Quiz Success Report (p. 236)
- *READ 180* Student Reading Report (p. 158)

Data in Action

Regular Reading Accountability Students benefit from consistent monitoring of work completed in the Modeled and Independent Reading Rotation. Implement daily goals for pages read or quarterly goals for books read or quizzes passed. Help students track progress on daily reading logs.

Parent Report I

Purpose

This report introduces parents or caregivers to the *Scholastic Reading Counts!* program and includes their child's independent reading goal, if established in SAM. It also includes recommendations for supporting reading at home.

SCHOOL-TO-HOME

STUDENT: IMRAN, KHALEEL

School: Lincoln Middle School
Teacher: Margaret Schirmer
Grade: 7
Class: Schirmer 3

September 4, 2011

Dear Parent or Caregiver,

Khaleel will be participating in *Scholastic Reading Counts!*, an independent reading program with a library of thousands of best-loved titles. Through *Scholastic Reading Counts!* we will be able to track what Khaleel is reading independently. Khaleel will also be encouraged and rewarded for reading more and achieving more!

Participating in *Scholastic Reading Counts!* includes:

· Choosing books to read.

· Taking quizzes on the computer to check comprehension.

· Receiving instant feedback, including reward points and congratulations screens for passing quizzes successfully.

Personal Goal (# of books or points/year)

Name	Grade	Lexile®	Personal Goal
Imran, Khaleel	7	710	20 Books / Year

Supporting reading at home will help Khaleel become a lifelong reader. Here are some useful tips:

· If Khaleel has an interest in a specific sport or hobby, encourage him/her to read about it.

· Talk about what your child is reading. Ask questions about the plot or about fun facts if it's nonfiction.

· Try to find a variety of reading materials for your child to experience: fiction, nonfiction, magazines, newspapers, humorous books, recipes, maps, etc.

Thank you for making Reading Count! for Khaleel this school year and always.

Sincerely,

_____

How It Helps

I send Parent Report I home at the beginning of the year to introduce parents to the program and suggest ways they can help with reading at home.

Parent Reports II and III

Purpose

Parent Report II updates parents or caregivers on their child's progress in *Scholastic Reading Counts!*
Parent Report III provides a final summary of a student's performance. Both reports include tips on encouraging reading at home.

SCHOOL-TO-HOME

STUDENT: IMRAN, KHALEEL

School: Lincoln Middle School
Teacher: Margaret Schirmer
Grade: 7
Class: Schirmer 3

February 2, 2012

Dear Parent or Caregiver,

Khaleel is currently participating in Scholastic *Reading Counts!*, an independent reading program with a library of thousands of best-loved titles. Congratulations on Khaleel's reading success so far this school year.

The following indicates that Khaleel is reading and succeeding:

Name	Grade	Lexile®	Personal Goal	Quizzes Passed	Average Quiz Score
Imran, Khaleel	7	719	20 Books / Year	9	89%

Some of the books Khaleel has read successfully are:

Title	Author
Tunnel Of Terror & Other...	Stamper, J.B.
Hear Me (Read 180)	Olson, Amy
Oh Yuck! (Read 180)	
All In a Day's Work & Ot	
Cyber Pranks (Read 180	
Love Letters And Other	
New Moon	
Twilight	
Adventures Of Capt. Un	

The more Khaleel rea

Here are some ways

· Make connect

· Make reading

· Celebrate Kha

Thank you for makin

Sincerely,

SCHOOL-TO-HOME

STUDENT: IMRAN, KHALEEL

School: Lincoln Middle School
Teacher: Margaret Schirmer
Grade: 7
Class: Schirmer 3

February 2, 2012

Dear Parent or Caregiver,

Congratulations on Khaleel's terrific reading achievement!

The following information shows that Khaleel is a successful reader:

Name	Grade	Lexile®	Personal Goal	Quizzes Passed	Average Quiz Score
Imran, Khaleel	7	719	20 Books / Year	9	89%

Some of the books Khaleel has read successfully are:

Title	Author
Tunnel Of Terror & Other...	Stamper, J.B.
Hear Me (Read 180)	Olson, Amy
Oh Yuck! (Read 180)	Masoff, Joy
All In a Day's Work & Other...	Stine, Megan
Cyber Pranks (Read 180)	Zarkh, Evelina
Love Letters And Other Stories	Walker, Kate
New Moon	Meyer, Stephenie
Twilight	Meyer, Stephenie
Adventures Of Capt. Underpants	Pilkey, Dav

Here are some tips to use at home to keep Khaleel reading and succeeding:

· Encourage Khaleel to write letters, postcards, or emails.

Reports for Administrators

READ 180 Reports

rSkills Tests Reports

Scholastic Reading Inventory Reports

Scholastic Reading Counts! Reports

Meeting Administrators' Reporting Needs

As students participate in *READ 180,* the Scholastic Achievement Manager (SAM) gathers data about program usage and performance. This data enables you to monitor the effectiveness of program implementation within your school or district. Using this information, you will be able to track program usage and reading progress for classes, teachers, grades, schools, or your entire district to ensure that students are getting the maximum benefits from *READ 180.*

SAM reports are available for the following components:

- *READ 180* Topic Software
- *rSkills Tests*
- *Scholastic Reading Inventory (SRI)*
- *Scholastic Reading Counts! (SRC!)*

Putting Reports Data to Work

SAM reports are designed for flexible use. You can specify a time period for data you wish to view, sort, save, and print. In addition, reports viewed onscreen contain links to accompanying instructional resources available through SAM. The *READ 180* Software Manual contains detailed instructions on how to adjust SAM settings and access SAM resources. You can also review aggregated SAM results in Data Snapshots on the Leadership Dashboard.

Each SAM report is linked to a specific instructional task. Data can be used to diagnose student needs, track progress, determine instructional pacing, and differentiate instruction. Each SAM report contains an icon that identifies its main instructional purpose. The following table briefly describes each report type.

DIAGNOSTIC	INSTRUCTIONAL PLANNING	PROGRESS MONITORING	SCHOOL-TO-HOME	ACKNOWLEDGMENT
Diagnostic Reports review details of student strengths and weaknesses and determine appropriate placement.	**Instructional Planning Reports** help teachers plan targeted, data-driven instruction for Whole- and Small-Group.	**Progress Monitoring Reports** monitor reading performance over time for students, teachers, grades, and schools.	**School-to-Home Reports** help teachers communicate student results to families.	**Acknowledgment Reports** celebrate student reading achievement.

Proven Results for Student Groups

READ 180 is proven to meet the needs of students across a range of demographic groups whose reading achievement is below the proficient level. The program provides concrete, reliable information that will enable you to track progress for groups of students across a school or district. More specifically, to help meet your state requirements, *READ 180* offers:

- A reliable mechanism for monitoring, evaluating, and reporting progress.
- Differentiated instruction to meet student needs.
- Reports that disaggregate student data by demographic group.
- The ability to export data to demonstrate performance across schools and districts.

The Compendium of READ 180 Research summarizes the results from 30 studies conducted over a decade. Several studies in this document illustrate the impact on student achievement when *READ 180* is implemented "on model." The Compendium can be downloaded at (**www.scholastic.com/research**).

Setting Usage and Performance Goals

Extensive efficacy research has shown that *READ 180* can improve reading performance and help students achieve grade-level proficiency when the program is used with fidelity, according to the *READ 180* Instructional Model.

READ 180 reports enable you to correlate software usage and participation rates with levels of performance in grades, classes, and schools within your district. This information can help you support *READ 180* teachers to ensure that their students receive maximum benefits from the program.

Usage and performance goals may include:

- ***READ 180:*** average session length; average sessions per week
- ***rSkills Tests:*** tests administered; strand scores; average test score growth
- ***SRI:*** Lexile growth; total tests administered
- ***SRC! books read; quizzes passed; words read; points earned***

Reports also enable you to review students' reading results in context. These results can help you monitor student response to intervention and determine where to provide additional implementation support.

Managing Reports in SAM

As students work on software, SAM stores the results of their work. This information is organized into a variety of reports that can be generated for each of the four software components—*READ 180, rSkills Tests, Scholastic Reading Inventory (SRI),* and *Scholastic Reading Counts (SRC!).*

Select a Group for Reporting

1. Use the SmartBar on the left side of the Reports screen to select whether to run a student, group, class, school, or district report.
2. Select the report you want to run.
3. If desired, click on the **Apply Demographic Filters** link to review results for certain populations of students. Applying demographic filters will re-create the report with only students who fall into selected subgroups.

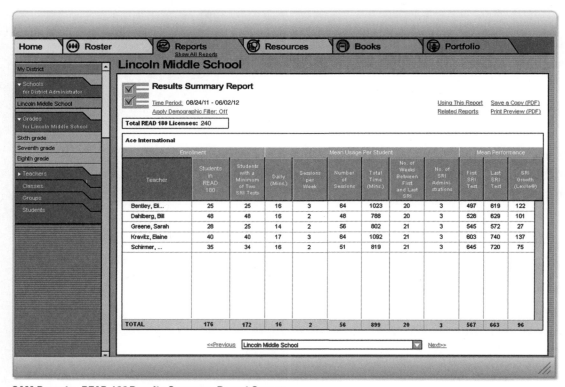

SAM Reports: *READ 180* **Results Summary Report Screen**

Customize Time Period

1. Determine the time period settings you wish to apply to review results.

2. Select from a variety of preset time period settings or choose to customize time period settings by selecing **Custom** in the Time Period Settings window.

3. Ensure that grading periods are set up in SAM so that "Grading Period" setting will match this year's grading calendar.

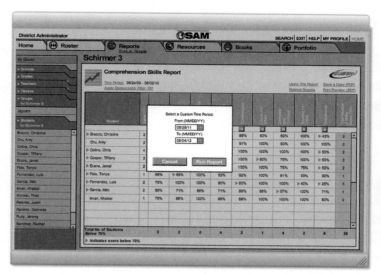

SAM Reports: Customize Time Period

School or District Reports

Depending on your leadership role within a district and your district's SAM setup, you may be able to review district results, or results just for one particular school in the district. Clicking on the SmartBar on the left side of the SAM Reports screen will allow you to review results at different levels. Reports will be structured in the same way, but will provide differing levels of granularity, depending on the type of report selected.

Select the appropriate district, school, or grade to view administrator reports in SAM.

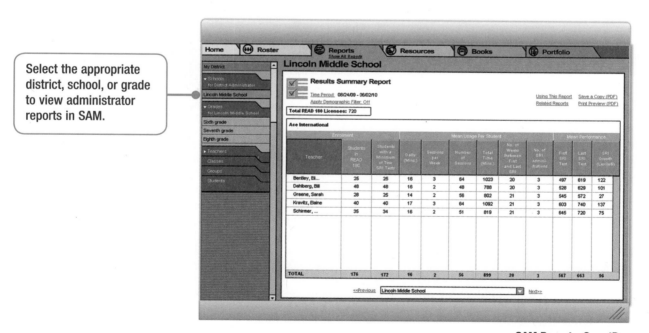

SAM Reports: SmartBar

Administrator Reports

Using the Leadership Dashboard

The Leadership Dashboard streamlines the process of progress monitoring and determining where to provide strategic implementation support. Use your Leadership Dashboard to monitor student progress, set up weekly notifications, and identify factors critical to a successful implementation.

① Receive Notifications and Schedule Reports

Manage **weekly notifications** or schedule SAM reports to be sent to your inbox.

② Review Aggregated Results

Review **aggregated student results** by school or district.

③ Support Implementation

Provide **strategic implementation support** by quickly identifying schools or classes that are experiencing challenges.

④ Review Student Results

Review results from each component of *READ 180* for all schools or classes.

Leadership Dashboard: Home Page

Leadership Dashboard Notifications

Use the Leadership Dashboard to manage weekly notification digests. Review the notifications and use the information to determine which SAM reports to schedule for further analysis.

Launch the Notifications Wizard

Log in to the Leadership Dashboard any time to set or modify notifications settings.

From the Leadership Dashboard Home Page, click **Notifications** to launch the Notifications Wizard.

Leadership Dashboard: Home Page

Manage Notifications

1. Click on the **Notifications** link on the Home Page of the Leadership Dashboard.

2. Place a check mark next to any notifications you wish to receive. Uncheck any you do not wish to receive.

3. Click **Save** to schedule the notifications.

4. A notification digest will be sent to your inbox once a week and will contain information for all notifications you selected.

5. Return to this screen to adjust notifications options at any time.

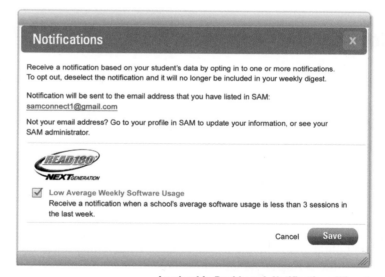

Leadership Dashboard: Notifications Wizard

Using the Leadership Dashboard to Schedule Reports

The Leadership Dashboard can simplify the reports analysis process. Review the aggregated SAM data on the Leadership Dashboard and schedule SAM reports to be sent to your email inbox.

Scheduling SAM Reports

Review aggregated data on the Leadership Dashboard Home Page. These data snapshots provide an overview of student participation in each component of the software. Identify any areas of concern and schedule accompanying SAM reports for detailed analysis of student performance.

Use the Report Scheduler to run the following reports:

- *READ 180* Results Summary Report
- *SRI* Growth Summary Report

Launch the Report Scheduler

1. Log in to the Leadership Dashboard any time to schedule a SAM report.
2. Review the Data Snapshots for your district or school. Use results to determine which reports to review.
3. From the Leadership Dashboard Home Page, click **Schedule a Report** to launch the Report Scheduler.

Leadership Dashboard: Home Page

Using the Leadership Dashboard Report Scheduler

The Report Scheduler on the Leadership Dashboard contains many of the same features and functions as reports settings found in SAM. Use these settings to schedule a report.

Schedule a Report

1. **Who:** Select the district or a school.
2. **What:** Select a program and a report.
3. **Time Period:** Select whether to run the report for the last two weeks or the school year. The selected time period is dependent on the date you schedule the report to be run.
4. **When:** Select the date to run the report.
5. **Confirm:** Review your selections. Click **DONE** to schedule the report.

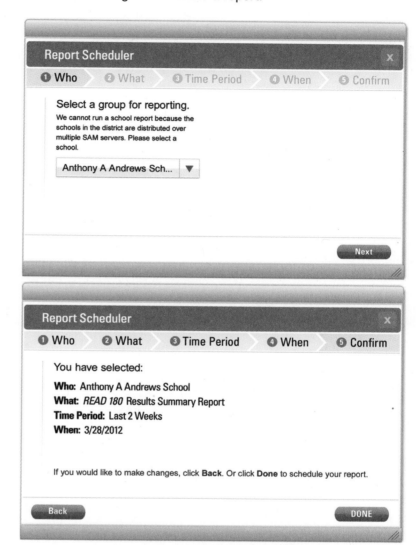

Leadership Dashboard: Report Scheduler

Review a Report

When the report is ready, you will receive an email notification. The report will be available in the Report Scheduler as a PDF. Use the report section of this guide to analyze student results. Use that analysis to provide instructional support and implementation feedback. For more information about implementation, review the Implementation Success Factors section of the Leadership Dashboard.

READ 180 Reports Overview

Students in your school or district who participate in *READ 180* use the *READ 180* Topic Software each day to practice reading and to build comprehension, fluency, writing, and other key skills. Each time students log on to the *READ 180* program, the Scholastic Achievement Manager (SAM) captures information about their participation and usage.

You can access this data for groups, classes, teachers, grades, schools, or entire districts by using the *READ 180* Reports in SAM. The information in these reports will help you monitor reading growth. You can also choose to filter results by demographic group to review performance of specific groups of students.

The following table summarizes how to use each *READ 180* Report.

If You Want to …	Run This Report
…track *READ 180* participation, performance, and reading progress for specific demographic groups	*READ 180* Demographic Results Summary Report (p. 254)
…compare *READ 180* participation, performance, and reading progress for schools, grades, or classes	*READ 180* Results Summary Report (p. 256)

Demographic Results Summary Report

Purpose

Use this report to compare *READ 180* usage data with *SRI* growth results for schools or groups.

Demographic Results Summary Report
SCHOOL: LINCOLN MIDDLE SCHOOL

Time Period: 08/24/11 – 02/02/12

Total READ 180 Licenses: 240

Lincoln Middle School

	① ENROLLMENT		**② DAILY (MINUTES)**	**③ SESSIONS PER WEEK**	**④ NUMBER OF SESSIONS**	**⑤ TOTAL TIME (MINUTES)**	**⑥ NO. OF WEEKS BETWEEN FIRST AND LAST SRI**	**⑦ NO. OF SRI ADMINIS-TRATIONS**	**⑧ FIRST SRI TEST**	**⑨ LAST SRI TEST**	**⑩ SRI GROWTH (LEXILE)**
DEMOGRAPHIC	STUDENTS IN READ 180	STUDENTS WITH A MINIMUM OF TWO SRI TESTS									
All READ 180 Students	184	179	16	2	47	759	20	3	554	649	95
Economically Disadvantaged	58	58	17	2	51	835	20	3	524	640	117
Limited English Proficiency	4	4	18	2	45	796	21	3	513	572	59
Students with Disabilities	45	44	17	2	48	797	21	3	405	519	114
Female	61	61	16	2	49	802	20	3	587	675	88
Male	78	77	16	2	50	804	20	3	513	638	126
Asian	3	3	17	2	46	768	21	3	485	634	149
Black/African American	70	69	16	3	52	834	20	3	551	659	109
Hispanic	6	6	17	2	45	736	21	3	576	644	68
White/Caucasian	64	64	16	2	47	767	21	3	549	653	104

MEAN USAGE PER STUDENT (columns ②–⑦) · **MEAN PERFORMANCE** (columns ⑧–⑩)

How It Helps

This report helps monitor student progress. I can see whether various demographic groups are meeting performance and participation benchmarks.

Using This Report

Purpose: Use this report to compare READ 180 usage data with SRI growth results for schools or groups.

Follow-Up: Run this report at the end of each test window to track performance progress within a school or district.

Understand the Data

① Enrollment

Number of students in a demographic group enrolled in *READ 180* who have completed at least one software session and the number of students with two or more *SRI* tests. Students enrolled in *READ 180* may appear in multiple demographic groups.

② Daily (Minutes)

Average number of minutes that students in a demographic group spent on the Topic Software each session (day). Students should average 15–19 minutes per session.

③ Sessions Per Week

Average number of sessions (days) for all students in a demographic group.

④ Number of Sessions

Number of sessions (days) logged on to the Topic Software.

⑤ Total Time (Minutes)

Average number of minutes all students in a demographic group (who have completed at least one *READ 180* session) have used the Topic Software.

⑥ No. of Weeks Between First and Last *SRI*

Average number of weeks between the first *SRI* test and the last *SRI* test for students in a demographic group who have taken two or more *SRI* tests.

⑦ Number of *SRI* Administrations

Average number of *SRI* tests taken by students in a demographic group enrolled in *READ 180*.

⑧ First *SRI* Test

Average first *SRI* score for all students in a demographic group who have taken two or more *SRI* tests.

⑨ Last *SRI* Test

Average last *SRI* score for all students in a demographic group who have taken two or more *SRI* tests.

⑩ *SRI* Growth (Lexile)

Average increase in Lexiles for all students in a demographic group who have taken two or more *SRI* tests within the selected time frame.

Use the Data

Who: School- and district-level administrators

When: Run this report monthly or after each SRI test.

How: You can apply the information in this report in the following way:

Establish Participation Criteria

- If your school or district has implemented *READ 180* for a full year, the total time benchmark is 1400–1500 minutes (3 days per week × 15 minutes per day × 32 weeks). Work with *READ 180* coordinators and teachers to set benchmarks for specific time periods.

Follow Up

- If average usage is below 15 minutes per day or 3 sessions per week, check in with schools or individual teachers to explore implementation issues. Ensure that all classrooms have access to fully functioning technology.
- Conference with teachers whose classes are not meeting minimum participation benchmarks. Discuss classroom management techniques to ensure that students log on to the Topic Software every day.

Review Related Reports

- *READ 180* Results Summary Report (p. 256)
- *READ 180* Reading Progress Report (p. 150)
- *SRI* Demographic Growth Report (p. 262)

Results Summary Report

Purpose

This report compares *READ 180* usage data with *SRI* results for schools or classes.

Results Summary Report
SCHOOL: LINCOLN MIDDLE SCHOOL

Time Period: 08/24/11 – 02/02/12 **①**

Total READ 180 Licenses: 240

Lincoln Middle School

ENROLLMENT			MEAN USAGE PER STUDENT						MEAN PERFORMANCE		
②			**③**	**④**	**⑤**	**⑥**	**⑦**	**⑧**	**⑨**	**⑩**	**⑪**
TEACHER	STUDENTS IN READ 180	STUDENTS WITH A MINIMUM OF TWO SRI TESTS	DAILY (MINUTES)	SESSIONS PER WEEK	NUMBER OF SESSIONS	TOTAL TIME (MINUTES)	NO. OF WEEKS BETWEEN FIRST AND LAST SRI	NO. OF SRI ADMINIS- TRATIONS	FIRST SRI TEST	LAST SRI TEST	SRI GROWTH (LEXILE)
Bentley, Elizabeth	30	30	16	3	53	856	17	3	481	605	124
Dahlberg, Bill	52	52	16	2	41	656	20	3	540	645	105
Greene, Sarah	29	24	14	2	31	545	21	3	562	580	19
Kravitz, Elaine	43	43	17	3	54	925	21	3	599	731	131
Schirmer, Margaret	42	41	16	2	44	702	20	3	658	728	70
TOTAL	195	190	16	2	48	767	20	3	567	664	97

Elizabeth Bentley

ENROLLMENT			MEAN USAGE PER STUDENT						MEAN PERFORMANCE		
CLASS	STUDENTS IN READ 180	STUDENTS WITH A MINIMUM OF TWO SRI TESTS	DAILY (MINUTES)	SESSIONS PER WEEK	NUMBER OF SESSIONS	TOTAL TIME (MINUTES)	NO. OF WEEKS BETWEEN FIRST AND LAST SRI	NO. OF SRI ADMINIS- TRATIONS	FIRST SRI TEST	LAST SRI TEST	SRI GROWTH (LEXILE)
Bentley 1	15	14	16	3	52	824	19	3	472	632	160
Bentley 2	9	9	16	3	55	910	15	2	494	564	69
TOTAL	24	23	16	3	53	856	17	3	481	605	124

Using This Report

Purpose: Use this report to compare READ 180 usage data with SRI growth results for schools or classes.

Follow-Up: Run this report at the end of each SRI test window to track progress and usage within a school or district.

> ## How It Helps
> *This report provides an overview of school and class participation in READ 180 and helps monitor fidelity of implementation.*

Understand the Data

1 Time Period

To view cumulative progress, set the time period to This School Year. Customize date ranges for a more targeted review of usage.

2 Enrollment

Total number of students enrolled in *READ 180* who have completed at least one software session. Also includes total number of students with two or more *SRI* test scores.

3 Daily (Minutes)

Average number of minutes that students spent on the Topic Software each session (day). Students should average 15–19 minutes per session.

4 Sessions Per Week

Average number of sessions (days) that students logged on to *READ 180* each week. Students should average 2–4 sessions per week.

5 Number of Sessions

Average total number of sessions (days) that students logged on to the Topic Software.

6 Total Time (Minutes)

Average total number of minutes that students spent on the Topic Software.

7 No. of Weeks Betweeen First and Last *SRI*

Average number of weeks between the first *SRI* test and the last *SRI* test within the selected time period for students who have taken two or more *SRI* tests.

8 Number of *SRI* Administrations

Average number of *SRI* tests taken by all students enrolled in *READ 180*.

9 First *SRI* Test

Average first *SRI* score for students who have taken at least one *SRI* test.

10 Last *SRI* Test

Average last *SRI* score for students who have taken two or more *SRI* tests.

11 *SRI* Growth (Lexile)

Change in Lexile from first *SRI* test to last *SRI* test for each school or class.

Use the Data

Who: School- and district-level administrators

When: Run this report monthly or after every *SRI* test administration.

How: You can apply the information in this report in the following ways:

Establish Participation Criteria

- If your school or district has implemented *READ 180* for a full year, the total time benchmark is 1400–1500 minutes (3 days per week × 15 minutes per day × 32 weeks). Work with *READ 180* coordinators and teachers to set benchmarks for specific time periods.

Follow Up

- If average usage is below 15 minutes per day or 3 sessions per week, check in with schools or individual teachers to explore implementation issues. Ensure that all classrooms have access to fully functioning technology.
- Conference with teachers whose classes are not meeting minimum participation benchmarks. Discuss classroom management techniques to ensure that students log on to the Topic Software every day.

Review Related Reports

- *READ 180* Demographic Results Summary Report (p. 254)
- *READ 180* Reading Progress Report (p. 150)
- *SRI* Growth Summary Report (p. 268)

Data in Action

Monitoring *SRI* Growth The overall *SRI* Growth (Lexile) includes students with only one *SRI* test score in the calculation. To monitor results for students with two or more SRI test scores, run the SRI Growth Summary Report (p. 268).

rSkills Tests Reports Overview

During Whole- and Small-Group Instruction, teachers use the *READ 180 rBook* to teach specific comprehension, vocabulary/word study, and conventions skills. At the end of each *rBook* Workshop, *READ 180* students take an *rSkills Test.* These tests give students an opportunity to demonstrate their ability to apply the skills they learned during the *rBook* Workshop.

When students take an *rSkills Test* on the computer, the Scholastic Achievement Manager (SAM) captures their test results. You can access these results for groups, classes, grades, teachers, or schools using the *rSkills Tests* reports.

The *rSkills Test* Summary Skills Report allows you to view scores on one *rSkills Test* for a group, class, teacher, or school.

To review additional results, consider running one of the following *rSkills Tests* Reports for teachers.

- *rSkills Tests* Grading Report
- *rSkills Tests* Grouping Report

rSkills Tests Summary Skills Report

Purpose

This report shows *rSkills Test* results for one test by skill area. The skill-by-skill score breakdown shows areas of strength and weakness.

Summary Skills Report
CLASS: SCHIRMER 3

School: Lincoln Middle School
Teacher: Margaret Schirmer
Grade: 7

Time Period: 01/15/12 – 01/30/12

TEST 4b (Stage B)
Average Test Score: 76%
Number of Students Tested: 7

SKILLS	SCORE RANGE	AVG. SCORE*	NO. OF ITEMS
Comprehension	**17% - 100%**	**63%**	**10**
Sequence of Events		64%	4
Summarize		61%	6
Vocabulary/Word Study	**25% - 100%**	**77%**	**8**
Multiple-Meaning Words		79%	4
Using a Dictionary		75%	4
Conventions	**50% - 100%**	**88%**	**7**
Using Correct Verb Tense		89%	4
Using Commas in a Series		86%	3

* Open-response scores are not included.

* Writing Prompt scores are not included.

Using This Report

Purpose: This report shows aggregated rSkills Test scores on one test for a class or group. The skill-by-skill score breakdown shows strengths and weaknesses.

Follow-Up: Target specific skills for Whole- and Small-Group Instruction that a majority of your students are having difficulty with.

How It Helps

"I use this report to monitor how students perform on skills learned during Whole-and Small-Group Instruction."

Page 1 of 1

Printed on: 02/02/12

Administrator Reports

SRI Reports Overview

Teachers use the *Scholastic Reading Inventory (SRI)* at the beginning of the year to screen and place students in the appropriate *READ 180* level. They also administer *SRI* three times during the year to monitor *READ 180* students' progress toward grade-level proficiency.

When students take *SRI*, the Scholastic Achievement Manager (SAM) captures their test results. You can review these results for classes, grades, teachers, schools, or an entire district using the SRI reports. These reports can help you to ensure that *SRI* is administered appropriately throughout the year and to monitor students' reading growth and response to intervention.

The following table briefly describes how you can use *SRI* reports.

If You Want to ...	Run This Report
...monitor reading growth for demographic subgroups	*SRI* Demographic Growth Report (p. 262)
...track reading performance across AYP student demographic groups	*SRI* Demographic Proficiency Report (p. 264)
...view *SRI* reading performance standards for a school, grade, or class	*SRI* District/School Proficiency Report (p. 266)
...examine reading growth between two *SRI* tests	*SRI* Growth Summary Report (p. 268)
...note changes in reading proficiency distribution across performance standards over time	*SRI* Proficiency Growth Report (p. 270)
...analyze overall current reading performance	*SRI* Proficiency Summary Report (p. 272)
...track *SRI* testing frequency by teacher or grade	*SRI* Teacher Roster (p. 274)
...view test activity by school or teacher	*SRI* Test Activity Report (p. 275)

Demographic Growth Summary Report

Purpose

This report provides a demographic summary of *SRI* performance over time.

Demographic Growth Report
SCHOOL: LINCOLN MIDDLE SCHOOL

Time Period: 08/24/11 – 02/02/12 **(1)**

Total Students: 190 **(2)**

Lincoln Middle School (190 total students)

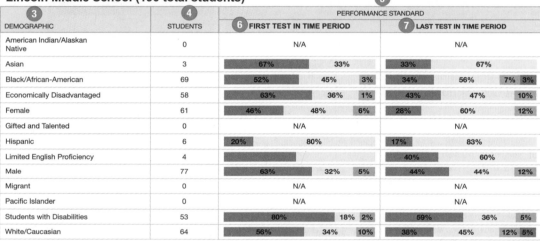

DEMOGRAPHIC **(3)**	STUDENTS **(4)**	PERFORMANCE STANDARD **(5)**	
		(6) FIRST TEST IN TIME PERIOD	**(7)** LAST TEST IN TIME PERIOD
American Indian/Alaskan Native	0	N/A	N/A
Asian	3	67% / 33%	33% / 67%
Black/African-American	69	52% / 45% / 3%	34% / 56% / 7% 3%
Economically Disadvantaged	58	63% / 36% / 1%	43% / 47% / 10%
Female	61	46% / 48% / 6%	28% / 60% / 12%
Gifted and Talented	0	N/A	N/A
Hispanic	6	20% / 80%	17% / 83%
Limited English Proficiency	4		40% / 60%
Male	77	63% / 32% / 5%	44% / 44% / 12%
Migrant	0	N/A	N/A
Pacific Islander	0	N/A	N/A
Students with Disabilities	53	80% / 18% / 2%	59% / 36% / 5%
White/Caucasian	64	56% / 34% / 10%	38% / 45% / 12% 5%

Legend: ■ Below Basic ■ Basic ■ Proficient ■ Advanced

Using This Report

Purpose: This report provides a demographic breakdown of SRI performance over time.

Follow-Up: Identify demographic groups that are in need of extra help based on their SRI performance standard percentages.

How It Helps

Identify demographic groups that are in need of extra help based on their SRI performance standard results.

Understand the Data

1 Time Period

Default time period setting of This School Year displays results from the first and most recent *SRI* administrations. Customize time period settings to compare results between any two *SRI* test administrations.

2 Total Students

Total students for each class, grade, or school who have taken at least two *SRI* tests within the selected time frame.

3 Demographic

Demographic subgroups established during student enrollment in SAM Roster. Students included in this report may appear in more than one subgroup.

4 Students

Total students in each demographic group who have taken at least two *SRI* tests within selected time periods.

5 Performance Standard

Percentage of students in each *SRI* performance standard: Advanced, Proficient, Basic, and Below Basic. Performance standards are color-coded according to the key at the bottom of the report.

6 First Test Score in Time Period

Percentage of students who fall within each performance standard on the first test within the selected time period for each demographic group.

7 Last Test Score in Time Period

Percentage of students who fall within each performance standard on the last test within the selected time period for each demographic group.

Use the Data

Who: School- and district-level administrators

When: Run this report after at least two *SRI* administrations.

How: Apply the information in this report in the following ways:

Monitor Progress

- During the year, track performance standard changes to ensure that students' reading results are improving.

Acknowledge Success

- If students in a particular school or class are doing especially well, explore the instructional strategies being used and share them with other teachers or schools.

Provide Additional Support

- Provide additional implementation training and in-classroom support for classes or schools who continue to fall below expectations.

Review Related Reports

- *SRI* Demographic Proficiency Report (p. 264)
- *SRI* Growth Summary Report (p. 268)
- *SRI* Proficiency Summary Report (p. 272)

Demographic Proficiency Report

Purpose

This report provides a demographic breakdown of *SRI* performance for schools, grades, and classes.

Demographic Proficiency Report
SCHOOL: LINCOLN MIDDLE SCHOOL

Time Period: 08/24/11 – 02/02/12 **1**

Total Students: 194 **2**

Lincoln Middle School (194 total students)

3 DEMOGRAPHIC	**4** STUDENTS	**5** PERFORMANCE STANDARD
American Indian/Alaskan Native	0	N/A
Asian	3	33% / 67%
Black/African-American	70	34% / 56% / 7% / 3%
Economically Disadvantaged	58	43% / 47% / 10%
Female	61	28% / 60% / 12%
Gifted and Talented	0	N/A
Hispanic	6	17% / 83%
Limited English Proficiency	4	40% / 60%
Male	78	44% / 44% / 12%
Migrant	0	N/A
Pacific Islander	0	N/A
Students with Disabilities	54	59% / 36% / 5%
White/Caucasian	64	38% / 45% / 12% / 5%

■ Below Basic   ■ Basic   ■ Proficient   ■ Advanced

Using This Report

Purpose: This report provides a demographic breakdown of SRI performance.

Follow-Up: Identify demographic groups that are in need of extra help based on their SRI performance standard percentages.

How It Helps

Use the SRI *Demographic Proficiency Report to identify demographic groups that are in need of extra support based on* SRI *performance.*

Understand the Data

1 Time Period

Default time period setting of This School Year displays results from most recent *SRI* administration. Customize time period settings to review results from previous tests.

2 Total Students

Total number of students who have taken at least one *SRI* test within the selected time period.

3 Demographic

Student demographic groups for Adequate Yearly Progress. Note that students may be included in more than one subgroup.

4 Students

Total students within each Demographic Group.

5 Performance Standard

Percentages of students within each of the four performance standards: Advanced, Proficient, Basic, and Below Basic. Performance standard results are color-coded according to the key at the bottom of the report.

Use the Data

Who: School- and district-level administrators

When: Run this report after each *SRI* administration, usually 4 times per year.

How: You can apply the information in this report in the following ways:

Monitor Progress

- Establish expected annual proficiency goals. Communicate expectations for students moving from lower to higher performance standards throughout the year.

Acknowledge Success

- If students in a particular school or class are doing especially well, explore the instructional strategies being used and share them with other teachers or schools.

Provide Additional Support

- Provide additional implementation training and in-classroom support for classes or schools who fall below expectations.

Review Related Reports

- *SRI* Demographic Growth Summary Report (p. 262)
- *SRI* Growth Summary Report (p. 268)
- *SRI* Proficiency Summary Report (p. 272)

Data in Action

Setting Up Demographic Subgroups To review results by demographic group, add demographic information when creating student accounts in the SAM Roster. This can be done during initial student data import or can be completed manually by modifying student profiles.

District/School Proficiency Report

Purpose

This report provides an overview of the performance of students who completed an *SRI* test.

PROGRESS MONITORING

District/School Proficiency Report
SCHOOL: LINCOLN MIDDLE SCHOOL

Time Period: 08/24/11 – 02/02/12 **1**

2 **Total Grades:** 3
3 **Total SRI Students:** 195

Lincoln Middle School (195 total students)

4 PERFORMANCE STANDARD	**5** STUDENTS	**6** PERCENTAGE OF STUDENTS	
Advanced	5	3%	
Proficient	24	12%	
Basic	94	48%	
Below Basic	72	37%	

Grade 6 (43 total students)

PERFORMANCE STANDARD	STUDENTS	PERCENTAGE OF STUDENTS	
Advanced	0	0%	
Proficient	4	8%	
Basic	22	51%	
Below Basic	17	40%	

Grade 7 (78 total students)

PERFORMANCE STANDARD	STUDENTS	PERCENTAGE OF STUDENTS	
Advanced	1	1%	
Proficient	14	17%	
Basic	30	38%	
Below Basic	41	53%	

7 YEAR-END PROFICIENCY LEXILE® RANGE

GRADE 1	GRADE 2	GRADE 3	GRADE 4	GRADE 5	GRADE 6	GRADE 7	GRADE 8	GRADE 9	GRADE 10	GRADE 11	GRADE 12
100-400	300-600	500-800	600-900	700-1000	800-1050	850-1100	900-1150	1000-1200	1025-1250	1050-1300	1050-1300

Using This Report

Purpose: This report allows administrators or principals to review the performance of students using SRI on a district-wide or school-wide basis.

Follow-Up: Identify schools or classes whose performance on SRI is less than optimal. Review SRI usage with the respective principal or teacher.

How It Helps

I use this report to review SRI usage and performance results within my school.

Understand the Data

① Time Period

Default time period setting of This School Year displays results from the most recently completed *SRI* test. Customize time period settings to review results from other *SRI* tests.

② Total Schools/Grades

Total number of schools or grade levels with students who have completed at least one *SRI* test.

③ Total *SRI* Students

Total number of students who have completed at least one *SRI* test.

④ Performance Standard

Students are grouped into four performance standards based on their *SRI* results: Advanced, Proficient, Basic, or Below Basic. Performance standard bands vary based on grade level.

⑤ Students

Total students within each performance standard based on results from most recent *SRI* test completed within selected time period.

⑥ Percentage of Students

Percentage of students within each performance standard based on results from most recent *SRI* test completed within selected time period.

⑦ Year-End Proficiency Lexile Range

Expected year-end Lexile range for reading proficiency. Proficiency Lexile ranges vary by grade level. Shaded grade levels indicate the grade levels of students included in the report.

Use the Data

Who: Administrators

When: After each *SRI* test, usually four times a year

How: Apply the information from this report in the following ways:

Monitor Progress

- Establish expected annual proficiency goals. Communicate expectations for student moving from lower to higher performance standards throughout the school year.

Acknowledge Success

- If students in a particular school or class are doing especially well, explore the instructional strategies being used and share them with other teachers or schools.

Provide Additional Support

- Provide additional implementation training and in-classroom support for classes or schools who fall below expectations.

Review Related Reports

- *SRI* Demographic Proficiency Report (p. 264)
- *SRI* Proficiency Growth Report (p. 270)
- *SRI* Proficiency Summary Report (p. 272)

Growth Summary Report

Purpose

This report measures Lexile growth between two *SRI* test dates in a selected time period.

PROGRESS MONITORING

Growth Summary Report
SCHOOL: LINCOLN MIDDLE SCHOOL

SCHOLASTIC SRI

Time Period: 08/24/11 – 02/02/12

Total Grades: 3
Total Students: 190
Average Lexile Growth: 102

Lincoln Middle School (190 total students)

GRADE	② TOTAL STUDENTS	③ FIRST TEST SCORE (AVG.) IN SELECTED TIME PERIOD	④ LAST TEST SCORE (AVG.) IN SELECTED TIME PERIOD	⑤ AVERAGE GROWTH IN LEXILE
6	43	354	470	116
7	78	539	624	85
8	69	598	707	109

Grade 6 (43 total students)

CLASS	TOTAL STUDENTS	FIRST TEST SCORE (AVG.) IN SELECTED TIME PERIOD	LAST TEST SCORE (AVG.) IN SELECTED TIME PERIOD	AVERAGE GROWTH IN LEXILE
Bentley 1	17	398	541	143
Bentley 2	9	494	577	83
Dahlberg 1	13	313	382	69
Dahlberg 4	4	585	657	72

Using This Report

Purpose: This report measures Lexile growth over time, between two SRI test dates in a selected time period, by district broken down by school, and by school broken down by grade and teacher/class.

Follow-Up: Identify schools, or individual grades or classes within a school, that are not showing adequate growth over time and provide extra help to optimize SRI performance.

How It Helps

Monitor reading growth for schools, grades, or classes. Provide additional support in areas that are not showing adequate growth over time.

Understand the Data

1 **Time Period**
Default time period setting of This School Year displays results from most recent *SRI* administration. Customize time period settings to compare results between any two *SRI* tests.

2 **Total Students**
Total number of students in each school, grade, or class who have taken at least two *SRI* tests within selected time period.

3 **First Test Score (Avg.) in Selected Time Period**
Average student Lexile measures for the first test within the selected time period.

4 **Last Test Score (Avg.) in Selected Time Period**
Average student Lexile measures for the last test within the selected time period.

5 **Average Growth in Lexile**
Average increase in Lexile score between the first test and the last test for all students who have completed at least two *SRI* tests within the selected time period.

Use the Data

Who: School- and district-level administrators

When: Run this report after at least two *SRI* tests have been administered.

How: Apply the information in this report in the following ways:

Monitor Progress

- Establish and communicate expected annual growth goals. In general, one year's growth is between 50 and 100 Lexile points, depending on grade level and initial *SRI* results. For more information, see Establishing *SRI* Growth Targets on **page 64.**
- Monitor growth rates to ensure that schools or classes are on track to meet annual growth benchmarks.
- To track growth for specific groups of students, apply applicable student demographic filters on the SAM Reports screen.

Acknowledge Success

- If students in a particular school or class are doing especially well, explore the instructional strategies being used and share them with other teachers or schools.

Provide Additional Support

- Investigate results for classes or schools whose data indicate that they are not meeting expected growth benchmarks.
- Provide additional implementation training and in-classroom support for classes or schools who continue to fall below growth expectations.

Review Related Reports

- *SRI* Demographic Growth Summary Report (p. 262)
- *SRI* Demographic Proficiency Report (p. 264)
- *SRI* Proficiency Summary Report (p. 272)

Administrator Reports

Proficiency Growth Report

Purpose

This report tracks changes in performance standards over time by district, school, grade, and teacher.

Proficiency Growth Report
SCHOOL: LINCOLN MIDDLE SCHOOL

Time Period: 08/24/11 – 02/02/12 **1**

Total Students: 190 **2**

Lincoln Middle School (190 total students)

PERFORMANCE STANDARD **3**	FIRST TEST IN TIME PERIOD		LAST TEST IN TIME PERIOD	
	STUDENTS **4**	PERCENTAGE OF STUDENTS **5**	STUDENTS	PERCENTAGE OF STUDENTS
Advanced	0	0%	5	3%
Proficient	12	6%	24	12%
Basic	82	39%	94	48%
Below Basic	116	55%	72	37%

Grade 6 (43 total students)

PERFORMANCE STANDARD	FIRST TEST IN TIME PERIOD		LAST TEST IN TIME PERIOD	
	STUDENTS	PERCENTAGE OF STUDENTS	STUDENTS	PERCENTAGE OF STUDENTS
Advanced	0	0%	0	0%
Proficient	1	2%	4	8%
Basic	22	51%	22	51%
Below Basic	20	47%	17	40%

Grade 7 (78 total students)

PERFORMANCE STANDARD	FIRST TEST IN TIME PERIOD		LAST TEST IN TIME PERIOD	
	STUDENTS	PERCENTAGE OF STUDENTS	STUDENTS	PERCENTAGE OF STUDENTS
Advanced	0	0%	1	1%
Proficient	9	12%	14	17%
Basic	30	38%	30	38%
Below Basic	39	50%	41	53%

Using This Report

Purpose: This report shows changes in distribution across performance standards over time by district, school, grade, and teacher.

Follow-Up: Identify schools (or grades within a school, or classes for individual teachers) that are not showing adequate growth over time and provide extra help to optimize SRI performance.

How It Helps

Identify schools or classes that are not showing adequate growth and provide extra support to optimize SRI performance.

Understand the Data

1 **Time Period**

Default time period setting of This School Year displays results from first and most recent *SRI* administrations. Customize time period settings to compare results between any two *SRI* tests.

2 **Total Students**

Total students for each class, grade, or school who have taken at least two *SRI* tests within the selected time period.

3 **Performance Standard**

Students are grouped into four performance standards based on *SRI* test results and grade level: Advanced, Proficient, Basic, and Below Basic. Lexile ranges for performance standards vary based on grade level.

4 **Students**

Number of students in each performance standard. Only students who have taken at least two *SRI* tests within the selected time period will appear on this report.

5 **Percentage of Students**

Percentage of students within each performance standard.

Use the Data

Who: School- and district-level administrators

When: Run this report after at least two *SRI* test administrations.

How: Apply the information in this report in the following ways:

Monitor Progress

- Establish expected annual proficiency growth goals. Communicate expectations for students moving from lower to higher performance standards throughout the year. See Establishing *SRI* Growth Targets on **page 62** for more information.

- During the year, track performance standard changes to ensure that students' reading results are improving.

Acknowledge Success

- If students in a particular school or class are doing especially well, explore the instructional strategies being used and share them with other teachers or schools.

Provide Additional Support

- Investigate results for classes or schools whose data indicate that they are not meeting expected benchmarks.

- Provide additional implementation training and in-classroom support for classes or schools who continue to fall below expectations.

Review Related Reports

- *SRI* Proficiency Summary Report (p. 272)
- *SRI* Demographic Growth Summary Report (p. 262)
- *SRI* Growth Summary Report (p. 268)

Data in Action

Tracking Growth The total number of students in Basic and Below Basic should decrease throughout the year as students move to higher *SRI* performance standards.

Administrator Reports

Proficiency Summary Report

Purpose

This report displays the reading performance of students within a district, school, or grade.

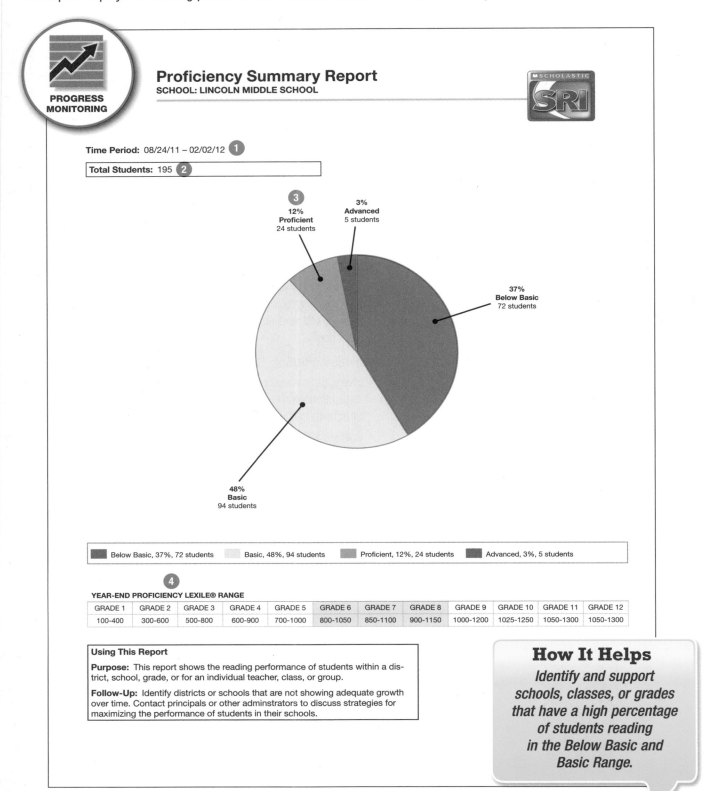

PROGRESS MONITORING

Proficiency Summary Report
SCHOOL: LINCOLN MIDDLE SCHOOL

SCHOLASTIC SRI

Time Period: 08/24/11 – 02/02/12 ①

Total Students: 195 ②

③
12%
Proficient
24 students

3%
Advanced
5 students

37%
Below Basic
72 students

48%
Basic
94 students

| Below Basic, 37%, 72 students | Basic, 48%, 94 students | Proficient, 12%, 24 students | Advanced, 3%, 5 students |

④

YEAR-END PROFICIENCY LEXILE® RANGE

GRADE 1	GRADE 2	GRADE 3	GRADE 4	GRADE 5	GRADE 6	GRADE 7	GRADE 8	GRADE 9	GRADE 10	GRADE 11	GRADE 12
100-400	300-600	500-800	600-900	700-1000	800-1050	850-1100	900-1150	1000-1200	1025-1250	1050-1300	1050-1300

Using This Report

Purpose: This report shows the reading performance of students within a district, school, grade, or for an individual teacher, class, or group.

Follow-Up: Identify districts or schools that are not showing adequate growth over time. Contact principals or other administrators to discuss strategies for maximizing the performance of students in their schools.

How It Helps

Identify and support schools, classes, or grades that have a high percentage of students reading in the Below Basic and Basic Range.

Understand the Data

1 Time Period

Default time period setting of This School Year displays results from most recent *SRI* administration. Customize time period settings to review results from previous tests.

2 Total Students

The total number of students who have completed at least one *SRI* within the selected time period.

3 Percentages

Percentages of students within each *SRI* performance standard: Advanced, Proficient, Basic, and Below Basic. Lexile ranges for each performance standard vary by grade level.

4 Year-End Proficiency Lexile Ranges

Expected year-end student Lexile ranges for reading proficiency in each grade. Lexile ranges vary by grade level. Grades included in the data are highlighted on the chart.

Use the Data

Who: School- and district-level administrators

When: Run this report after each *SRI* administration, usually 4 times per year.

How: You can apply the information in this report in the following ways:

Monitor Progress

- Establish expected annual proficiency goals. Communicate expectations for students moving from lower to higher performance standards throughout the year.

Acknowledge Success

- If students in a particular school or class are doing especially well, explore the instructional strategies being used and share them with other teachers or schools.

Provide Additional Support

- Provide additional implementation training and in-classroom support for classes or schools who fall below expectations.

Review Related Reports

- *SRI* Proficiency Growth Report (p. 270)
- *SRI* Growth Summary Report (p. 268)
- *SRI* Demographic Growth Summary Report (p. 262)

Data in Action

Monitoring Progress The information in this report can help you assess proficiency progress and track trends across an entire school or district.

Teacher Roster

Purpose

This report shows *SRI* usage by teacher. Correlate the results from this report with district testing windows to ensure that all classrooms are following established testing procedures.

Teacher Roster

SCHOOL: LINCOLN MIDDLE SCHOOL

Time Period: 08/24/11 – 02/02/12

TEACHER	GRADE	STUDENTS ENROLLED IN SRI	STUDENTS TESTED ONCE	STUDENTS TESTED TWICE	STUDENTS TESTED THREE OR MORE TIMES	STUDENTS NOT TESTED
Bentley, Elizabeth	6	30	0	5	25	0
Dahlberg, Bill	6, 7, 8	52	0	6	46	0
Greene, Sarah	7	29	4	2	23	1
Kravitz, Elaine	7, 8	43	0	1	42	0
Schirmer, Margaret	7, 8	42	1	3	36	0
TOTAL TEACHERS = 5		**195**	**5**	**17**	**172**	**1**

How It Helps

Monitor test activity during and after SRI *testing windows. Follow up with teachers or administrators when report indicates that* SRI *use is not meeting district expectations.*

Using This Report

Purpose: This report shows SRI usage by teacher. It lists the number of students enrolled per teacher and how often students have been tested.

Follow-Up: Use the report to review SRI usage per teacher. Investigate instances where SRI is not being implemented according to the district or school plan.

Test Activity Report

Purpose

This report provides information on how each school or classroom utilizes *SRI*. Correlate the results from this report with district testing windows to ensure that all classrooms are following established testing procedures.

INSTRUCTIONAL PLANNING

Test Activity Report
SCHOOL: LINCOLN MIDDLE SCHOOL

Time Period: 08/24/11 – 02/02/12

TOTAL STUDENTS: 195

GRADE	TEACHERS	STUDENTS ENROLLED IN SRI	STUDENTS TESTED ONCE	STUDENTS TESTED TWICE	STUDENTS TESTED THREE OR MORE TIMES	STUDENTS NOT TESTED
6	2	43	0	8	35	0
7	4	83	4	5	73	1
8	3	69	0	4	64	0

How It Helps

Review SRI *usage for teachers within a school or district. Investigate instances where the* SRI *is not being implemented according to district or school plans.*

Using This Report

Purpose: This report provides data on how each school in a district is utilizing SRI.

Follow-Up: Contact principals or other administrators in schools where student SRI use is not meeting district plans or expectations.

Scholastic Reading Counts! Reports Overview

When *READ 180* students in your school or district finish reading a book or an eReads in the Modeled and Independent Reading rotation, they take a *Scholastic Reading Counts!* quiz to demonstrate comprehension on what they read.

As students take quizzes, the Scholastic Achievement Manager (SAM) stores data about their independent reading performance and progress. You can access this data for classes, grades, schools, or an entire district through the *Scholastic Reading Counts!* reports.

The following table briefly describes how you can use the *Scholastic Reading Counts! (SRC!)* reports.

If You Want to ...	Run This Report
...monitor independent reading progress based on total quizzes passed and reading level	*SRC!* Books Read Summary Report (p. 278)
...review data on student enrollment, quizzes taken, and quizzes passed	*SRC!* Participation Summary Report (p. 280)
...monitor independent reading progress based on number of points students earned for quizzes passed	*SRC!* Points Summary Report (p. 282)

Books Read Summary Report

Purpose

This report provides data on *Scholastic Reading Counts!* quiz success rate by grade, class, or group.

PROGRESS MONITORING

Books Read Summary Report
SCHOOL: LINCOLN MIDDLE SCHOOL

SCHOLASTIC READING COUNTS!

Time Period: 08/24/11 – 02/02/12 ①

Grades: 3
Students: 195

Lincoln Middle School   ②   ③   ④   ⑤   ⑥   ⑦

GRADE	NUMBER OF QUIZZES PASSED	STUDENTS	AVG. STUDENT LEXILE®	AVG. BOOK LEXILE®	AVG. BOOKS PER STUDENT	TOTAL WORDS READ
6	189 ▇▇▇	43	470	513	5.0	1,120,462
7	322 ▇▇▇▇	83	549	546	3.4	2,632,037
8	450 ▇▇▇▇▇▇	69	707	573	6.4	4,243,536
TOTALS	**1,031**	**195**	**567 (AVG.)**	**533 (AVG.)**	**4.6 (AVG.)**	**7,996,035**

Grade 6

TEACHER	NUMBER OF QUIZZES PASSED	STUDENTS	AVG. STUDENT LEXILE®	AVG. BOOK LEXILE®	AVG. BOOKS PER STUDENT	TOTAL WORDS READ
Bentley, Elizabeth	168 ▇▇▇▇▇	30	380	484	7.0	735,663
Dahlberg, Bill	21 ▇	13	600	738	1.5	384,799
TOTALS	**189**	**43**	**470 (AVG.)**	**513 (AVG.)**	**5.0 (AVG.)**	**1,120,462**

Using This Report

Purpose: This report provides data on the number of books read by a district, school, grade, or class.

Follow-Up: Identify groups that are performing less than optimally in the SRC! program and intervene accordingly. Congratulate and offer further encouragement to groups that are doing well.

How It Helps

Get an overview of Scholastic Reading Counts! *performance in the district.*

Understand the Data

1 Time Period

Time period settings can be adjusted to view year-to-date or month-by-month results.

2 Number of Quizzes Passed

Total *Scholastic Reading Counts!* quizzes passed, shown numerically and graphically.

3 Students

Total students who are enrolled in *Scholastic Reading Counts!* in each school, grade, or class.

4 Average Student Lexile

Average current *SRI* Lexile scores for students who are enrolled in *Scholastic Reading Counts!* in each school, grade, or class.

5 Average Book Lexile

Average Lexile of all books and eReads articles for which students have passed a quiz. Students should strive to read books and articles within 100 Lexile points of their current Lexile level.

6 Average Books per Student

Average number of *Scholastic Reading Counts!* quizzes passed per student.

7 Total Words Read

Total words read for all books and eReads articles when each *Scholastic Reading Counts!* quiz is passed.

Use the Data

Who: School- and district-level administrators

When: Run this report once a month.

How: You can apply the information in this report in the following ways:

Acknowledge Success

- Establish and communicate quarterly or annual goals for quizzes passed per student. Congratulate teachers or principals on quiz success rate.
- Hold reading celebrations. Visit classrooms to congratulate students who have met or exceeded reading goals.

Monitor Progress

- Ensure appropriate reading goals. See the Modeled and Independent Reading goal guideline chart on **page 89** for more information about setting reading goals.
- Monitor quizzes passed, average books per student, and compare average book Lexile with average student Lexile. Follow up with teachers or administrators whose students are not taking or passing quizzes.

Review Related Reports

- *SRC!* Points Summary Report (p. 282)
- *SRC!* Participation Summary Report (p. 280)
- *SRC!* Books Read Report (p. 220)

Data in Action

Progress Monitoring This report shows independent reading progress, as measured by the number of books read. For classes or schools using points to motivate students' reading performance, run the Points Summary Report.

Participation Summary Report

Purpose

This report provides district and school-wide data on *Scholastic Reading Counts!* participation.

INSTRUCTIONAL PLANNING

Participation Summary Report
SCHOOL: LINCOLN MIDDLE SCHOOL

Time Period: 08/24/11 – 02/02/12

Teachers: 9
Students: 195

GRADE	TEACHERS	STUDENTS ENROLLED ③	QUIZZES TAKEN ④	QUIZZES PASSED ⑤
6	2	43	472	189
7	4	83	646	322
8	3	69	843	450
TOTALS	**9**	**195**	**1,961**	**961**

Using This Report

Purpose: This report provides district- and school-wide information on the number of teachers using the program, students enrolled, quizzes taken, and quizzes passed.

Follow-Up: Identify schools or classes that are not participating in the program according to expectations.

How It Helps

Quickly and effectively track Scholastic Reading Counts! *participation across the district and within individual schools—including total quizzes attempted and passed.*

Understand the Data

1 **Time Period**

Time period settings can be adjusted to view year-to-date or month-by-month results.

2 **Teachers**

Number of teachers in each grade with students participating in *Scholastic Reading Counts!*

3 **Students Enrolled**

Number of students enrolled in *Scholastic Reading Counts!*

4 **Quizzes Taken**

Total quizzes attempted in each grade. Students may attempt a quiz on the same book up to three times, with different questions presented in each quiz attempt.

5 **Quizzes Passed**

Total quizzes passed in each grade level. Optimally, the total number of quizzes passed should be close to the total number of quizzes taken.

Use the Data

Who: School- and district-level administrators

When: Run this report once a month.

How: You can apply the information in this report in the following ways:

Monitor Program Implementation

- Establish quarterly or annual participation goals for grades, classes, teachers, or schools. Communicate expectations and celebrate successes. See the Modeled and Independent Reading goal guideline chart on **page 93** for more information about setting reading goals.

- If a particular school, teacher, or grade level does not appear to be fully using the program, investigate further by running the *Scholastic Reading Counts!* Books Read Summary Report.

Address Needs

- If quiz pass rates in a particular grade, school, or class are low, schedule a meeting with teachers and program coordinators to discuss methods for optimizing program use.

- Ensure that all classrooms have the technology and print materials necessary to maximize usage.

Review Related Reports

- *SRC!* Books Read Summary Report (p. 278)
- *SRC!* Points Summary Report (p. 282)
- *SRC!* Books Read Report (p. 220)

Points Summary Report

Purpose

This report provides data on *Scholastic Reading Counts!* quiz points earned for quizzes passed.

PROGRESS MONITORING

Points Summary Report
SCHOOL: LINCOLN MIDDLE SCHOOL

Time Period: 08/24/11 – 02/02/12

Grades: 3
Students: 195

Lincoln Middle School

GRADE	NUMBER OF POINTS	STUDENTS	AVG. STUDENT LEXILE®	AVG. BOOK LEXILE®	AVG. POINTS PER STUDENT	TOTAL WORDS READ
6	942	43	470	4513	21.7	1,120,462
7	1,430	83	549	546	15.1	2,632,037
8	2,250	69	707	573	32.1	4,243,536
TOTALS	**4,622**	**195**	**567 (AVG.)**	**533 (AVG.)**	**20.7 (AVG.)**	**7,996,035**

Grade 6

TEACHER	NUMBER OF POINTS	STUDENTS	AVG. STUDENT LEXILE®	AVG. BOOK LEXILE®	AVG. POINTS PER STUDENT	TOTAL WORDS READ
Bentley, Elizabeth	701	30	380	484	29.2	735,663
Dahlberg, Bill	122	13	600	738	8.7	384,799
TOTALS	**823**	**43**	**470 (AVG.)**	**513 (AVG.)**	**21.7 (AVG.)**	**1,120,462**

Using This Report

Purpose: This report provides data on the number of points earned by a district, school, grade, or class.

Follow-Up: Identify groups that are performing less than optimally in the SRC! program and intervene accordingly. Congratulate and offer further encouragement to groups that are doing well.

How It Helps

The number of points students earn in Scholastic Reading Counts! *is a good indicator of their progress in Modeled and Independent Reading.*

Understand the Data

1 Time Period

Time period settings can be adjusted to view year-to-date or month-by-month data on program usage.

2 Number of Points

Total *Scholastic Reading Counts!* points earned, shown numerically and graphically.

3 Students

Total students who have passed at least one *Scholastic Reading Counts!* quiz.

4 Average Student Lexile

Average current *SRI* Lexile scores for students who are enrolled in *Scholastic Reading Counts!* in each school, grade, or class.

5 Average Book Lexile

Average Lexile of all books and eReads articles for which students have passed a quiz. Students should strive to read within 100 Lexile points of their current Lexile level.

6 Average Points per Student

Average number of quiz points earned per student. Students earn points only for quizzes passed. Point values for each book and eReads article vary based on word count and interest.

7 Total Words Read

Total words read for all books and eReads articles when each *Scholastic Reading Counts!* quiz is passed.

Use the Data

Who: School- and district-level administrators

When: Run this report once a month.

How: You can use the information in this report in the following ways:

Acknowledge Success

- Establish and communicate quarterly or annual goals for quizzes passed per student. Congratulate teachers or principals on quiz success rates.
- Hold reading celebrations. Visit classrooms to congratulate students who have met or exceeded reading goals.

Monitor Progress

- Monitor quizzes passed and average books per student, and compare average book Lexile with average student Lexile. Provide additional support to teachers or administrators who are not optimizing program usage.
- Ensure appropriate point goals. Points earned for passing quizzes vary by book. Review the Modeled and Independent Reading goal guideline chart on **page 93** for more information about reading goals.

Review Related Reports

- *SRC!* Books Read Summary Report (p. 278)
- *SRC!* Participation Summary Report (p. 280)
- *SRC!* Points Report (p. 226)

Data in Action

Recognizing Reading Successg Students enrolled in *READ 180* may have experienced reading challenges in the past. Help build confidence and reading success by implementing awards or celebrations for success in *Scholastic Reading Counts!* Establish goals for points earned, books read, or quizzes passed and celebrate students, classes, or schools who meet or exceed these expectations.

Reports Glossary

Common terms associated with *READ 180* data.

Average Session Length

The average number of minutes a student spends each day on the *READ 180* Topic Software. Students should have an average session length of 15–19 minutes.

CheckPoints

Opportunities during each *rBook* Workshop to use data to regroup students and provide differentiated support based on common areas of student need. Each *rBook* Workshop has three CheckPoints: Reading CheckPoint, Writing CheckPoint, and End-of-Workshop CheckPoint.

Comprehension Score

Percentage of Reading Zone comprehension questions a student answered correctly on the first attempt.

Context Passage

An activity students complete during the Success Zone in the *READ 180* Topic Software. The activity asks students to use context clues to complete a cloze activity—filling in the blanks in a passage with word choices that best fit the passage.

Differentiated Instruction

The process of modifying instructional content or process to meet the varying learning needs and learning styles of all students. Opportunities for differentiated instruction in *READ 180* are included in each area of the Instructional Mode.

Discrepancy Passage

An activity students complete during the Success Zone in the *READ 180* Topic Software. Students are asked to select which of the passages most closely matches the information provided in the Anchor video.

Groupinator

A feature of the Teacher Dashboard that provides recommended *rBook* CheckPoint grouping based on data from student performance in various areas of the software. The Groupinator correlates with the Teacher Dashboard lesson by connecting student groups with corresponding lessons correlated to common areas of student need.

Independent Reading Goal

Total annual *Scholastic Reading Counts!* quizzes passed or points earned for quizzes passed. Goals can be established for an entire class or individual students in the SAM Roster. Progress toward goal will then be tracked in SAM reports.

Leadership Dashboard

A web-based gateway to review student performance and implementation results for a class, grade, school, or district.

Level

A student's *READ 180* reading level, assigned based on *SRI* test results. There are four possible levels in each stage of *READ 180*.

Lexile

A measure of determining the readability of a text and a student's current reading ability. A Lexile is assigned to each text in a *READ 180* classroom. Students take the *SRI* test four times a year to determine initial Lexile scores and track Lexile gains throughout the year.

Manual Promotion

Using SAM to promote students to a new *READ 180* software level based on data and classroom results.

Notifications

A component of the Teacher Dashboard and Leadership Dashboard that allows you to opt in to receive weekly updates when student performance results fall below benchmarks.

Open Response

A type of *rSkills Test* question. These require students to respond in writing to a critical reading question focused on one of the three critical reading skills taught during the *rBook* Workshops: synthesize, analyze, or evaluate. Each *rSkills Test* includes two optional Open Response questions.

Oral Fluency

A student's ability to read text aloud with appropriate speed, accuracy, and prosody. Oral fluency is practiced in the *READ 180* Topic Software Success Zone. It can be assessed three times a year using formal Oral Fluency Assessment (OFA) resources.

Performance Standard

One of four proficiency bands used to report student *SRI* results: Advanced, Proficient, Basic, and Below Basic. Each performance standard includes a range of Lexile scores. The range of results depends on the student's grade level.

Quiz Points

Recognition a student receives for passing a *Scholastic Reading Counts!* quiz. Each book is assigned a specific number of points, and students earn points for passing quizzes. Track points earned on *Scholastic Reading Counts!* reports.

READ 180 Topic Software

The software students use daily during the Instructional Software rotation. The *READ 180* Topic Software offers practice and performance tracking for comprehension, vocabulary, fluency, phonics, spelling, and writing.

Reading Zone

One of five activities, or zones, in the *READ 180* Topic Software. Students watch anchor video footage, read passages, and answer comprehension and vocabulary questions in the Reading Zone.

Report Scheduler

A feature of the Teacher Dashboard and Leadership Dashboard that allows you to schedule a SAM report to be run and sent to your e-mail inbox.

rSkills Tests

Tests that assess student ability to apply skills taught in each *rBook* Workshop. There is one *rSkills Test* for each Workshop. The *rSkills Tests* are comprised of 25 multiple choice, 2 optional open response, and 1 optional writing prompt questions.

SAM

The Scholastic Achievement Manager allows teachers and administrators to manage and review student enrollment and performance data, and access data-driven resources for customizing students' learning experiences.

Scholastic Reading Counts!

A component of the *READ 180* software suite that allows students to demonstrate comprehension of the book by taking a quiz on books read during Modeled and Independent Reading. Quiz results can be tracked with SAM reports.

Scholastic Reading Inventory

A component of the *READ 180* software suite that measures a student's reading ability. *READ 180* students take an SRI test four times a year and receive a Lexile score that assists with placement and measures growth.

Segment

One section of a topic from the *READ 180* Topic Software. Each of the 15 topics include 4 segments. Each segment includes activities from five zones: Reading Zone, Word Zone, Spelling Zone, Success Zone, and Writing Zone.

Session

One day of work in the *READ 180* Topic Software. Each day of school is considered one session, regardless of the number of times during that day a student logs in to the software.

Spelling Zone

One of five activities, or zones, in the *READ 180* Topic Software. Students complete activities that build spelling skills, using words from the reading passages in their segment.

Success Zone

One of five activities, or zones, in the *READ 180* Topic Software. Students review everything they have learned in the current segment. Students can only access the Success Zone after they have completed the required work in the Reading, Word, and Spelling Zones.

Teacher Dashboard

A web-based gateway to review student performance and implementation results for a class, grade, school, or district.

Topic

A group of four software segments that share a common theme. There are 15 total topics in the *READ 180* software.

Word Zone

One of five activities, or zones, in the *READ 180* Topic Software. Students complete activities that build word recognition and fluency, using words from the reading passages in their segment.

Writing Zone

One of five activities, or zones, in the *READ 180* Topic Software. Students respond to a writing prompt based on the topic studied during the current segment.

Using Reports Effectively: Frequently Asked Questions

Which report helps me diagnose individual student needs so that I can differentiate instruction?

The *READ 180* **Student Diagnostic Report** (p. 156) shows student progress and recent errors to help you identify and prioritize a student's needs in comprehension, word recognition, spelling, and fluency. Use this data to target student needs using *Resources for Differentiated Instruction.*

Which reports help me decide which comprehension skills to target at Reading CheckPoints?

Use the *READ 180* **Comprehension Skills Grouping Report** (p. 142) to identify specific comprehension needs and to assign students to small groups for targeted instruction. To adjust groups in the Teacher Dashboard Groupinator, see the *READ 180* **Comprehension Skills Report** (p. 140). Scan the "Total" row at the bottom of the report to identify skills that a significant number of students are struggling with.

Which report can help me make instructional decisions about phonics and word study?

The *READ 180* **Phonics and Word Study Grouping Report** (p. 148) shows the most frequent types of word-recognition errors for a selected group. Use this data to identify skills to target for Small-Group Instruction, if results indicate that a majority of students are struggling with phonics and decoding.

Are there ways to monitor and hold my students accountable for independent reading?

Yes. Be sure to have your students take a *Scholastic Reading Counts!* quiz upon completion of each Audiobook or Paperback. Then use the *Scholastic Reading Counts!* **Student Reading Report** (p. 238) to track the number of books read and quiz scores for each student. For a group snapshot of reading progress, see the *Scholastic Reading Counts!* **Reading Progress Report** (p. 230).

How can I quickly assess how my class is progressing in the *READ 180* Topic Software?

The *READ 180* **Reading Progress Report** (p. 150) gives a record of skills progress and time spent on Software for a group or class. This is an effective way to compare progress among students and to identify areas for further investigation.

Which reports show how my students are doing in each Topic Software Zone?

The *READ 180* **Student Segment Status Report** (p. 162) provides useful data about students' work in the Reading, Word, and Spelling Zones. This information can help you to monitor each student's skills progress, completion status, and time spent in each zone. See the *READ 180* **Student Spelling Zone Report** (p. 164) and **Student Word Zone Report** (p. 166) for specific Study Words a student is working on. You can use these reports to set up review and practice assignments.

How are Spelling scores calculated?

Spelling scores are calculated with CLS. CLS stands for correct letter-sequences. It is a spelling performance indicator that is sensitive enough to measure the short-term gains of students' spelling skills. In *READ 180*, CLS is used to measure spelling skills on both the Spelling Assessment and Spelling Challenge. Results of CLS impact the percentage score you will see in the following *READ 180* reports:

- **Grading Report**—Spelling Score
- **Skills Alert**—Avg. Spelling Zone Assessment Score
- **Student Segment Status Report**—Spelling Zone Status: Assessment Score

The goal of CLS is to give students partial credit for spelling a word with close approximation to the correct orthographic pattern. For instance, consider two students who spell the word "America" as follows:

- Student 1—Amrka
- Student 2—Amereca

Although in traditional spelling tests both students would be scored as incorrect, Student 2 demonstrates a much closer approximation to the correct spelling of the word. Instead of giving credit for words only when all letters are correct, CLS views spelling words as including smaller units known as letter-sequences. Correct letter-sequences are pairs of letters in a word that are placed in proper sequence. Therefore, if a student is able to write at least some letters in a word in proper sequence, that student will receive partial credit for spelling the word.

How does the *READ 180* software compute Spelling scores?

The *READ 180* software automatically generates CLS (correct letter-sequences) scores. To compute the number of correct letter-sequences in a word, CLS first assumes there is a space-holder at the beginning and end of the word. Each letter pair (including the first space + first letter and last space + last letter as letter pairs) are counted as letter-sequences. As a shortcut, when computing the possible number of correct letter-sequences in a word, count the number of letters in that word and add 1 to that value. For example, "America" has 7 letters. By adding 1 to that value, we see that it contains 8 letter-sequences.

In addition, the following rules apply when scoring with CLS:

- Omitted letters decrease the letter-sequence and CLS score.
- Inserted letters are not included in the letter-sequence count.
- In words with double letters, if one of the double letters is omitted, only the first letter written counts as a correct letter-sequence.
- Initial letters of proper nouns must be capitalized to be included in the letter-sequence count.
- Internal punctuation marks (e.g., apostrophes, hyphens) are counted as separate letters when calculating CLS.

Where can I find help with assigning grades?

You can use the *READ 180* Grading Report (p. 144) and the *rSkills Tests* Grading Report (p. 174) to incorporate multiple aspects of a student's performance when determining grades. It is important to calculate information from each rotation when determining grades. Use both reports results and classroom performance to assign grades to each student. For more information see Grading in *READ 180* on page 110.

Which reports are best to share with my students?

You can share reports with your students to address concerns, help them to set goals, and celebrate their successes. The *READ 180* Student Reading Report (p. 158), the *rSkills Tests* Student Skills Report (p. 184) and *Scholastic Reading Counts!* Student Reading Report (p. 238) show individual skills progress. Often, seeing a record of their performance can motivate students. You can also show students their *SRI* Student Progress Report (p. 208) to share evidence of reading growth and overall performance levels.

Which reports are best to share with my students' parents?

The *READ 180*, *SRI*, and *Scholastic Reading Counts!* **Parent Reports** (pp. 168, 170, 216, 240, and 241) include student-specific progress data that you can share and send home.

Which are the best reports to share with my principal?

Principals are most interested in big-picture progress—specifically, how much improvement your students make over a given time period and how they are performing in general. Share the *SRI* **Growth Report** (p. 190) with your principal to demonstrate how students within a group, class, or grade are performing on SRI compared to their grade-level proficiency range. Your principal may also want to ensure that *READ 180* students are using the program as directed—spending at least 20 minutes each day on the Topic Software, as your school schedule permits. The *READ 180* **Participation Report** (p. 146), which shows frequency of student software use, may be of interest to your principal.

Reports Index

Report Types

Alerts and Acknowledgments

Appendix 1

Growth on *SRI* median and upper and lower quartiles, by grade.

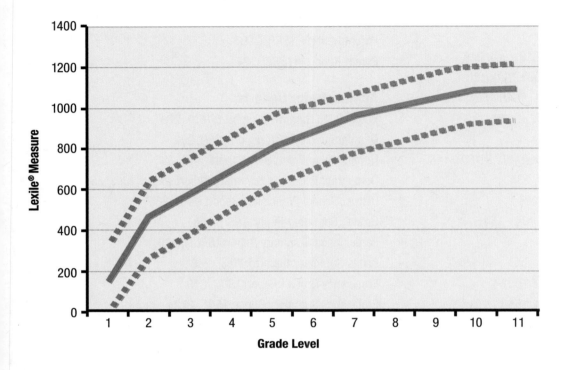

Appendix 2

State assessments linked to the Lexile Framework for Reading

State Assessment
Arizona's Instrument to Measure Standards (AIMS)
California English-Language Arts Standards Test
Florida Assessments for Instruction in Reading (FAIR)
Georgia Criterion-Referenced Competency Test (CRCT)
Georgia High School Graduation Tests (GHSGT)
Hawaii State Assessment
Illinois Standards Achievement Test (ISAT)
Kansas State Assessments of Reading
Kentucky Core Curriculum Test (KCCT)
Minnesota Comprehensive Assessments (MCA)
New Mexico Standards-Based Assessment (SBA)
North Carolina End-of-Grade (NCEOG)
North Carolina English I End-of-Course (NCEOC)
Oklahoma Core Curriculum Test (OCCT)
Oregon Assessment of Knowledge and Skills (OAKS)
South Carolina Palmetto Assessment of State Standards (PASS)
South Dakota Test of Educational Progress (DSTEP)
Tennessee Comprehensive Assessment Program (TCAP) Achievement Test
Texas Assessment of Knowledge and Skills (TAKS)
Virginia Standards of Learning Tests (SOL)
West Virginia WESTEST 2
Proficiency Assessments for Wyoming Students (PAWS)

Appendix 3

SRI was developed to measure growth, so it is better to under-target than over-target. Most *READ 180* students should be targeted at below grade level or far below grade level for their initial test.

On the SRI each student takes a unique test. Therefore, the Standard Error of Measurement (SEM) associated with any one score or student is also unique. The initial SEM, or uncertainty, for an *SRI* score is shown in the table below. When students are appropriately targeted, using both grade level and initial reading level, students can respond to fewer test questions and not increase the error associated with the measurement process. When only grade level of the student is known, the more questions the student answers, the more the SEM decreases.

Mean SEM on *SRI* by Extent of Prior Knowledge		
Number of Items	**SEM Grade Level Known**	**SEM Grade and Reading Level Known**
15	104L	58L
16	102L	57L
17	99L	57L
18	96L	57L
19	93L	57L
20	91L	56L
21	89L	56L
22	87L	55L
23	86L	54L
24	84L	54L